'Incredible . . . So brilliantly written, beautifully sewn together. A call to arms of sorts, pushing us to look ahead and understand and learn from the past instead of dwelling on it. I loved it'
MELISSA THOMPSON

'In *Between Two Waters*, Pam Brunton attempts to reconcile history and modernity without flinching at how colonialism, capitalism and extraction have determined the globalised ways we eat today – and shows that we could change our menus for the better. Using her native Scotland as the lens, Brunton tears through the weeds of the global food system with aplomb'
ALICIA KENNEDY

'A wild ride of a book mixing memoir, political manifesto and philosophy to examine the past and suggest a new way forward for the future. Like a delicious meal, this book will stimulate your mind and linger long after you have finished'
LOUISE GRAY

BETWEEN

TWO

WATERS

BETWEEN TWO WATERS

Heritage, landscape and the modern cook

PAM BRUNTON

CANONGATE

First published in Great Britain, the USA and Canada in 2024
by Canongate Books Ltd, 14 High Street, Edinburgh EH1 1TE

Distributed in the USA by Publishers Group West and in Canada by
Publishers Group Canada

canongate.co.uk

1

Copyright © Pamela Brunton, 2024

The right of Pamela Brunton to be identified as the
author of this work has been asserted by her in accordance
with the Copyright, Designs and Patents Act 1988

For permission credits see p. 272

Every effort has been made to trace copyright holders and obtain their permission
for the use of copyright material. The publisher apologises for any errors or
omissions and would be grateful if notified of any corrections that should
be incorporated in future reprints or editions of this book.

British Library Cataloguing-in-Publication Data
A catalogue record for this book is available on
request from the British Library

ISBN 978 1 805301 77 6

Typeset in Garamond Premier Pro by Palimpsest Book Production Ltd,
Falkirk, Stirlingshire

Printed and bound by CPI Group (UK) Ltd, Croydon CR0 4YY

To families, of all kinds

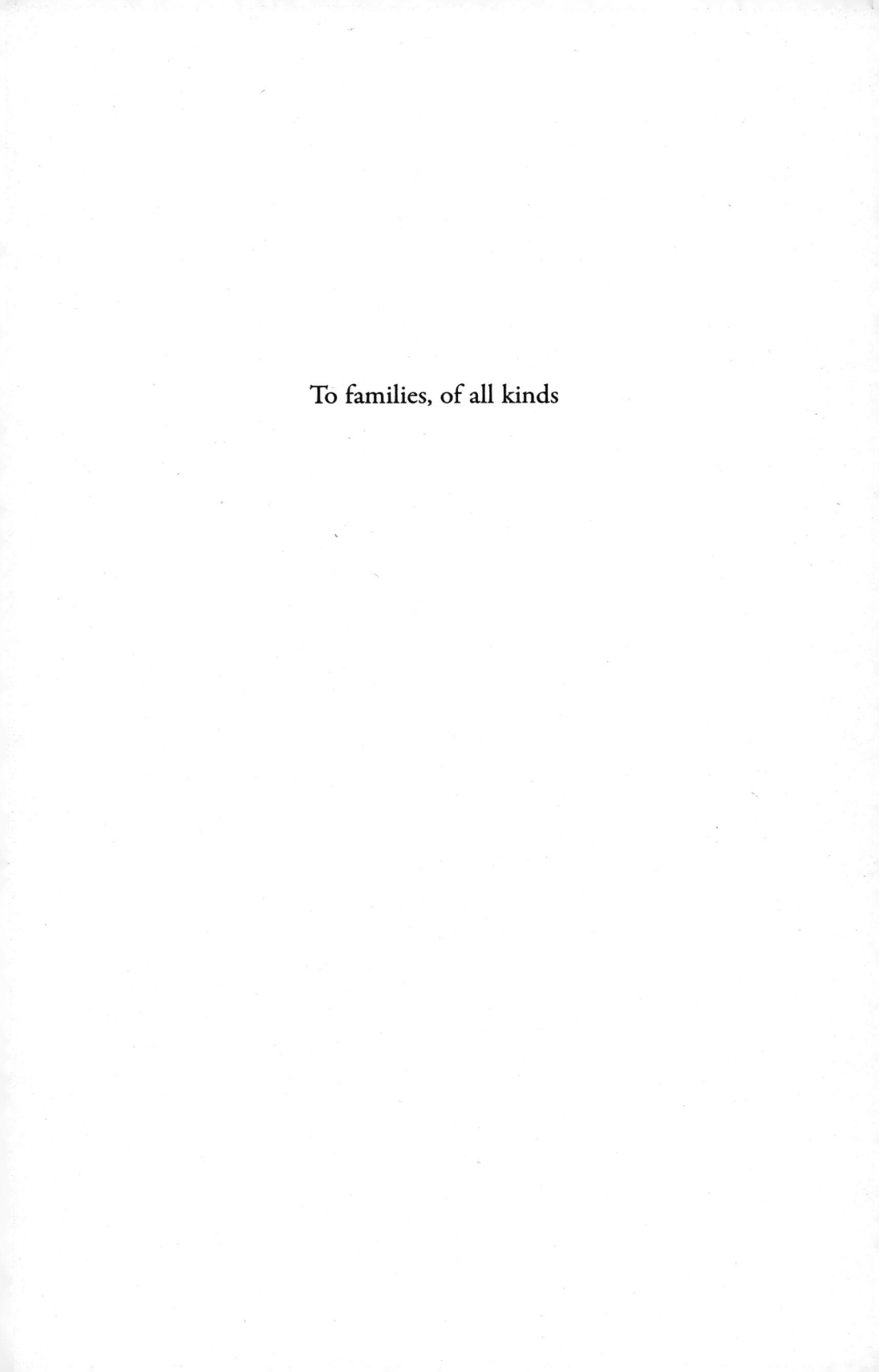

'Adopt, adapt, improve – don't forget yer heritidj'
— My dad, inscription inside a
Scottish cookbook, 1999

'Tradition is never static . . . this is an aspect of human psychology that touches on the question of communal identity . . . to identify such movements it is important to examine the food of the Scots . . . over the longest possible time span.'
— Alexander Fenton, *Food of the Scots*, 2007

'Nothing is true but change . . . nothing endured at all, nothing but the land she passed across.'
— Lewis Grassic Gibbon, *Sunset Song*, 1932

CONTENTS

Chapter One: The Road Less Travelled   1

Chapter Two: Modern   29

Chapter Three: Scottish / *people*   83

Chapter Four: Scottish / *land*   156

Chapter Five: A Modern Scottish Cook   201

Chapter Six: A War for the Human Imagination   240

Acknowledgements   269

Notes   273

List of Recipes   293

Chapter One:

THE ROAD LESS TRAVELLED

In March 2015, on the shores of a great tidal sea loch, Loch Fyne, my partner Rob and I opened a restaurant called Inver.

Opening a fragile small business anywhere is terrifying. Immediately the pressures pile up: Inver drained all our life's savings, leaving a rattling-empty post-purchase bank account. There were not nearly enough staff to do the job. Consider the public exposure of your most intimate creative thoughts, bared in the choice of menus, decor, drinks, table settings, uniforms... Add to this the intensity of living, working and socialising with your romantic partner through 100-hour, 6-day working weeks with nowhere near enough sleep. Then imagine all this happens under the steady, unerring, hawk-eyed judgement of media, colleagues and friends, and you get close to feeling how I felt that spring. The many-armed terrors don't just keep you up at night, they claw screeching through your waking mind, filling your lungs with their broken bloody fingernails and making actual nightmares feel like an ad break.

In the early weeks of Inver, the dining room was mostly empty but for the glisten on the gold rims of the vintage glassware we'd collected during the dreaming years. Bright spring light shafted through the windows, bounced from the surface of the loch outside. The dust motes were illuminated, tumbling upwards as waitress Siobhan straightened forks and added another log to the fire. One such empty lunchtime the phone rang. I got to it first. 'Hello', said a voice. The man on the line explained he was watching us from the far shore of the loch. 'I often see your lights on at night . . . and we've been thinking of visiting, my wife and I.'

'Oh, but you should!' I urged, star-struck by this nameless, faceless stranger.

'Well, now . . . but what is it you're doing over there? *What sort of food is it you do?*'

Breathe.

'Erm . . . so, *modernScottishfood*.' I tried to tie the words together into something cohesive.

'Oh, right. Right . . . Right. So. What's that, then?'

'Well, today on the specials board we have a lamb-bone broth with mussels and turnip and seaweed, kind of like a Scotch broth, you know? Just a really nice one. It's like the lamb is seasoned with all the things it's been eating. The lamb is from Ian on the island of Bute, it's really hogget, super-flavourful, we like to use all of it, even the bones, and we have this amazing slow-grown chicken from St Brides Farm with wild garlic from just round the corner and a sauce made from the chicken liver with oloroso sherry and a bowl of skirlie on the side. You know skirlie? Oatmeal and onions cooked in chicken fat . . . It's like one of my favourite things to eat. Lots of black pepper. And we have salad and radishes from Kate's garden in Strachur and oh there's dessert, it's rhubarb, kind of raw but not really cos it's fermented in sugar so it tastes like when you're a kid and you dip the rhubarb in sugar and we serve it with whipkull, like a rich custard, but whipped up, you know? It's a traditional Hogmanay thing in Shetland. And the halibut is from Gigha but all the fish are actually born right here in the hatchery near the restaurant, and there's scones. We have scones. We bake them fresh every morning and we've made the butter and the jam.'

There's no tumbleweed in Scotland and I don't know what the local equivalent is. Maybe dandelion clocks? By now, the noise on the other end of the phone was like an ethereal dandelion seed head glancing past the receiver strewing fluffy skelfs along the line. Finally, he spoke.

'But not, you know, just *normal Scottish food*? Fish and chips? Steak pie? *Lasagne?*'*

It would be wrong to say that phone call has stayed with me all this time. The first years of running Inver were too full for any excess information to stick in the mind for long. But now the emotional tsunami of those early years is receding, it's one of the odd dislodged pieces of furniture left strewn on the shore. You have to approach it, stalk it from different angles, try to see it for what it is.

Normal.

Scottish.

---

* No, we don't do fish and chips. Actually, that's not true. Partly in response to that phone call, we did a raw fish and chips: Gigha halibut, lightly cured, with shredded pickled potato and a bold horseradish cream with chive oil, loosely suggesting tartare sauce or wasabi. It got reviewed in the *Guardian* newspaper, in our first serious bit of media, the rope thrown down into our dark pit of self-doubt. Food critic Marina O'Loughlin exhorted her readers to grab the nearest helicopter and get to Inver. Since then, in the Covid-19 lockdown, I've taken the fryers home and made fish and chips for the fifteen or so residents in our small hamlet of four inhabited houses. Alastair, the Gigha halibut farmer, brought the haddock back from the fish market for us all.

Food.

Normalscottishfood.

Modern Scottish food.

And now, almost ten years later, I find myself asking the question: what kind of food *do* we serve? What *do* I do every day?

I know that when we opened Inver, we set out to cook and serve something we called 'modern Scottish' food – in part as a reference to the current 'modern British' trend we'd left behind in London, and in part because we didn't know what else to call it. We were in the midst of this most iconic of Scottish scenery, using produce from local farms, gardens, hills and waters, and taking inspiration from traditional food culture and historic recipes (including a century-long handwritten cookbook collection inherited from my great-aunt, Ann Simpson). It seemed like a fair claim.

We have spent the last decade explaining ourselves to each other, to the press and to our guests. But something hasn't quite settled in my mind. Like jolting a bucket of new vinegar as you rack off the clear liquid from the murky sediment at the bottom, fragmentary thoughts are stirred up every time the phrase comes up. Modern Scottish food. Normal Scottish food. The two are not the same. But why?

I guess we had some things in common with the guy on the phone. We both thought we knew what the words 'Scottish' and 'food' meant. 'Normal' gave our neighbour the more secure footing; he stood solidly in the present with the current culture's consensus bunched around his shoulders as in a rugby scrum. 'Normal' is the popular opinion. To name our food 'modern Scottish' I must have known that there was this 'normal Scottish' food I was distinguishing us from. But the specials-board dishes I'd recited to the guy on the phone – the broth, the whipkull, the scones – are very securely Scottish.

Recipe books document their presence in the Scots culinary canon since – well, at least since the advent of the printing press allowed the literate population a way of documenting and articulating their own food culture to themselves and each other 500 years ago. Probably from way before then. And yet, they are not what our neighbour meant by 'normal'. It's no longer the norm to eat broths made from real bones left over from butchering a whole, carefully raised animal, and simmered with vegetables grown in ground nearby; to eat seaweed; to serve niche Shetlandic winter specialities, or to be offered warm scones made from 'heritage' varieties of wheat, freshly milled into flour and served with newly churned cultured butter made from good cream and homemade jam made from fruit you've picked at the farm.

What constitutes 'normal' in Scotland these days are dishes from countries whose links to Scotland are via their people or their trade relationships, not their immediate geography. Lasagne and spaghetti bolognaise have been normalised by generations of Italian immigrants who settled in Britain a century or more ago and opened Italian restaurants, fish-and-chip shops, and ice-cream parlours. Routinely voted 'Britain's most popular dish', chicken tikka masala was originally a foothold in the British economy in the 1960s and '70s for Bangladeshi and Pakistani immigrants from former British colonies struggling to find work elsewhere in racist, factional Britain. Burger and chips appears to be Scotland's new mince and tatties: one street corner in central Glasgow has seven burger shops in as many paces. Hamburgers themselves may have originated as the German frikadelle in the seventeenth century, possibly first served between bread at an American World's Fair in the early twentieth century. Franchised fast-food chains, the forerunners of our globalised food system, spread the hamburger worldwide: Wimpy was the first to bring the industrial American burger to Britain in the post-war 1950s.

None of these foods are dishes you'd find in Bologna, Dhaka or Hamburg. They are produced with the peculiar British palate in mind, and are served in environments that appeal to the sensibility of a dining public in the UK. Meanwhile, in the supermarket, fresh produce sections are brimming with bananas, pineapples and mangoes from Africa and the Americas, year-round Peruvian asparagus and Kenyan sugar-snap peas. This is the 'normal Scottish' our neighbour was asking for. Not a restaurant menu that serves flavours with centuries-old traditions in Scotland, made with excellent produce grown nearby and seasoned at times with flavours brought here by 'new Scots' over the last century or two. But if so few people would identify with it, can I even call this 'modern Scottish' food? Which of us is right?

Autumn is peaking outside my window. First, in the sheep field, burnished pheasants dart through worn green marsh grasses, evading the staccato march of black crows. Highland cattle, the colour of spice, slouch over mossy stone dykes and turn their scratchy red heads slowly over black-faced white sheep. There's a flit of dead leaf and a sudden drop of small birds. Beyond the field a buzzard lifts heavily off a fence post and is momentarily framed by the still, slate-grey water. At the far shore of the loch, the long low line of the land tapers away as if drawn by a skimmed stone. The near hills are rawest rust-orange, layered beyond with deep blues the colour of ancient royalty. The far bank of the loch is bolted with stone castles. Breezes glance white on the water, eddying round fishing boats drawing up creels of crabs and prawns, nets of herring and mackerel lines. Time and tide for no man bide, but here they slow. The small ferry drags through the water like a metronome.

Directly over the loch in a traditional pre-Clearances farming township, the walls stand still. This is Auchindrain (from the Gaelic 'Achadh an Droighinn', the blackthorn field). On mornings like this one, thick white frost seizing the long-shadowed fields, women like me once lit fires from last night's embers, scraping cold sticks from the byre floor and banking peat in a stone hearth. Through the reek of smoke and animal hides, the warming scent of boiling oats drifts like a thin winter sun. It's the landscape of Jacobite rebels, commando-crawling like adders through bracken; nascent dreams of nationhood flowering with the summer heather on the hills and in the glens. It's where tweed-swathed clan chiefs ruled and riderless horses returned home faithful from ancient battles on faraway fields. It's the dark, antlered head of a red stag mounted high against white snow and pine-green shadows. It's the island-blistered horizon-lines in ballad and lyric and poem; murmured round hearths and campfires, chanted at weddings and rugby matches, seized in hotel brochures and charity-shop calendars. It's the cloud-swaddled sunset that has sold a gazillion whisky bottles, shortbread tins and plastic-wrapped portions of colour-coded pink salmon. It's a popular tourist destination. It's home. Seeing the landscape like this is like looking through binoculars with a colander hanging off the end. There is more shadow than light. The picture is fragmented. The story is full of holes.

We are in Argyll, on the raggedy, frayed western edge of Scotland. Argyll stretches on the mainland from Campbeltown in the south to Oban in the north, and encompasses twenty-three of Scotland's ninety-three inhabited islands, from Bute, Islay and Jura to the Inner Hebridean islands of Mull and Iona, Coll and Tiree. It was torn from the rock currently known as Ireland some time in prehistory: the Dalradian strata found across much of northern Scotland also appears in north and west Ireland. The youngest of these rocks are at least 470 million years old. They were named by geologists relatively recently – after Dál Riata, the ancient Celtic kingdom formed in the fourth century, when Irish Gaelic monks made it across the sea in their coracles, set up monasteries and spread Celtic Christianity along the western seaboard of Scotland and through the north-west Highlands. The Celts populated landscapes and displaced languages. Their most famous monastery is the one on the tiny Inner Hebridean island of Iona, population around a hundred souls, where Rob and I first lived when we moved back to Scotland from London.

Through the last two millennia, the natural and social landscapes of Highland Scotland have changed beyond recognition. It was in Dál Riata that the peoples that became modern Scots were first introduced. The invading Celts battled the powerful Picts, the 'painted people' who had already repelled the Roman armies. The Roman Empire had subsumed England, but the Romans were reduced to building a wall to keep back the fierce northern hordes, whom they named Scotti. The etymology is unclear, but it became the Roman name for all the tribes north of Hadrian's Wall, and the origin of the word 'Scotland'.

When the Celts arrived, the land was covered in ancient, diverse Caledonian forest. Deer and wild boar roamed freely. Beavers built their dams on rivers that ran with silver salmon in the spring. Grouse, woodcock and capercaillie coexisted with their predators: hawks, eagles, lynx and wildcats. Now, wild salmon are so scarce that sport fishermen aren't allowed to land any fish that they actually catch. Osprey, golden eagles, salmon and a range of hawks and harriers are critically endangered. There are as few as thirty true wildcats left in Scotland and the lynx is extinct. The great herring waters of our own Loch Fyne are emptied of these 'silver darlings'. The valuable game animals, like grouse and deer, have proliferated.

Very little of the country's famed natural larder is enjoyed at home. The majority of our shellfish is shipped to London and Spain. Despite a landscape that is well suited to extensive animal husbandry, we import New Zealand lamb, Argentinian beef, and venison from Poland. Our food culture is popularly represented abroad by deep-fried Mars bars, a hi-vis orange drink called Irn-Bru, and the dish of haggis, neeps and tatties, whose key ingredients originally come from India, the West Indies, Anatolia, Sweden and Peru.

To an invading fifth-century Celt, the current social landscape would be almost unrecognisable. The periods of starvation and the diseases of under-nutrition (like rickets), common throughout the Middle Ages, are lessened, but Scots in the twenty-first century still have an uneasy relationship with their dinner. Poor diet contributes significantly to the main causes of death and poor health in Scotland, including heart disease, diet-related cancers and type 2 diabetes. Children's diets are particularly poor, and the proportion of adults in Scotland that are overweight or obese is 64 per cent and rising.[1]

The pretty picture on your postcard from Scotland is a snapshot of only a fragment of our story, a hasty scribbled message from one time and one place. There is a lot left outside the frame. For holidaymakers, the silhouetted hills might be enough. Tweed-clad stalkers bag their brace of grouse and ask no questions. But I can't ignore the rest of the story. For me, an investigation of our country's historic food culture would be about understanding my place in it.

In between the formation of Scotland the nation and the food we eat today is the period of time called 'modernity'. It's during the few hundred years from the 1500s that the words 'normal' and 'modern' have been given their contemporary meanings. We are all modern Scots and our daily food choices collectively create our normal. But even the name of our small country came from other people. Who or what is it guiding our choices today? Did we Scots *really* choose poor human health and ecological decay to be the norm? What am I not seeing between the holes?

Inver Restaurant is housed in a renovated crofting cottage right on the shore of Scotland's deepest, longest sea loch, Loch Fyne. The oldest part was built around 300 years ago (though there has been a dwelling on the site since around the fourteenth century). That one-room cottage was originally home to the loch's ferryman and his family, with one attic bedroom and an open fire in the kitchen-living area (now the fireside bar). The burn to the side of the cottage – the one you cross to reach the four cabins we call 'luxury bothies' – was the family's supply of fresh water. Part of the family's rent to the Strathlachlan estate was paid in herring.

History lives for us here. Our landlords at the restaurant, the Maclachlan family, are descended from a powerful chieftain called Lachlan Mor, who lived on the shores of Loch Fyne in the thirteenth century. ('Mor' means 'big' or 'great' in

Gaelic, so he was 'Big Lachlan'.) The Maclachlans own the cottage and the acres of rolling land in which it sits. It was the clan's foresighted 24th chief, Madam Marjorie Maclachlan – the only woman to have led the clan – who originally opened a restaurant here, Inver Cottage, in 1968.* Marjorie's son Euan, current laird of the estate, and 25th hereditary Chief of Clan Maclachlan,† lives in New Castle Lachlan, a short walk from Inver.

Inver is a common place name all over Scotland, especially in the west and the Grampians: Inverness, Inveraray, Inverkip, Invergowrie, Lochinver. It's an anglicisation of the Gaelic word inbhir, 'a meeting of two waters', and often used to mark a point where a river meets a loch, or a loch meets the sea. These liminal shores, where ecosystems ripple and swirl, are fertile, abundant places, full of opportunity.

Inver Cottage, the old crofter's home, stands on Lachlan Bay, where the small River Lachlan meets Loch Fyne. Flowing waters mean movement; a flow from a rooted past, itself with branched roots steeped in deeper histories, to an unformed future. Meanwhile at Inver, our restaurant, the present eddies in the lee of 300-year-old walls.

* * *

---

* Marjorie commissioned the restaurant's open, airy design from the architect and pioneering conservationist Geoffrey Jarvis. Jarvis united the old croft house and its boatshed with a light, bright extension that became the main restaurant, making the most of the views out to the loch and bay.

† Euan's sister Gina and her late husband, Tony Wignall, took over the running of the restaurant from Marjorie herself in the 1980s. Tony's 'phenomenal' porridge, enriched with whisky, demerara and cream, gets a mention in Catherine Brown's book *A Year in a Scots Kitchen*. Gina's daughter Jasmine and her husband, the musician Joe McAlinden, ran Inver Cottage from 2003.

Anyone who goes anywhere is looking for something. I didn't know what we were searching for when Rob and I first arrived at Lachlan Bay one ice-cold day in early November 2014. We thought we were looking for a venue for a restaurant, somewhere we could create something beautiful, together, and finally unload the boxes that we'd packed and unpacked for years. What we found was not the destination but the start of the journey of our lives. Everything we had done up until then was like the part where you pack the cases and stow them away in the boot of the car. We would use everything we had in the next few years; every bit of imagination and our creative educations; all the goodwill we'd accumulated with family and friends; every last penny and scrap of sanity.

When we arrived, it was sleety-grey cold. White horses were cruising the loch and tripping up the bay. The restaurant had been shut since the end of the summer season. The cold clamoured at you as soon as you entered the back door. The kitchen is a big open space, surrounded by ancient thick stone walls which hold the cold and radiate it inwards; in the winter months the inside feels colder than out. The wooden shelves were covered in decades of white paint, and sloped enough that you could roll a salt cellar from one end to the other. The plaster walls were peeling. Jasmine, then-owner, was leading us through, musing on whether or not the new folks would want her pot of broken biros. I was captivated by the space. You could almost run. We'd been working in a city restaurant in Belgium, and as in city restaurants everywhere, the land had been the most expensive part of the building and floor space was dedicated first to tables where paying customers could eat away at the bills. City restaurant kitchens are mostly tiny, cramped. I couldn't even imagine having enough staff to fill these workstations. I was all in before we even stepped through the swing doors into the restaurant itself.

Even in winter's greys, the light brims into the Inver dining room. The mist and crashing waves outside seem to dissolve the windows; the restaurant merges into the landscape. Pacing through to the little bar – still with a wicker basket of Tunnock's tea cakes on display – it was too easy to imagine unpacking the bone-handled butter knives, our antique books with the dripping wax candles on top, and that gold-tipped glassware from warm summer months brocante-shopping in France. The bar was transporting – it was 1968 again. From their smoke-stained paintings, two old ladies stared into the middle distance from their respective perches either side of the open fireplace, gazes meeting like crossed swords above the deep, battered red couches. The crescent of yellow from the choking wood fire spread like a sepia rainbow over the mantelpiece. (Later, inspecting the chimney, we found sooty iron hooks on either side which would have been used for hanging and smoking lamb legs or hams.) Our dreams were quietly coming to rest on the window ledges and the beer taps, the wicker armchairs and the original Ercol tables.

My and Rob's glances kept snagging on each other. Jasmine wandered back through to the kitchen and I remember hearing myself saying, as if from outside the windows, 'Well, if it's not here, I don't know where it is.' So we said yes, and started the conversations that would take us from Ghent, Belgium, back to Argyll, Scotland. We drove through a January blizzard, moved into a static caravan a ten-minute walk from the restaurant, and got ready to open Inver in March 2015, six weeks later. Six weeks. I think of what we achieved in those six weeks and I am incredulous and fearful. I think of what came next and my stomach still knots like the moment you reach the top of the rollercoaster.

We had no investors, nor backing from an established restaurant group with recourse to PR firms, HR departments, book-keepers and banks, so there was no more money until the old restaurant till ratcheted itself open. We planned everything ourselves. The retiree family workforce was mobilised to paint the walls. Mum and Aunt Elaine sewed the bench-seat covers using organic Hebridean tweed from Ardalanish on the Isle of Mull. Our friend Rebecca Proctor was starting a pottery studio and created our first range of bowls and plates. We'd done the food for our friends' wedding at a former hunting lodge on Mull a couple of years previously, and groom Iain did us the website and branding in exchange. I found the owners of a polytunnel we'd spotted, Kate and Russell, who grew fruit and veg. I tried to clean the kitchen using an old paint scraper to remove yellow stalactites of grease from the asbestos panel behind the double fryers.

We had no budget for decor, so after the dads and Uncle Gordon had finished the paint job, we hung all the prints and paintings we'd amassed for our various homes over the years: our East London Georgian terraced house, the Belgian 1940s art deco apartment block, our lean-to cottage at the back of the craft shop on the Isle of Iona. Suddenly, Inver felt like home.

Here's an interesting thing about restaurants like ours. They are a kind of liminal space between public and private. Someone owns them, someone made those design decisions and someone's personal taste shaped that menu. Restaurants don't have the same necessity to your daily life as does, say, the workplace canteen, the school dinner hall, or the prison mess. If you don't

THE ROAD LESS TRAVELLED

like a restaurant, you don't have to go to it! But restaurant guests are paying money for an experience, and feel they're in a position to judge whether or not that experience is worth the price. Part of what they're paying for is the decor, the smiling man at the door, and whether or not the words on the menu resonate with their own ideas of what should be served in this place at this time. In between the chaos of accumulating half-finished jobs, we got snatches of clarity in which we glimpsed what we ourselves were doing. We were inviting the public into our home, to partake of our deepest hopes and most vivid dreams. It was exactly what we had been planning to do. It was terrifying.

We posted recruitment notices for staff: we had no reputation, few contacts, and were setting ourselves up to do something that really hadn't been done before quite like this, in rural Scotland. We didn't really have money to pay wages until the restaurant started making some cash. In my years working in high-end London kitchens, long hours were just the norm. Seventy hours was an easy week; ninety hours or more over five days was not unusual. I just assumed that's what we'd have to do – more if we needed to – to get the place up and running. We'd worry about sleep later. I said yes straight away to a friend who was up for coming to help: that was Ally. Like a bolt of sudden sunshine through stormy skies came a CV from Siobhan. Articulate, engaging, and keen to relocate to the middle of nowhere – mostly to get out of her parents' house – she became our first waitress. And that was it, the entirety of the staff for our opening days. Now, Inver employs nineteen people, not counting me and Rob.

But in the meantime, there was the tonic syrup to make for

the house G&T, the butter to culture and churn, vegetables to ferment and pickle. Our friend, the baker Ben Glazer, who had worked with us in Belgium, came up for a few days to sort out our 'bread schedule' (and also painted some of the bar ceiling, which got repainted shortly after). There was no artisan bakery or butter producer around to help lighten the load; if we wanted to serve it, we had to make it.

There was no time or money to renovate the kitchen or buy much new kit, so we started Inver with the two ancient grease-clogged six-burner stoves, with as much carbon chipped off with the paint scraper as I could manage. On one of those stoves only three of the burners worked, with tiny thumbnail flames; on the other, the flames rose so high the sides of all the old dented aluminium pans were scorched almost to the handles. I quickly bought new stainless-steel pots and developed a technique of temperature control that involved switching pans quickly from one range to the other to raise or lower the heat.

And there were the menus to write. This wasn't the first time I'd tried to articulate myself through the medium of a menu: while living on Iona we ran a series of one-off dinners in various locations across the Hebrides and Highlands of Scotland under the moniker 'The Painting School', and it had given us some confidence that people did understand our nascent language. In Belgium too, as part of running the kitchen there, negotiating items on and off the menu was part of my role. Some of our now-typical flavour combinations were already familiar when we first set the Inver tables. But there was little time to think and reflect creatively. Anxiety and stress are dampers for all but the fiercest flames.

* * *

THE ROAD LESS TRAVELLED

Inver has always been a very personal project. It's like a multi-sensory installation. It is all about Rob and me creating a world within the world, full of the things that we like, and inviting you to come and share it. However, this level of personal emotional investment is perhaps a greater risk even than the deep financial commitment. You leave yourself very vulnerable to the smallest attack. And the general public don't do small attacks; they go all in, too.

People have been making the journey to the restaurant for decades. Guests who have been coming here since they were children now bring their own kids. There have been weddings and engagements, funeral teas and Easter gatherings, birthday parties and family reunions. How many layers of emotion have accumulated with the paintwork? Food memories are some of the most powerful we have; they engage all the senses. The wisp of a scent or a single sharp spoonful, and a time and a place spin back into focus quicker than you can open a photo album or scroll through a phone. Compound that sensual density with a table full of your closest friends at moments of heightened emotion, and there is a lot invested in people's memories of a decades-old restaurant. People don't just come to Inver for dinner. There are easier ways to feed the family than by booking the tickets, packing the bags and making the journey all the way here. So when I wrote a whole new menu I wasn't just presenting something new, I was also erasing the deeply dug old.

It was a Thursday night in early April, not yet Easter holidays. We'd been open maybe two or three weeks in our first year of business. There were no customers booked, and at 7.30 p.m. we were thinking perhaps we would shut up early. Ally and I were cleaning down the kitchen and organising the fridges when an elderly couple stepped carefully in the front door, one toe's tip at a time, as if we had set up an obstacle course in the bar. (I suppose for them, we had.) Delighted, smiling broadly, Siobhan offered them a menu, sat them down on the couch, got them their ginger beer and a glass of water. The spectacles went on like a shield and from behind them the short menu was scanned. It was found all to be an error. The lady approached the bar. By this time I was also behind the bar, in my white chef's jacket, beaming. 'Hello! I'm Pam. What can I help you with?'

'What is all this?'

'What . . . do you mean? The menu? Well, it's all from round here. Really amazing produce, we're so delighted to be able to cook with it . . .'

This time there was no time for the tumbleweed. She slammed her palms flat on the old bar top and growled: 'We have been coming here for *years*!'

The entitlement seethed through her teeth like snakes. Fangs out.

'We used to have *steak*.'

She pounced. '*WE USED TO HAVE LOBSTER!*'

'Uhhh . . . okay, okay, well, if it's seafood you're after, we have just *literally* finished steaming some crabs, straight from the loch! Like, they have really just come in the back door . . . In the creel, of course, they didn't walk themselves . . . hahaha . . . We were going to save them for tomorrow lunch but I'd be really happy to prepare you one now! We have fresh sourdough bread just baked this morning, and we can do you the crab cold, with our mayonnaise, or I could knock you up a hollandaise or something? It would be really quick.'

'NO. We are LEAVING. And MAY I SUGGEST, Miss, that if you have things in the kitchen you would like to sell, YOU. PUT. THEM. ON. A. BOARD!'

'We do have a board – well, it's a mirror . . . it's right here in front of you. Look: "Specials". It's just the crabs have really only just got here . . .'

They left. I made mental plans to sell enough fish and chips to get our money back and return to my office job.

As that first couple revolved out through the door, a second couple turned in – a few years younger, bustling, looking around, eyes wide like they were koalas that had just dropped from a eucalyptus in Australia and landed on a heather-clad hillside in Argyll. Oh god, I thought, here we go. I took over the menu, offered them a drink, made sure to mention the crabs. Went back a few minutes later to ask if there was anything I could help with, any questions they had. She looked at me with wide eyes and said, 'I just don't know what to order! We've been coming here for years and . . . and, well, the last few times the menu was always just the *same*, we just had the *same thing* all the time. Now . . . well, now I just want to eat it all!'

I went back into the kitchen and opened the fridge. I turned on the crazy gas rings, and I didn't cry.

It's hard to fully understand what that first couple were so upset about. The level of anger on display didn't appear to be directly connected to the simplest telling of what had happened: new owners at a restaurant had changed the menu. You wouldn't go into a newly opened restaurant on a city high street and expect it to be serving the exact same food as the previous restaurant (in fact, you'd think it was really odd if they'd chosen to). So why at Inver was it such a provocation? The couple's fury had come from a much deeper place than that of a simple commercial transaction.

I've browsed our early menus, wondering what could possibly have offended folk back then. That day the flavour combinations were straightforward and intelligible, the main ingredients almost all Scottish, the cooking itself perfectly capable. But they were not the same as what had been on offer at Inver Cottage, and this is perhaps the key. It didn't much matter if it was better or worse, or fashionable or traditional. It wasn't what Inver Cottage customers recognised as Inver Cottage food, and to some people, for whom a summer trip to Lachlan Bay was a time-honoured tradition, this change was a personal affront. It jarred their expectations, disrupted the comfort of familiar routine and the bonding with self and surrounds that comes with upholding a tradition. It was perhaps all the more acute because the location outside – so integral to the experience of coming to Inver – was unchanged. As if in visiting your dearly loved aunt, you found the last ten Christmases of your hand-knitted cardigans discarded in the wheelie bin and her newly bared arms covered in gang tattoos.

'Normal' comes from continuity. But norms must change too, or lamb broth and barley bannocks would still be familiar foods to the majority. Food culture is not an easy thing to shift – the forces that move it must be powerful ones.

THE ROAD LESS TRAVELLED

Inver is not only about what goes on within the restaurant's stone walls. It's not only about what goes on in my head; me, the creative cook. Rather, it's about the connection we have – all of us – to all the landscapes that buoy us. About acknowledging the collaboration it takes to get any dish onto a restaurant table: cooperation between the microbiota and insects in the soil, the aquatic life in the loch; with the gardener and farmer, fisher and gamekeeper. The constant recombining of our personal internal landscape, peopled by family and fellows, with other landscapes; broader cultural landscapes laid over the shifting geographical ones. All the journeys made before us have brought us all to these shores. People ask sometimes if there will be another Inver, in a city maybe, nearer them. And of course we say no, this restaurant could only happen in this spot right here, right now.

So, let's say you take the car. Wherever you're coming from, the part of the journey that I feel is 'coming to Inver' starts from Loch Lomond, just leaving Glasgow, probably because this is the journey Rob and I most often make. Let's say it's . . . spring. Spring because today I am writing in two woollen jumpers with a blanket on my knees in the depths of winter. One last phone call home before the mobile reception begins to flicker; check the kids are doing their homework, the dog's eating from the right tin, and the office has your email with the instructions for the daily minutiae that is someone else's to-do list for a day or two.

Houses fall away and the lochside flashes through trees still thin from winter, green shoots barely softening their webbed black lines. From the passenger window your gaze drags across the fluttering landscape like fingers trailed over a wire fence. Beyond the trees, the surface of the loch flickers like a reel of old cine film rattling in a gloaming room. The dark spaces between the lit frames are where the truth lies. Your breathing slows. Beyond the shore, layered hills make forms of the mist like half-kept promises. At the top of the loch, the car turns a corner, carving suddenly left onto another loch. The flappering film catches and unwinds from the spool in a final rattle, drops like an adder from a rock to the floor, and the whole screen before you is quickly bright.

And now you are climbing. Hills assert their forms and engulf the road. For us, driving home with a car full of city-visit essentials (a takeaway curry, a mended tooth, newly clipped hair), this road is landmarked by the edible: we stop at the frothing elderflower trees, the verdant banks of wild garlic swaying with needle-white tips, and later, as summer scrolls on, the ditches full of burbling, heady meadowsweet. With scissors from the car boot we fill supermarket shopping bags with the harvest from abundant roadsides.

At Arrochar the road goes through a pass between hills, as if the land itself grudgingly concedes passage through a half-opened door. The new road, called the Rest and Be Thankful, was completed in 1941 as an alternative (faster, bolder) to the slower, thinly winding road you can still see below you. The Old Military Road that doodles past cowsheds and patched fields at the foot of glacial valley Glen Croe was originally built by Major William Caulfeild's British soldiers as they penetrated the Highlands in the 1740s. At the end of the climbing road a stone bids travellers 'Rest and Be Thankful'. Back up on the pass, to your right, there are banks of boulders restrained with heavy wire mesh, like the boundaries of a war zone. The battle is ongoing; every run of small pebbles in heavy wet weather starts an earthly slide that threatens the road and its travellers. Millions of pounds have been spent restraining the hills: man against mountains.

In the long open straight beyond the hill called the Cobbler, the landscape widens like arms. You sit up, roll down the window. There is a wind that gathers pace down one hill and swoops up from the riverbed. Cool-water scent swirls through the car, coasts gently over the hairs on your arm and eddies at the driver's window like the will of a trapped bird. Now you are awake.

There is another turn. At a corner flanked by pretty pastel cottages you turn right, through the village, past the Post Office. The loch is open here, and you can see the moorings, bright hi-vis orange like modernity itself curled tight into balls. The pier and a few white sailboats and wooden dinghies are bobbing on the tide. There is one more turn in the road, a sharp right and round an S-bend onto a single track: our road, the B8000. In the early years of Inver, when this was not yet home, this turn constricted my throat: whatever respite we'd had from the all-consuming world that we had built here was over, and we were back in its choking hold. Today I think I share the view that others see.

Now, the senses are on high alert. The tension is more tightly wound the closer you get – sea air, shuttling water, the rattle of pebbles on the riverbed. The spring air, heavy with the musk of unseen lives, drapes your nose with trilling, hidden bird song. The trickling chill and heavy sulphurous drift of seaweed follows a warming day's retreating tide. Before you step into the restaurant, into the elemental scent of baking bread and of food cooking on fire, it is these sensations that ready the imagination for the meal to come.

What we seek on any journey we find around the dinner table. Sustenance, physical and imaginative. Sometimes we find challenge, and adventure. Most of all, we find communion with others: with those we care about; with the strangers who show us what we are. Communion with ourselves and with the land around us. In eating familiar food we find belonging; in sharing food we show affection; in eating together we forge bonds. The more significant the food, the deeper the bonds. A companion is, literally, a person with whom you break bread.*

Food is one of the most intimate ways we have of accepting the world around us. It's one of very few things we permit entry to our physical body. Sharing food can be an exploration of the new or a way of showing inclusion. The partial fusing of one food to another is a potential way to meld cultures and compromise divergent ways of thinking. In the Christian faith, communion is the symbolic act of internalising Jesus Christ's teachings by ingesting bread, his body, and wine, his blood. Other religions have similar practices connecting food with the spiritual nourishment given by their teachers, and the creation of community by sharing food. Refusing food, leaving the table (or walking out of a restaurant), is one of the most powerful ways we have of rejecting the people behind the plate.

Your companions at Inver are all of us here. All of us who will cook and serve; your fellow diners; the farmers and gardeners, fisherfolk and cheesemakers. Their names and their histories are shared with you. Their stories are broken open like a fresh loaf of bread. When you sit in the bar before dinner you join the tenants of Inver Cottage centuries ago. As you

---

* From Old French 'compaignon', literally 'one who breaks bread with another', based on Latin 'com', 'together with', and 'panis', 'bread'.

walk from the bar to your table you cross the same ground as they did on the way to their boat, off to catch herring. Glancing out the window you see a similar view. It's peopled by Highland chiefs, their wives and their neighbours, scouting for wild herbs and cockles in the bay. Travellers and traders from centuries back look back at you.

Around Inver the restaurant swirl all the forces shaping life in a small modern country. Scotland is not isolated. We're part of a big, globalised world, where the way people choose to use their landscapes is determining the future of all of humankind. A recent report says that soil erosion from fields used for intensive farming is estimated to be more than 100 times higher than the rate at which soil forms.[2] We are running out of actual *soil*, from which everything we eat – *everything* – comes. Land provides the basis for human livelihoods and well-being everywhere, including the supply of food, fresh water and biodiversity, all essential to human survival. Land also plays an important role in the climate system; it's both a source of greenhouse gases (for instance, when farmland is dug up and plants are felled or harvested) and, conversely, a sink for carbon (when, say, Highland peat bogs are left undisturbed). More than one-third of all greenhouse gases are attributed to the world's food system,* but currently 25–30 per cent of the total food produced globally is wasted.

The year 2000 marked the first time in human history that the number of people on the planet suffering from diseases of

---

* The UN's Intergovernmental Panel on Climate Change recently reported that the way we choose to grow, store, eat and distribute food is responsible for between 21 and 37 per cent of greenhouse gas emissions.

over-nutrition (obesity, type 2 diabetes, diet-related cancers) equalled the number suffering diseases of under-nutrition, from rickets to starvation. Meanwhile, Coca-Cola spend $4 billion a year just on advertising – *double* the World Health Organization's whole annual budget, and *twelve times* the WHO's health promotion budget (i.e., their counter-advertising budget).[3]

Scotland's long coastline has shaped Scots' character and culture for centuries, and now unseen shifts in the seascape influence both again. The Firth of Forth once held the largest native oyster bed in the world – now it has none. At the fishery's peak, 11,000 tonnes of cod were caught each year off Scotland's west coast. Now, it's 500 tonnes, and just nineteen super-trawlers catch two-thirds of Scotland's landed fish.

This is the 'normal' food culture that the Scots people wake up to every day. In 2014 the Scottish government went as far as to publish a food and drink policy in which they said they had 'strong ambitions' for the country to be a 'Good Food Nation, where people from every walk of life take pride and pleasure in, and benefit from, the food they produce, buy, cook, serve, and eat each day' (and in 2022 passed the Good Food Nation Act, putting in place the legislation to realise this vision).[4] The policy also acknowledged that one of the problems in achieving this shimmering vision is low *expectations* of food and a disengagement from where food comes from. As if instead of cooking and sharing food, or travelling to a restaurant, we could just pop vitamin pills equivalent to the nutritional content of those meals – bullet points for our bodies that would satisfy our physical needs.

Nothing is isolated; everything affects who we are and how we sense ourselves. There is current research that suggests human beings have a second brain in our bellies.⁵ There is less known about this gut-brain than about some planets in space and the chasms at the bottom of the sea. This second brain is manned by billions of microbes, a Stalingrad office block of civil servants, who trade biochemical signals with our head-brain to control our mood, emotional well-being, immune system, digestion, and the physical health of our organs and muscles. We are ourselves a multitude, an ecosystem with an ecosystem. The way we eat, the emotional situation in which we ready ourselves to consume, is as important to our well-being as the nutrients we ingest.

With this book, I will honour my role as a cook: I will consider in its composition all of your senses and imagination. I'll try to find a way to satisfy our need for communion with each other and the world in which we live. We'll have tactile cupped bowls to hold your meal, warming broths, mollifying custards, then cooling, sharp ices to follow the elemental meat and bread. We can wonder together what it is to serve 'Scottish' food, in an old building steeped in local and personal histories, in these 'modern' times. What could learning to read the landscape itself add to your understanding of this simple menu? What other journeys have brought these ideas and ingredients to this table? How do we decide which of our invented traditions serve the future? Any Scottish food served today, normal or otherwise, is the answer to these questions, whether you know the question was asked or not. As a cook I want to know what the ingredients I'm cooking with say to others about me, and to me about myself.

Around a table, we are travelling companions. In the pages to come we share our table with poets and philosophers, scientists and inventors. Revolutions come and go. On our journey to dinner there are tragic deaths and historic events, and orphaned children ask for our hands to hold. There is grand injustice and personal guilt. There are heroes, using their lives to fight for ours. There is, in the end, a new start.

Bon appétit! / Good appetite!

Slàinte mhath! / Good health!

باهلنا واشلفاء / Bil-hanā' wa ash-shifā' / May you have your meal with gladness and health!

Smacznego! / Enjoy your meal!*

---

* Is it only in the English language that there is no greeting for eaters embarking on a meal?

Chapter Two:

MODERN

It's true that modernity *is* normality for all of us alive in Scotland today. 'Normal' food *is* modern food. But what the hell is 'modernity'? Tracing backwards from today's normality, we find a trail of crumbs strewn through books on philosophy, economics and literature: the ideas that we consider the essence of modern life all came from specific influential individuals. Throughout modernity, an economic trend called capitalism played out in the colonisation of lands and people overseas. This same trend shaped Scotland's social and natural landscapes at home, as the novel financial fashion took hold in Highland estate ledgers and city merchants' offices. Watching these landscapes shift, we can see the soft bones of contemporary Scottish food culture emerging through the cobbles and bracken like a skeleton through X-ray.

Thoughts make real things happen. Philosophers, and their colleagues in literature, the arts and modern media, are like society's computer programmers, writing the code that structures our minds. Early 'Enlightenment' thinkers believed that the natural world existed quite apart from human beings, that natural 'resources' were infinite, and that we humans were above and beyond nature's influences. (That exact same rationale places men above women and considers white people superior to Black and brown.) The normal food we eat today is still produced and traded according to this logic. But natural resources are running out and the planet's physical limits are breached. The way the world's power and privilege are skewed today, and the climate crisis we are living through, are the parallel results of the last 500 years of philosophical and economic fashion. If thoughts make real things happen, we need to tell new stories.

As a disillusioned nineteen-year-old, I quit a degree in philosophy and started cooking for a living instead. Since then I've been strung between the immediate sensual gratification of a day in the kitchen – the physicality of rolling kilos of butter pastry, scrubbing floors and hefting lamb carcasses – and the theory of life. This book is a product of that tension, hung from the centre of the tightrope.

I've spent my adult life working with food in some capacity or other, including through a degree in food policy. But I had no idea about the medieval divine right of kings, which was the great organising force for society prior to the rise of capitalism, and how this assumption would have affected the diet of every person in the European Middle Ages, including Scots (and most significantly, how it still does in the twenty-first century). Nor had I ever even considered how we got from there to today's normal: the brutal transition from a communal management of landscapes, with rights to their produce shared by every commoner, to enclosed, privatised property, and the massive shift in thinking that entailed. And yet this shift determines how very ordinary lives just *are,* today. It's *this* contemporary reasoning that influences how you get to eat what you eat, or don't get to eat at all.

'Modern', then, has two meanings relevant to our story, this investigation of Scots food history: as a reference to the period of time called 'modernity' and to society's 'most current ideas and practices'.[1] As historian Chris Bayley explains: 'Modernisation is both a process by which those who aspire to be modern borrow from and emulate those they believe to be modern, and a period in which the centralised nation-state, increasing global, commercial and intellectual links, industrialisation and urban living go hand in hand.'[2]

One of the events that heralded the modern era was the invention of the printing press by Johannes Gutenberg in around 1436. Having a machine that could print hundreds or thousands of copies of a document – a cookbook, say – meant suddenly knowledge and information could spread, contagious as a virus, and unite ordinary people across broad space and long time.* Stories united 'imagined communities'[3] across countries and continents, through the spread of literature and newspapers. This was also the start of national identity – actually the start of 'nations' themselves. The printing press was the single greatest precursor to the greatest social shift in over 1,000 years. Without it, there could be no Enlightenment; no light bulbs and no light-bulb moments.

As societies shift, so does the way they eat. Before the printing

---

* Gutenberg's greatest achievement was the first print run of the Bible, in Latin. He died penniless, without a ready market for most of the books.

press, when grand civilisations died or dispersed their ways of cooking often died with them. In pre-industrial civilisations, wealth was the exclusive preserve of those with political or religious power, so the employers of professional cooks were kings, aristocrats or priests. The most highly developed cuisines were those of the upper classes, who would have had the power and money to ensure things were written down, laboriously, by scribes. But reliance on written documents made these elaborate cuisines vulnerable. In fact, one way that European colonisers achieved dominance in the lands they invaded was by burning hand-written books and documents. With few alternative copies in existence, cultural eradication was easy enough to achieve.

By contrast, peasant food culture worldwide was better preserved because the knowledge was spoken, and real living skills were handed down through generations: herring-salting, mole-pounding, dough-folding; pickling vegetables and hanging hams. Ordinary cuisines were practised daily from breakfast to suppertime. Peasant society made the kitchen a repository for skills and knowledge.

The printing press would invert this power balance. Throughout modernity, from the 1500s till the twentieth century, the cooking techniques and recipes that were most securely archived document the practices of the literate classes, in Scotland as elsewhere. You had to be able to cook fairly elaborate dishes to need a cookbook; you had to have a kitchen, or employ a cook, or both. You also need to be able to read to have use for a book, and it took until the twentieth century for literacy to be available for all.

Meanwhile, back in the fifteenth century the scribes were in open rebellion. Their way of life, skills and income were in jeopardy! In reality, the printing press gave rise to many more industries than the scribes could've imagined. Graphic designers, illustrators, typesetters, book-binders and booksellers, professional readers, journalists, teachers, cookery and food-writers – and every literate person alive today – can all be grateful that the scribes' campaigns to suppress the printing press failed. Just because we can't predict the outcome of technological change doesn't mean we should fear it. Rather, perhaps, we should be wary of who's holding the levers.

Around the same time as the printing press was rolling out its first sheets, merchants and the moneyed class were starting to think differently about how to trade with an increasingly wide world.

Capitalism now feels so much part of normality that it is hard to tease it apart from our culture and sense of self. And it is hard to see what else there would be: if I critique capitalism, must I be arguing *for* communism? Must I be arguing for a back-to-the-land pastoral idyll that couldn't possibly feed the world's 8 billion people (and rising – if you want to see how quickly, check out the Worldometer)?[4]

Take a normal trip to the modern supermarket. You go in, you choose what you want, you leave. Right? Except . . . how free *is* that choice? The goods aren't dumped arbitrarily in the aisles – their presence, appearance and positioning are a result of hundreds of decisions made by people, back through supply chains linking your shopping basket to farms in Africa, shipping containers in China, oilfields in Iraq, design studios in London, offices in Brussels, boardrooms in Switzerland and walls of computers on Wall Street. Everyone wants a say in what you eat. And they're in it for the money.

But capitalism, it turns out, is not trade itself; trade has been around for as long as humans. Trade is about cooperation and shared values, what we have versus what we need.

When people ask us if we'd open 'other Invers', they are asking us if we'd engage in the thing that makes capitalism its peculiar self. Capitalism is a system for concentrating wealth. Profit from one venture is invested in new ventures in order to keep producing more profit, a process called accumulation. Profit is achieved partly by paying workers less than the value of their work, so that the 'work' (meaning a bottle of wine, a bag of potatoes, your dinner in a restaurant) can be sold, and the excess harvested by the owner of the means of production (the farm, factory, supermarket or restaurant) to be invested yet again. An alternative is to pay workers *exactly* the value of their work, meaning profit is spread equitably between workers rather than reinvested to the benefit of owners only. It's a profit-share, social enterprise or employee-ownership model of generating wealth.

Once a year our accountant judges our performance based on how much money we have made. He's not interested in how much we spent on the staff summer day out, or that we put wages up well ahead of inflation. In capitalism, profit itself is given its own worth (an 'exchange value'), rather than being appreciated for what we humans need money to *do* for us (a 'use value': such as building the Pyramids or Edinburgh Castle, farms or hospitals or schools). When the value of money is unhitched from what we need it *for*, there is no such thing as *enough*; all of the earth's resources, including human beings, are fair game. Contrast with how nature does growth: to maturity, ripeness and natural limits.[5]

* * *

Capitalism was the first draft of an economic system for a globalised, industrialised planet, and like most first drafts, it's far from perfect.

The Scottish economist Adam Smith (known as the 'Father of Capitalism') published his treatise *The Wealth of Nations*, the starting point of modern economic theory, in 1776. It was Smith who first articulated Gross Domestic Product (GDP) as a measurement of a country's 'output', expanding the measures of a country's wealth from simply its gold and silver stores to include all the products of its nascent industries, which these days means everything from primary production (like farming or energy) to factories, supermarkets and restaurants. Of course, in 1776 it was easier to believe that the natural world had unlimited resources to feed the factories, and no one knew what all that unleashed carbon was doing to the climate. Diet-related ill health was mainly down to a lack of nutrients, not too many of the wrong ones.

We know now that the planet can't handle all we're throwing at it, and natural resources are not infinite. Even before Smith penned his treatise, the growth of capitalism had its detractors. Swiss-French philosopher Jean-Jacques Rousseau (1712–78) wrote:

> The first man who, having fenced in a piece of land, said 'This is mine', and found people naive enough to believe him, that man was the true founder of civil society . . . From how many crimes, wars, and murders, from how many horrors and misfortunes might not any one have saved mankind, by pulling up the stakes, or filling up the ditch, and crying to his fellows: Beware of listening to this impostor; you are undone if you once forget that the

fruits of the earth belong to us all, and the earth itself to nobody.[6]

Adam Smith may have fathered capitalism, but no parent knows crib-side what havoc or joy their child will wreak. Even Smith had concerns about where capitalism seemed to be headed; he warned about income equality and that capitalist owners and landlords would become rich at the expense of the workers' quality of life. He spoke out against unregulated workplaces, child labour and long working hours. Smith knew that short-term profit maximisation could jeopardise longer-term, sustainable behaviour.

The government, said Smith, should provide public goods that the 'market' might not safeguard; ensure a fair legal system; hold corporations accountable and enforce contracts. Without laws to restrict them, monopolies of powerful companies could dominate a market and reduce competition, manipulate prices, and ultimately harm consumers. Smith knew that a capitalist system needed to be properly regulated and guided by ethics to lead to prosperity for *all*. He knew that the marketplace's 'invisible hands', turning individual self-interest to collective well-being, needed some pretty sturdy legislative and regulatory gloves. Maybe in fact this father knew his son too well.

Back at Inver, I prefer to buy organic produce wherever possible, to ensure that climate, wildlife, topsoil and waterways are protected from the effects of nitrogen fertilisers and pesticides, even though this produce costs our business more. I look on the higher price as a way of incorporating all the environmental costs of production and paying a more honest price, rather than extracting freebies from the soil. This is where the price on our menu comes from: the whole cost of our ingredients (and of our labour, because the staff are also treated fairly).

'Externalities' is an economist's term for the side effects of production whose costs are not factored into the sale price of a good. Artificial nitrogen fertiliser and chemical pesticides – key ingredients in modern industrial food and farming – take a huge amount of energy to produce and distribute. They are kept relatively cheap because the fossil fuels they depend on are also kept artificially cheap, by the use of government subsidies and other favours to the gas and oil industries.[7] The fossil fuel industry, however, has enormous adverse effects on society and our environment: air pollution, greenhouse gas emissions and related climate collapse, the destruction of fragile ecosystems and disruption to human lives. The costs of all these things are not factored into the price of gas, oil, petrol, diesel, coal – or into any of the things these fuels produce, such as plastic packaging, chemical fertiliser and pesticides. So food produced in large-scale industrial farming systems appears cheap, but when *all* the costs are counted, it's anything but.

Fuel and farming subsidies like this are actually a transfer from the 'public purse' – citizens' own money – to the individuals who make money from the production and distribution of cheap food: industrial farming corporations, food processing companies, energy companies and supermarkets. 'Intensive agriculture has been subsidised to help wreck ecosystems,' says my old professor of food policy, Tim Lang.[8] If the full price of industrial food production was factored into the bill, low-input 'organic' systems would not seem elitist; they'd be cheaper than industrialised farming. The problem isn't that organic food is expensive – it's that non-organic food is unrealistically cheap.

And then take trees. We do every day. We take all the things trees do that human beings literally couldn't live without – air and water purification, carbon storage, habitat creation; not to mention the beauty in wooded landscapes and their deep cool shade on a sunny day. 'Centuries of their falling leaves have built this soil,' says professor of environmental biology and member of the Potawatomi Nation, Robin Wall Kimmerer. Without the soil, there are no farms, no food. Yet these 'ecosystem services' are given no representation in our economy. What should we give the trees back? asks Professor Kimmerer.[9]

Even capitalism's winners think the system isn't working. Jeremy Grantham, the British hedge-fund Goliath who predicted the last two major market bubbles, believes that 'the capitalist beast is out of control, and it doesn't owe any responsibility to the society it lives in, the town, the state or the country even'.[10] Capitalism, says Grantham, is killing the planet and needs to change. He feels that the economy has lost its social bonds. 'We deforest the land, we degrade our soils, we pollute and overuse our water and treat air like an open sewer, and we do it all off the balance sheet. Capitalism and mainstream economics simply cannot deal with these problems.'[11]

What we have on this planet is already more than we need for everyone on it to live comfortably. The richest 1 per cent capture 25 per cent of global GDP each year. This means a quarter of all economic 'growth' (the labour, resources and energy) happens to make the richest people even richer.[12] Meanwhile 50 per cent of the global population – mostly in the global south – get just 5 per cent of that global profit. With this inequitable access to wealth comes terrible consequences: chasms in life expectancy, health and well-being, and a living planet that is struggling to process all the shit we throw at it – a planet we all need to stay healthy in order for humankind to function, never mind thrive.

In his *Theory of Moral Sentiments*, Adam Smith stated that the value of any government is 'judged in proportion to the extent that it makes its people happy'. But GDP is about quantity of wealth – not quality of life. Today, unlimited growth is an outdated proxy for measuring societies who have already passed the point of having *enough*. The problem now is how to distribute what we have better, so *everybody* is better off.

All food production needs land. All living things need food. So land is power. Land, it turns out, was the kindling for the earliest capitalist fires. The first 'free' ingredient.

A capitalist needs free or very cheap inputs in order to generate substantial profit – it's the free stuff that essentially becomes the profit. The land enclosures of medieval Europe transformed the countryside from 'the commons', where the ordinary people had entitlement to make their own living, into private property. The medieval enclosures created a condition of 'artificial scarcity': suddenly there wasn't land enough to go round, so those without had to pay those who had the thing they needed, be that food, housing or water – all the things you need land *for*. The enclosures did two things to boost capitalism: the theft of land was the original accumulation that allowed some people to reinvest their wealth. (Karl Marx called this 'primitive accumulation' to honour its barbaric, inelegant violence.) And it provided lots and lots of cheap, desperate labour for whatever happened next.

After enclosure, rural peasants who were still on the land now had no rights to it, written or unwritten. For the first time, the words 'poverty', 'pauper' and 'vagabond' appeared in common use in the English language. No longer was food production about satisfying human needs within the limits of the land; instead, it was about extracting what could be taken in the cheapest way possible to allow the greatest profit for the 'owners' of the land. Meanwhile, in the swelling cities, economic migrants and refugees were many and jobs were few, driving down the cost of labour. The new urban peasants had to work sixteen hours a day, sometimes seven days a week, significantly more than under feudalism.[13] Health records plummeted.

And how did this play out in the food culture of the time? After nascent capitalists enclosed the land at home, they turned to land and lives abroad.* Colonialism's first thefts were land and people, then the spices, sugar, tea, cotton and tobacco,[14] which in turn fuelled the factories and their workers back home – a win-win for the new owner class.

For over 200 years, stolen human lives stoked capitalism's growth, and there are monuments to this brutality in our recipe books and food culture, as in our street signs and statues. They're rippled through Scots' famed baking heritage and sweet tooth: black bun, Dundee cake, shortbread, tablet; the cup of

---

* Socialist and communist countries founded empires on stolen land too – though 'for the good of their people' rather than private gain.

tea that goes with it all. We Scots are indebted to stolen land and labour for ingredients that have defined what Scotland *tastes* like. We owe thanks to unimaginable human suffering for our 'comfort foods'.

Scotland played a significant part in the transatlantic slave trade. Glasgow was a busy river port with an established shipbuilding industry, well-placed to exploit this new overseas market and become Britain's second economic centre: the Merchant City. Glasgow and Greenock became major sugar refining locations. Glasgow (with London, Bristol and Liverpool) formed the third corner of the 'triangular trade' in which sailing ships following the trade winds took enslaved people from Africa to the Americas and West Indies; sugar, tobacco and cotton from the American and Caribbean colonies to European factories; and goods like linen, rum, porcelain, salt pork and herring on the return journey from Europe to markets in the colonies.

From the first crossing to the Americas in 1525 till the slave trade was abolished in the late nineteenth century, the slave ships transported an estimated 12.5 million people across the Atlantic Ocean between the west coast of Africa and the Americas – the notorious 'middle passage'. These traumatic journeys were full of squalor and horror. In his book *The Interesting Narrative of the Life of Olaudah Equiano*, former enslaved man Equiano spoke of hundreds of men, women and children in dark confinement, chained by leg clamps ('bilboes'), most having never been on the sea before, for months at a time. The wooden boards were awash with vomit, urine and faeces, open sores festered and damp flesh rotted. Constant moans and wailing were indistinguishable from the whipping winds and groaning timbers. Disease spread rapidly, suicide was a form of resistance, and uprisings were common. The voyage was part of the process of dehumanisation, a necessary step to ensure that people were 'seasoned' to their new lives. Torture, abuse and rape continued on the plantations. A child born into slavery became a slave.

Glasgow's Jamaica Street and Virginia Street, Buchanan Street, Ingram Street, Glassford Street, George Square and Merchant City, amongst others, were all named for the link to the slave trade.[15] In Edinburgh, streets are named for Henry Dundas, one of the most powerful Tory politicians of the late eighteenth century. He was first commissioner and then president of the East India Company, from 1784 to 1801, where he escalated appointments of crony Scots to Indian positions. Dundas was nicknamed 'the Great Tyrant'. Choosing his economic and political interests over the escalating head count of enslaved African people, he played a key part in delaying the abolition of slavery from 1792 until 1807.[16] Dundas Street and the 150-foot statue of the man himself in St Andrew Square commemorate someone who sanctioned atrocities across the Caribbean.

Scotland's involvement with enslavement has gone largely unacknowledged in Scottish culture. Glasgow University archaeologist and history lecturer Dr Peggy Brunache, who has lived in Scotland since 2006, reports that 'Scots were over-represented on sugar and coffee plantation landscapes, across all class boundaries . . . 70% of Scottish surnames belonging to modern Jamaicans descended from enslaved communities'.[17] The substantial profit made from enslavement contributed to turning Scotland from a relatively poor country prior to 1750, to an economy that rivalled (and briefly surpassed) England's, with Glasgow becoming the British Empire's second financial capital. Scots were up to their eyeballs in the slave trade. Profits from stolen land and labour overseas built modern Scotland – and enslaved labour built our food culture.

The trade in enslaved African people dovetailed with the tectonic shifts in land-ownership in the Highlands and Islands of Scotland during the eighteenth and nineteenth centuries – shifts that shape the landscape and culture you experience living and travelling in rural, modern Scotland today.[18] Under the terms of the Abolition of Slavery Act 1833, a pot of £16 billion (in today's money) was paid to enslavers for the loss of their 'property' (the freed people) by the British government,[19] and some of this money bought Highland land. In fact, one 2020 report found that two-thirds of the land in the Highlands and Islands was either bought or improved by wealth generated by enslaved labour.[20] The new wealthy elite who were buying the estates also escalated the eviction of the indigenous people – the Gaels, who had maintained the landscape and culture for centuries. Journalist Robert Somers visited one such area after the famine of 1847. After describing the 'miserable and filthy huts' of Glenshiel's inhabitants, and the labour they were obliged to give to the tacksmen (middle-management rent collectors), Somers concluded pointedly: 'It is preposterous to talk of slavery being abolished in the British dominions.'[21] Buying Highland estates was a way of 'laundering' ill-got money, purifying the cash and the capitalist both. The new romanticism of Highland life and land in the 1800s enabled successful merchants and 'owners' of enslaved people and lands overseas to give themselves an alternative identity and sense of self back home.

Meanwhile, Scotswomen slow-baked shortbread, jammed summer berries and stirred tablet into spoon-seizing clots. Floss Marian McNeill, author of *The Scots Kitchen* (1929), reckoned that 'one of the special skills in the Scots kitchen is sweet making and sugar work'. Sugar has always been desirable. We humans can't make sugar: plants make sugar (sucrose) photosynthetically, from sunshine. Sugarcane, the most important plant from which sucrose is extracted, was domesticated about twelve millennia ago, one of the very first plants to be intentionally grown by settling humans.

Originally, sweets in Britain were about showing off. The Countess of Sutherland,* ascribed the honour of having written Scotland's first personal, manuscript cookbook (1683), dedicated it to preserving fruits and jellies – all using masses of sugar. The 350-year-old book is barely legible but on every page there's a mention of sugar or syrup.[22] It's not a coincidence that the author was a member of a wealthy class; seventeenth-century sugar was expensive, rare and aspirational.

The popularity of cheaper cane sugar from the colonies saw an increase in baking and the start of a catalogue of recipes for cakes, biscuits and sweets. The cheap energy in a cup of sweet tea in turn kept the factory cogs churning at home. When the British government removed the import duty on sugar in 1874, it became cheap enough for most people to enjoy in their tea or coffee, or in the form of sweets or jam. Without the free labour of enslaved people to subsidise the cost of cane sugar, however, by the 1880s it was European-based sugar-beet farming that provided two-thirds of the world supply. Britons were soon consuming twice as much beet as cane sugar; and

---

* Helen, Countess of Sutherland (née Cochrane), was also associated with the most brutal and comprehensive clearances, in Sutherland. She and her vilified factor and sheep-farmer Patrick Sellar relocated nearly 15,000 people before Sellar was tried for culpable homicide (though acquitted).

MODERN

a third more total sugar in 1900 than in the twenty years previously.[23]

The traditional Scots 'high tea' dates from around the 1800s: an Arbroath smokie or boiled ham and buttered new potatoes, followed by scones, jams and fruit cakes full of imported dried fruit, sugar and spices. During my late-twentieth-century childhood, on a visit to Great Auntie Ann in Leven, Fife, the little tea trolley was wheeled in laden with lemon sponge, coffee and walnut cake, iced fruit slices, scones, pancakes and the occasional teacake. All home-baked, served with a pot of tea and with glass dishes of homemade soft-fruit jam. (It's only now that I realise how much time, money and effort went into this display of lavish hospitality from someone living in council-sponsored housing on a state pension.) I have inherited Auntie Ann's cookbooks: a collection of hand-written notebooks, spines slouched with age, stuffed with cuttings from magazines and newspaper supplements advertising Milk Marketing Board butter, weekly rations updates, Be-Ro flour or Stork margarine. They span one-fifth of modernity.

Sugar is a perfect example of a 'modern' ingredient. The sticky trail back from the sugar bowl shows the way capitalism disregards costs in pursuit of profit. Today, sugar in Scotland is easily accessible, and cheap. 'We eat too much, we sell too much, we grow too much, and we import too much,' says campaign group Action on Sugar. In the modern supermarket, sugary drinks, breakfast cereals and snacks are sold on promotion, in bright-coloured wrappers, strategically placed at the till and at children's eye level. Campaigners fight to get all the costs of sugar consumption onto the till receipt: soft drinks taxes, sugar levies and calorie counts on packaging hint at the unpaid health bills. This is where Adam Smith saw the role of government: setting the legal backdrop for what companies and countries are allowed to do, to balance profit with the well-being of people and planet.

In the UK, just two major players monopolise sugar. Tate & Lyle Sugars is the only importer of raw cane sugar to the UK. The other, British Sugar, uses sugar beet mostly grown industrially in East Anglia and the East Midlands, supplemented with sugar from EU and non-EU countries 'to meet demand'.[24] Historically Tate & Lyle has been a recipient of the largest EU Common Agricultural Policy farming subsidies, despite their billion-pound annual revenue.[25] In 2005, company secretary Robert Gibber explained that these payments go via Tate & Lyle to the sugar producers in least-developed countries – which means that, pre-Brexit, public money was routinely spent subsidising the price paid for cane sugar by a multinational corporation.[26] Tate & Lyle was one of the few large UK-based businesses to lobby for a 'hard' Brexit (meaning Britain would sign its own international trade deals after leaving Europe in 2020), and now benefits from the UK government's autonomous tariff quota, which allows tariff-free imports of cane sugar produced in Australia and Brazil – countries with far lower environmental standards than the UK and the EU.[27] Australia still uses toxic, bee-killing neonicotinoid pesticides, long banned in Europe, and Brazil has recently overturned a ban on growing sugar cane in the Amazon rainforest. This disadvantages UK sugar-beet farmers, and once more 'offshores' the UK's environmental responsibilities.[28] 'Common' land rights, health and cash are diverted to private profit. Tate & Lyle Sugars also sponsored the lanyards at the 2017 Conservative Party Conference.[29]

Buying sugar for the restaurant is difficult. My choice is

either organic-certified imported cane sugar or industrially grown British beet sugar. Both come with uncounted 'externalities'. A British Sugar report in 2004 showed that organically grown sugar beet was viable, but claimed that the demand was not there.[30] What I understand by this is that BS anticipates that consumers won't pay the organic premium for a product they expect to be cheap, and that BS are unwilling to sacrifice maximum profit to protect our common environment. Consumers can of course only buy what is available to them – it's hard to gauge demand for a product that doesn't exist.

Consigning the past to history serves to distract us from what is *still* going on. To see how globalisation is eating away at the commons, grabbing the freebies as it goes, take chocolate, one of Scotland's favourite treats.[31] Rainforests are a global common – all of us depend on them – but West African forests are cut down in great swathes for cocoa production.

The world's love of chocolate is a major cause of the destruction of tropical forests – and chocolate supply chains map the route that modern money travels from the global south to north, producing inequalities in wealth *and* health. Satellite imagery shows that, since 2000, cocoa has been responsible for 360,000 of a total 962,000 hectares (37.4 per cent) of the deforestation of protected areas in Ivory Coast, and 26,000 out of 193,000 hectares (13.5 per cent) of the deforestation of similar areas in Ghana.[32] Clearing West African tropical forests displaces massive amounts of climate-ravaging CO_2 from the soil.

These long and winding Big Cocoa supply chains also hide enslaved children. There are an estimated 2 million children working on chocolate farms on the west coast of Africa. Dr Michael Odijie of the London School of Economics explains that deforestation drives cocoa producers to resort to enslaved children for their labour needs.[33] How? Clearing forest initially exposes rich, fertile ground, while also displacing the communities who live there. As the soil is depleted, it takes more labour to produce the same amount of crop. When other competing plantations clear forest to plant cocoa, thus increasing cocoa availability and depressing prices, the struggling producers are pressured to clear more forest and start again. 'In sum, while deforestation leads to less labour availability, more labour is needed,' says Dr Odijie.[34] Unpaid adult and child labour is thus built in to the cocoa industry in the Ivory Coast and Ghana, from where nearly two-thirds of the world's cocoa now comes. So endemic is it that modern slavery is sometimes referred to as 'chocolate's hidden ingredient'.

In 2021, seven of the world's biggest chocolate companies, including Nestlé, Mars, Barry Callebaut and Hershey, were taken to court by eight former enslaved children. All eight, now young adults, relayed a story disturbingly similar to first-hand accounts of the transatlantic slave trade from centuries ago: they were kidnapped or coerced from their homes in Mali, trafficked to the Ivory Coast, and forced to work for several years without pay, doing dangerous jobs without protective clothing (such as using machetes, land clearing, and applying pesticides). They were kept without travel documents and isolated from anyone speaking their own language or dialect, with no clear idea of how they could return to their families.[35] The Washington court dismissed the case, citing concerns that locating culpability for child labour between the farms employing the children and the companies eventually buying the cocoa 'could leave too many people liable for forced child labor, including consumers and retailers who might benefit from lower prices'.[36]

The Ivory Coast alone produces around 45 per cent of the world's cocoa beans, but receives only around 4 per cent of the chocolate industry's estimated annual worth of $100 *billion*. The trade relies on a famously 'opaque' supply chain, full of middlemen who connect mostly small-scale cocoa farmers to the global marketplace. These farmers are vulnerable to the drought, pests and diseases that could destroy a harvest, plus global price fluctuations (meaning those rational or irrational reactions to world events by human traders). Farmers receive a pitiful 6 per cent of the chocolate bar's eventual retail price, despite doing the back-breaking, risky work of producing the essential ingredient of chocolate. The side-stepping of the real price paid for cocoa on this scale keeps the region artificially impoverished, the profits of Big Cocoa artificially high, and puts pressure on farmers to clear more rainforest. 'The bigger players in the chocolate and cocoa sector could easily pay farmers more . . . and still make a decent profit,' says Paul Schoenmakers, former Head of Impact at 'slave-free' Dutch chocolatier Tony's Chocolonely. 'In the end, it's a matter of choice, whether you want to maximise your profits at the expense of extreme poverty.'[37]

Chocolate-lovers who also value people can certainly avoid the big brands who buy untraceable West African cocoa, and support brands who buy direct from farmers or can certify their supply chain. But eradicating child slavery and ensuring profit is distributed more equally must also be the responsibility of governments, chocolate manufacturers of all scales, and cocoa commodity traders. In 2020, both the Ivory Coast and Ghana introduced the Living Income Differential (LID) – a $400 premium placed on every tonne of cocoa and transferred directly to the smallholder farmers. But chocolate companies such as Hershey are finding ways to avoid paying.[38] In a global-scale supply chain, robust international regulation is the force that should balance the capitalist's 'rational' pursuit of profit and put a price on the 'externality' of using a rainforest to produce a KitKat. Adam Smith says so, remember?

At Inver, we buy chocolate from Lara and Cameron at Bare Bones Chocolate in Glasgow, who buy cocoa direct from farmers' co-operatives in Madagascar, Honduras and the Dominican Republic, paying well over the market fair-trade price and avoiding the middlemen mark-ups. Every stage of the chocolate-making is done by hand in their small workshop in Glasgow, from the roasting of the organic cocoa beans to the folding of the recycled packaging, thus paying their dues to the planet. Unlike much industrial chocolate, which can contain as little as 20 per cent cocoa (bulked up and bound with even cheaper soy, vegetable fats and sugar), all Bare Bones chocolate is utterly delicious, with natural flavour profiles including dates, maple syrup, fudge and cherries. Connecting with Lara and Cameron and their network of global ingredients unites me and Inver with the kind of real-life economy the planet and its people could sustain, at home and overseas. The chocolate *is* relatively expensive. But chocolate is a treat, not a staple, and I don't feel that I'm entitled to treats at the expense of other people's and the planet's well-being. I'm buying for the restaurant, however, so the additional cost is written into the menu and recouped from paying customers. A step further would be to support chocolate-making in the countries that grow the cocoa: most of chocolate's 'added value' is in the making, not the growing, so more of this profit could stay where it's most needed.

In the early years of Inver, we created a dessert all about the chocolate and that iconic Scots ingredient, barley, in a collaboration with our local brewery Fyne Ales, using products and flavours from the brewery.* It was a warm chocolate mousse, with malted-barley ice cream, a beremeal and roasted-barley koji crumble (tasting like ripe bananas), and 'beer bubbles' – a bitter, frothy foam to counter all the fat and sweetness. It made it to the main menu too. Our local pig farmer, Bruce, took a particular liking to it. When Bruce died a few years later we reinstated it on the menu in his honour, and his wife, Rhona, came in for lunch to enjoy it again. Our menu is still deeply contoured by our own personal landscapes.

Right at the beginning of modernity, the French philosopher and mathematician René Descartes introduced the idea of mind–body 'dualism' into an already stratified society. And it's because of habitual Cartesian dualism that we still talk about 'nature' as something apart from us, rather than something we are inextricably entwined and co-dependent with. Cartesian dualism is a conceptual separation of mind ('thinking substance') and body ('extended substance'). Men, said Descartes, were unique in having a mind – this showed their closeness to the creator, God. Women, animals, uncivilised folk from other cultures, and nature itself, existed on a continuum away from God. Then, like Plato had before him, Descartes took the five physiological senses and listed them in order of importance, from eyes to fingertips, according to how reliably they relayed

---

* We'd just made the country's first (in recent times) spontaneously fermented sour beer, Beer Première, and used the dinner to launch it.

information to this thinking mind. Sight and hearing were top of the Cartesian pile. Touch, scent and taste were René's second-grade senses.

As a mathematician, Descartes saw the natural world as a matter of geometry, the line drawings of a machine. This mechanistic idea of both nature and body gave permission to tinker: if it's only a soulless machine, without consciousness or the ability to feel pain, or rights and presence in the world of its own, then it's just a 'resource' to use as we need. To prove his point, he nailed live dogs to boards and cut into them to see their workings, insisting that the writhing, screaming animals did not feel pain, that the movements were just the turning cogs in a machine. (Rumour has it one of these dogs belonged to his wife. I guess, as a woman, her pain wasn't real either.)

Descartes was highly influential in Europe and beyond. People began to see 'Mother Nature' as an insensate machine. The twentieth-century rise of the banana, now the world's favourite fruit, is a product of that conceptual transformation of nature.

'The story of the banana is really the story of modern agriculture exemplified in a single fruit,' says Daniel Bebber, who leads the BananEx research group at the University of Exeter. Almost all (99 per cent) of the bananas in global circulation are a variety called the Cavendish, but there are many, many more kinds of banana. Cavendish has qualities that suit global distribution, making it a poster-fruit for the modern world. It's high-yielding, can be picked while green and firm – making it easier to transport without bruising – and is relatively disease-resistant. Every Cavendish banana you pick up in a store, anywhere in the world, is also genetically identical to every other Cavendish banana. It's a clone: each new banana plant comes from a cutting from another banana plant.

The world's bananas are therefore a monoculture, and incredibly vulnerable to pest or disease. The last globalised banana, the Gros Michel, was wiped out in the 1950s by Panama disease. Sure enough, another strain of Panama disease was confirmed in Colombia in 2019, called Tropical Race 4 (TR4). Colombia's economy relies heavily on the crop (as do Ecuador, Costa Rica and Guatemala) and the country declared a national state of emergency in August 2019.[39] 'TR4 is a "doomsday" scenario for bananas,'[40] says filmmaker Jackie Turner, who produced a film about the emergency. The related 'Banana List' helps banana lovers find more unusual varieties, like Dwarf Red, Lady Fingers and Blue Java (which apparently tastes like vanilla ice cream).[41]

Bebber reports that organic farms in the Philippines have fared better against TR4 because the microbiota in the soil are able to fight the infection. He says banana farms should be looking at adding organic matter, and perhaps planting seasonal crops between rows to increase shelter and fertility, using microbes and insects rather than chemicals as 'biocontrols' and leaving more wild patches to encourage wildlife.[42] Mimicking what Mother Nature does herself, in other words.

Descartes claimed that the senses were a thing apart from mind and body, and that they could be teased apart and graded. Both this and his assertion that animals are less able to perceive the world intelligently have been well and truly quashed. The modern science of phenomenology shows our senses are in fact *all* interconnected, and it is through our physical brain that we experience them in all their glory. Scientific advances since Descartes' era show that, in fact, animals *do* have self-consciousness and an intimate, coherent intelligence, and can have emotions that are meaningfully similar to our own. In 2012, a prominent international group of cognitive neuroscientists, neuropharmacologists, neurophysiologists, neuroanatomists and computational neuroscientists gathered at the University of Cambridge to draft the Cambridge Declaration on Consciousness. 'The weight of evidence indicates that humans are not unique in possessing the neurological substrates that generate consciousness. Non-human animals, including all mammals and birds, and many other creatures, including octopuses, also possess these neurological substrates.'[43]

Even at the time Descartes was writing, the Dutch-Jewish philosopher Spinoza was calling him out. Spinoza reckoned that all matter (God, soul, human, nature) was made of the same stuff, and must have originated from the same place (these days we call it the Big Bang). He was promptly branded a heretic and expelled from both Jewish and Christian communities. The implications of Spinoza's theory for the powerful groups of the time were catastrophically castrating: if humans were made of the same stuff as nature and God, we'd have no rights to go plundering landscapes. It would be tantamount to raping and pillaging God. It is Spinoza that today gets recognition for being ahead of his time.

We live in a world shaped by this modern iteration of dualist assumptions: damage to languages and cultures worldwide, the ecological crisis and the accompanying imbalance of power and wealth can all be traced back to the musings of one man and his yowling dog. It's ironic that Descartes was actually attempting to philosophically *unify* human experience. Dualism has split the whole world in two.

Descartes was not, of course, alone – his voice is one of many that helped articulate and shape society's experience of itself in early modernity. Another voice still incredibly influential today is John Locke's.

I first heard the name during my political philosophy classes at Edinburgh University.* An English political philosopher, Locke was a young man when Descartes died. In Locke's time, the king or queen was God's representative on earth, and Church was closely intertwined with State: religious leaders played a crucial role in legitimising the rule of the monarch, who in turn chose them. Below the tiny aristocracy and a growing merchant class were the peasants and commoners who made up the bulky mass of society. Implicit in this was a value system: humans were not equal. Rights were not for all. There was no social mobility. The strata of society would stay separate, the rich floating like black oil on common waters.

The arguments about human rights that emerged in Locke's writings during this period had a very specific origin: they began as a repudiation of the divine right of kings. As a schoolboy in 1649, Locke had watched in the crowd as King Charles I was executed. As he grew up, King Charles II, King of Scotland, England and Ireland, and his brother James, were investing heavily in the slave trade. Locke joined the dots: slavery and monarchical rule were operating in tandem. His *Two Treatises of Government* (1689) argued against the very root of enslavement: 'Slavery is so vile and miserable an estate of man . . . that 'tis hardly to be conceived' that anyone would support it. Instead, the 'natural state' of man was to be free and equal. Locke's position on slavery (and social hierarchy)

---

* Political philosophy is all about the relationship between the individual and the state.

therefore seems pretty clear. The big 'but' comes when you remember that Descartes' philosophical legacy was simultaneously alive and well: all the people in question were not 'men' in the same way as Europeans were. It was the white male alone who had these rights.

This included a man's right to take land that was empty ('terra nullius'), and by his own labour transform this land into 'property'. Although Locke spoke about equality of men, he also talked about 'natural hierarchies' based on use of reason and intelligence, thus taking up Descartes' baton and handing it to the colonialists.

When the colonialists first landed on the shores of what is now called America and Australasia, they saw an empty land. Australian land was of course *not* empty to the 250 different Aboriginal peoples who had been living on it for 80,000 years prior to the arrival of the white European.[44] This is an indication of the colonists' ecological illiteracy, not an accurate reading of what was actually going on. Today we think of land as either 'farmed' (and we know what that looks like) or 'wild'. But there is another way, and it is the way that most peoples of the non-European world (the majority of the planet's population) were following for the several millennia prior to the start of capitalist land-grabs.

In *Tending the Wild*, M. Kat Anderson describes the abundance that greeted the first settler-colonialists in what is now called California: fertile valleys teeming with deer, elk and bison, wild edible plants and mushrooms; rivers full of great fishes, shorelines darkened by huge flocks of wild geese and ducks.[45] This was not agriculture as the Europeans knew it, but nor was it 'wilderness': the land had been *tended*. The indigenous Californian people had cultivated the vast landscapes using millennia-old techniques: by burning, by gathering in the right season and in the right quantity, by recycling nutrients and maintaining the fertility of the soil, by irrigating, pruning and coppicing, sowing, tilling, and controlling insects and pathogens. When you know how to read the land, you can see that Native Americans had, in fact, 'a sophisticated understanding of the inner workings of nature and acted deliberately to sustain, not degrade ecological systems'. Their interactions with nature were a true *relationship*, showing 'reciprocity, continuity, familiarity and continual learning'.[46]

Similarly, when the first prison ship landed on Australia, the settlers found an ancient, abundant, technologically advanced civilisation. Early observers documented communities using dams, wells, vast aquaculture complexes, fisheries, irrigation trenches, terracing, domesticated cereals, roots and vegetables, and preservation techniques for everything from grains to wild game.[47] There's evidence of baking, with grindstones found from as far back as 30,000 years, pre-dating the Egyptians (usually credited as the world's first bakers) by about 15,000 years.[48] But steeped in Cartesian bias, the colonisers refused to see. In his book *Dark Emu*, indigenous author Bruce Pascoe describes an ancient, ingenious sprung fish trap on a weir, which itself was specially constructed to divert fish from the main flow of the river. One settler-colonist, James Kirby, documented the fishing method in detail, with obvious approval of the efficiency of the operation. His interpretation, however, was clouded by dualist bias; a refusal to see objectively what was in front of him. 'I have often heard of the indolence of the Blacks and soon came to the conclusion after watching a Black fellow catch fish in such a lazy way, that what I had heard was perfectly true.'⁴⁹

Lifelong traveller and anthropologist-in-residence at *National Geographic*, Wade Davis, says emphatically that there is no sense in which any person can call a *culture* 'uncivilised'. Other cultures are not failed versions of modern western life and it is unfathomably ignorant and misleading to stare from that viewpoint. 'Consider the way we look at a mountain,' writes Davis. 'To [westerners], a mountain is a big pile of rock. To the Iskut [a First Nation community in British Columbia, Canada], it's a deity. It's not about who's right or who's wrong – there is no right or wrong. It's a series of cultural beliefs, and it changes the way we consider the mountain, and how we treat it.'

Ignoring the complexity of indigenous cultures is not only an insult to those native cultures, but also to western audiences. 'When you dumb down a program, you get a dumb audience,' says Davis.⁵⁰

A MOUSE FROM ZIMBABWE
(or what's this all got to do with me?)

Fast-forward a couple of centuries, and we see how the defining characteristics of 'modernity' become the features of individual lives, including my own. My mum was born Sheila Fraser in 1951 in what was then Salisbury, capital city of Rhodesia – modern-day Harare, in Zimbabwe – when the country was coming to the end of its time as a British colony. My mum's father, Don Fraser, was an RAF pilot stationed at the British airbase outside Salisbury during the Second World War. Novelist Doris Lessing's 'Children of War' series, written about the same place at the same time, talks of the dances at the airbase, flirtations with the young pilots, the parties in apartments and sundowners at hotels in the city. After the war, my grandfather, with his young wife and their infant son – now the Uncle Gordon who helped us paint the Inver walls – travelled from Dundee back to Salisbury to rejoin the life he had left there.

All I know of my grandparents on Mum's side fits into a small white vinyl suitcase. In it are black-and-white photos and Super 8 cinefilms in flickering shades of grey. So much hides between the frames. In one photo, my grandmother Jean (Georgina), a slight, elegant figure in a tailored skirt-suit and tapered sunglasses, with perfect lipstick and a cigarette draped from her lips, gathers her young daughter to her side. There are snaps of picnics on the banks of the Zambezi and holidays to Victoria Falls. There are hotels – Rhodes Hotel, Meikles Hotel – with sunny verandas and tables crowded with beer bottles, the sundowner gatherings that Lessing describes in her novels.

It's a strange thing, to feel loss for people you didn't know. Sifting through the photos, you stare at the smile, or the eyes staring back at you, and search for a hook that can drag you into the frame, suddenly give you substance in the same place as these strangers who have made you who you are. My great-grandmother, Don's mum Margaret Fraser, is already an older woman in these photos. She lived with them in Zimbabwe for six years, leaving her own husband behind in Dundee. It was she who fought the Edinburgh courts at age seventy-one to keep Mum and Uncle Gordon in her custody after her son and his wife were killed.

With my grandparents in the photos is a Zimbabwean

family who worked for them in the house. The housekeeper, Edward, helped with cooking, cleaning and gardening. He used my gran's recipes for mince and tatties or roast chicken with vegetables, and sometimes cooked Southern African food for the family too, like the pan-national bobotie, the aromatic minced meat dish baked with a savoury custard topping. There's pictures of his wife, Nannie, holding their baby, Susan. My great-gran was asked to name Susan: an honour for this tiny, thrawn woman, who often defended Edward from the Black police who came to the door, demanding he accompany them to the police station on nebulous pretexts. But it's Edward and Nannie's older son I stare at most. His name is Jackson: he's the same age as my mum and she calls him her best friend, her playmate. There are photos of the two of them playing together in the garden, of Jackson holding up a snake on a stick. If he is still alive, he's around seventy now, and his sister Susan is in her sixties. I have spent as much time with this family as I have with my own grandparents. I know their stories as well as I know anything from my mum's childhood.

 The last my mum saw of her parents was on the hot sticky tarmac of Lourenço Marques Airport (now Maputa Airport) in Mozambique. It was August 1961. Mum and Gordon were returning to Scotland so they could start the new school year on time, in a country Mum had never visited, and without her parents. The plane was shimmering in the heat haze, glaring white and unreal against the blue sky. Mum was holding her older brother's hand. In the other hand she held a small pink vanity case containing her pet white mouse, a companion for the long journey back to Scotland. The mouse made it all the way to Dundee, where it started its new life hiding under the bed in the cold grey city on the banks of the River Tay.

Six months later, Don and Jean Fraser had packed up their African lives and booked seats on the first airliner operated by the new Scottish airline, Caledonian Airways. The plane had been christened *Star of Robbie Burns* in honour of the Scots poet. Don and Jean travelled to Mozambique again to board the flight to Douala, Cameroon (then a French colony), first stop on the way to Europe. Don, the pilot, was entertained in the air. Jean hated flying, it terrified her, but she was buoyed with the thought of seeing her two children again.

It was a real shock to enter the few details I knew into Google and find the flight report so quickly. By the time I'd got to the end of it, the salty tears had wormed watercourses down my cheeks and were pooling in the corners of my mouth.

'The crew in charge of flight CA153 on 4 March 1962 were led by a very experienced aviator, Captain Arthur Williams,' the flight report reads. The description of the minutes leading up to the plane's take-off from its first transfer in Cameroon makes the hazy African evening crystal clear. Shortly before sunset, the passengers filed back on board. One by one the engines roared into life, and the flight deck recorded a normal take-off. All the plane's lights came on in the expected sequence but one. And the plane didn't climb as fast or high as anticipated. 'Sadly for the crew and those aboard, before the flaps could deploy, at approximately 18h22m45s the left wing crashed into a tree 70 feet above the runway elevation some 2040 meters from the end of the runway.'

British Caledonian Airways flight CA153 crashed in the jungle two kilometres from the runway at Douala Airport, Cameroon, in the early evening of 4 March 1962. Sundowner time. There had been one-tenth of a second between the wing-tip hitting the tree and the final impact. The end, the flight report notes, was 'mercifully quick'.

I have never been to Zimbabwe. My mum won't go back; the country is now so different she fears losing her parents, and her childhood memories, twice. She's looked for her old house online, but in place of the one bungalow with the tidy vegetable garden there's several, smaller homes. I have no way of knowing what happened to Edward and Nannie, Jackson and Susan after my family left Zimbabwe (yes, I've tried social media).

I want them to be okay. I want them to have felt about our family the affection and respect that Mum and her parents felt about them. It is, of course, my own conscience I am trying to salve, and my own identity I'm trying to validate. I know the relationship between the two families wasn't an equal one and that they were living in a time where white privilege was enshrined in law in a land that had belonged to Black Africans, if it belonged to anyone.

I often wonder what we Brits owe them for the riches that we took from the once-prosperous land. One group of economists estimated that from 1990 to 2015 the global north appropriated from the south land, raw materials, energy and labour totalling $10.8 trillion in northern prices – enough to end extreme poverty 70 times over.[51] Modern global food systems continue this trajectory.

Perhaps this book is my first gesture of personal reparations.

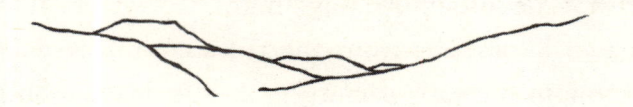

MODERN

From a lush, fertile, rich country at the time of its conquest on behalf of the British state, Zimbabwe now ranks 134 out of 137 nations in the UN's World Happiness Report – it's the fourth-saddest country in the world.[52] The last six decades in Zimbabwe have been characterised by the worst effects of post-colonial politics: genocide, government corruption, stratospheric inflation, droughts, famines, degrading and debilitated infrastructure and the AIDS pandemic.

Zimbabwe is a land-locked country, once known as the 'Jewel of Africa' for its great prosperity, its mines seamed with diamonds, gold and copper. There have been people on Zimbabwean soil for ten times as long as there have been people in Scotland – at least 100,000 years. Ancient states traded Zimbabwean gold, ivory and copper for Arabian and Portuguese cloth, glass and porcelain. With thriving farms on fecund soil, it was known as the 'bread basket' of Southern Africa. Over the last two centuries tourism has been a growing industry; national parks feature iconic African wildlife, and Victoria Falls, the huge waterfall on the great Zambezi River, is a World Heritage Site.

Enter Cecil Rhodes, the man who gave his name to the British colony my mum was born into. Cecil John Rhodes was a British mining magnate, politician and imperialist, and one of the richest men in the world: a millionaire by his mid-twenties and a multi-millionaire by thirty. Rhodes set up the De Beers diamond firm, which till very recently controlled the world trade in diamonds,* and followed that with successful prospecting for gold. In 1888 Rhodes wheedled permission to mine diamonds from the Matabele King Lobengula's mines in pres-

---

* It was De Beers who invented the tradition of the diamond engagement ring.

ent-day Zimbabwe, the move that kicked off British colonialism in Southern Africa. Controversial even in his own time, Rhodes went on to conceive the disastrous Jameson Raid of 1895, which prompted the Second Boer War, in which tens of thousands of African civilians and poorly fed British soldiers died.*

Rhodes was also the architect of the first legal, political and financial structures to systematically disadvantage native Black Africans in a British colony. These insidious laws limited the voting rights of Black 'Rhodesians', restricted their access to the most productive land, and forbade sexual relations between white and Black people. Their effects on racial inequality persist today. At Zimbabwe's eventual independence in 1980, 42 per cent of the land was owned by white Zimbabweans, the minority ethnic group – approximately 5.5 per cent of the population.

In December 1962, a few months after my grandparents' plane had crashed in the Cameroon jungle, Rhodesia's far-right, white Rhodesian Front party won a surprise victory. When he eventually became prime minister in 1965, Ian Smith quickly declared that Rhodesia would 'never in a million years' be ruled by a Black majority.† Smith's ensuing fifteen-year guerrilla war with Black nationalists, led by the Patriotic Front,‡ would claim the lives of thousands.

---

* It was as a result of defeat in the Boer Wars and difficulty in recruiting healthy troops back home that free school meals were introduced in Britain.
† In 1965, Smith's Rhodesia became the first colony to declare independence from Britain since the thirteen states of America in 1776. In response, the international community imposed economic sanctions and British prime minister Harold Wilson declared Rhodesia a 'rebel regime'.
‡ A coalition of Robert Mugabe's Shona ZANU party and Joshua Nkomo's Matabele ZAPU party.

MODERN

Back in Dundee, my mum was fourteen and she and my dad had just got together at a high school disco. 'That idiot Smith', as Mum calls him, remained in power till 1979, when negotiations brought an end to the guerrilla war, the international trade sanctions and white-minority rule in Rhodesia. In the country's first democratic elections of 1980, the ZANU-PF party won, Robert Mugabe became prime minister, and the country got its modern name, Zimbabwe. Mugabe stayed in power for 37 years, till, in November 2017, an army coup saw the 92-year-old dictator placed under house arrest.

As the well-known African idiom goes: 'When elephants fight, it is the grass that suffers.' Large parts of Africa are resource-poor and politically fractious because of extractive colonialism – not because things have 'always been that way'. Ordinary Zimbabweans endured the excesses of Mugabe's regime, characterised by corruption, nepotism and human-rights abuses. Estimates for the number of deaths during the five-year Gukurahundi campaign alone range from 20,000 to 80,000; thousands of others were tortured in military internment camps.

In 2001, Mugabe executed his radical 'Fast Track' Land Reform.* White Zimbabweans were now less than 1 per cent of the population but owned 70 per cent of productive arable land; within three years, war veterans backed by state security forces had seized 90 per cent of commercial farms totalling more than 10 million hectares. Despite Zimbabwe's constitution

---

* Ugandan political scientist Mahmood Mamdani calls it the 'greatest transfer of property in Southern Africa since colonisation'. Mamdani, Mahmoud, 'Lessons of Zimbabwe', *London Review of Books*, 2008, p. 24, at <https://www.lrb.co.uk/the-paper/v30/n23/mahmood-mamdani/lessons-of-zimbabwe>

explicitly stating that any one farmer couldn't own more than one farm, Mugabe himself managed to accumulate at least thirteen. These mismanaged land reforms, following decades of political turmoil and economic decline – plus the effects of Cyclone Eline in 1999 – turned Zimbabwe from a food-secure nation, with surplus to trade, into one requiring intervention by the World Food Programme.[53]

ADDING VALUES

Twenty years on, Zimbabwe struggles at the bottom of the world's well-being charts, but the UK is one of Zimbabwe's top export markets for fruit and veg. Citrus fruit (especially oranges), sweetcorn, baby corn, sugar-snap peas, bananas, passion fruits, avocados and strawberries are all exported from Zimbabwe to the UK. Zimbabwe can produce high-value crops in a period of the year when most countries are unable to, giving it a competitive advantage – and giving the UK the year-round supply of supermarket exotica that modern shoppers have come to expect. But when we buy imported green beans and oranges from Africa we gorge on African sunshine, and slug its water. And the highest earning supermarket chief executive in the UK will earn in five *days* what a woman picking grapes in Southern Africa will earn in her entire life.[54]

My old professor Tim Lang calls the current British government's food-supply strategy 'parasitic on other economies' lands and labour', and adds that 'to use food from countries potentially or already worse affected by climate change than Britain itself would be immoral'.[55] He reckons that Britain's reliance on importing so much of our food from far away is a hangover from the days of empire, suggesting that there remains in shoppers' minds 'a malign assumption that we deserve to be fed. We do not.'[56]

The inherent value of fruit, vegetables and other edible crops is their ability to feed people. This value doesn't shift with revolution, political upheaval, an investor's whims, or the managed fluctuation of global commodity markets. A thriving agriculture sector that sustains its home market before shipping nutrients overseas provides food security, and real independence from the demands of the foreign market – including the country's ex-colonial masters. Some extra cash in the economy is essential; in a capitalist economy, 'cash cropping' (i.e., growing things that are exchanged for cash such as maize or tomatoes for processing) is desirable for farmers if they are to exist above subsistence level. In fact, laws that denied access to cash cropping for Black Zimbabweans were historically used as a means of oppression, because it meant that these farmers couldn't participate in the world in the same way as whites. And, from our point of view, what would Scotland's food culture taste like without its spices, coffee, tea, chocolate and bananas? But a coherent approach by governments to balance export income with home security and food justice is essential to make sense of any land reform policy.

Land-ownership on foreign soil by European and American supermarkets and food processing corporations – which ties the whole supply chain into export-first legal structures – is modern-day colonialism. Nobel Prize-winning Indian economist Amartya Sen explains that it is not the presence or absence of food in a country that causes famine, but the hungry people's *entitlement* to it.[57] Farmers producing crops for export rely on foreign distributors, processors and certifiers to take their crops, and these companies don't prioritise starving people over profit. Scanning the 'country of origin' lines on supermarket labels and the columns on the restaurant's online order sheets, I wonder what gaps there are in African shopping baskets to enable my dinner menus. I wonder what it would take for some of the supermarkets' and Big Food corporations' extraordinary profits to be given to the farmers, so they don't need to export quite so much. And what kind of a government it would take to make that happen.

I wonder if my mum's childhood friend Jackson got a piece of land in the reforms and grows lemons, with which he makes the lemon curd that flavoured my childhood too. These naive fantasies of course enshrine my own values and my own idea of what a happy ending would look like. But the alternatives are bleak. I know my kitchen comfort has come at an unconscionably high price.

CORN-ON-THE-COB

For me, there's one vegetable that embodies everything that modernity has brought to my kitchen table: sweetcorn. Following this one plant across continents, I can trace the threads of capitalism as it re-weaves social and natural landscapes overseas and at home. Corn-on-the-cob is also one of the stitches securing my own personal food story to the world's wide cloth.

Every now and then when my brother and I were young, Dad would set the cine projector up. Sometimes we were allowed to put on one of the old rattling black-and-white films from Zimbabwe. In one of the films my mum and her brother play tag between rows of sweetcorn plants, throwing spent husks at each other, laughing at the unseen cameraman's antics. They are maybe six and nine years old. The rows of corn are in the family's back garden, in a vegetable patch that includes avocado, orange and peach trees, passion-fruit vines (granadillas) and banana palms. Three decades later, my childhood garden featured rows of corn too, grown against all the odds on the wind-battered edge of the North Sea. On the kitchen windowsill behind the sink, avocado pits were forever suspended over jam jars of water, held aloft by cocktail sticks. From the pit's bulbous bottom would come tentative white roots, and from a sudden split in the top would appear the tall green shoot. They never survived the transplant into cold soil. A new avocado was duly purchased and the cycle of hope started anew. Recently I returned to my childhood home and found an actual avocado plant, leaves and all, growing in a pot of actual soil in the living room. I don't think we yet have fruit.

Sweetcorn is best eaten straight from the plant, like peas or asparagus, before the simple snappy sugars revert to bland starches. It was our best summer treat, maybe even more than the herbal greenhouse tomatoes squashed onto toast with supermarket cottage cheese, or the fragrant, heady strawberries picked in nearby East Scryne Farm for pocket money (one for the punnet, one for me). The corn was stripped of its leaves and just-boiled, on the cob. It was eaten with elbows on the table, rolled bite by bite through a knife-smear of butter on the edge of the plate, dipped in the little pile of fine salt and peppered from the greasy grinder. The warm kernels left marks like tiny teeth in the cold butter. Little yellow plastic corn-handled forks were gripped by small fingers with dirt behind their nails, and the salty butter dripped onto grazed knees and stung.

I remember the secret pleasure of waking suddenly in the night to light filtering through the gaps in the wooden shutters.

Darkness is brief in Scottish summers. In the corn years, my night dreams were always slanted by the fleeting shadows of a past I didn't know. When I was the same age as Mum was when her parents died so suddenly, the fear of recurring loss would sneak with the light into my child's head and writhe there in the half-light till morning.

Corn is not an easy plant to grow in cold climates. I tried, in the back garden of a small rental cottage on Loch Fyne, during the 2020 lockdown. I trowelled in three small plants in a raised bed stuffed with fecund rotted manure and soil. Their companion leeks were delighted – fat sweet white stems, forked greens lifting skywards like open arms. By September the corn plants had grown taller than me (no great challenge) but the garden ran out of sunshine before the cobs could fully ripen. I kept hoping for too long, perhaps like Mum had, and lost the tiny cobs to frost and rot. Maybe we could have got something out of them if I'd harvested them sooner; a short, barely sweet crunch wrung from scant October light.

Mum's garden was on the east coast of Scotland, where there is more sunshine than in the west (and where most of the country's horticulture takes place). The corn plants were started from seed in mismatched tins in the greenhouse and potted on into a bed in the lee of the garden walls, a little shelter from the scouring North Sea winds. The plants all flourished, as if by will alone.

In Mum's box of black-and-white photos there's one with a spidery scrawl in fading biro on the back, writing I remember as my great-grandmother's: 'Severe lightning shows up the mealies ... It was completely dark when this was taken! One thing I don't like – the thunderstorms.' 'Mealies' is a Southern African name for corn, now a major African staple food. 'Mealie pap' is a corn porridge, similar to grits in the southern states of the US or polenta in Italy. It was instrumental in facilitating European invaders' colonisation of the African subcontinent.

Maize is the seed head of a tall annual grass, *Zea mays*. Picture the other grass crops in common cultivation (wheat, barley, oats and rye), and you see how far it has come from its first domestication 10,000 years ago. A sweetcorn is the seed head of the solid stem of the modern plant. It's around 1,000 times bigger than it was originally and is now found in around 200 varieties, from white through yellow to blue-black – different variations suitable for all uses, from fuel to food. Sweetcorn is 3.5 per cent sweeter and contains much less water than it used to, when there were eight known varieties cultivated only in Central America. Corn has always been selectively bred for human needs, but these days major crops of corn are also genetically modified to resist disease and coordinate with the application of engineered pesticides. The difference is that the genetic modification is done in a laboratory; it's not something farmers and gardeners can do for themselves in the field, by cross-pollination or grafting. The power is thus in food techs' hands, not farmers'. Plant chemists select corn for commercial profit, not for reasons of human nutrition, ease of nutrient extraction or flavour. Potential effects on the natural environment or the health of farm-workers are not factored into the equation.

Peel back the husks on a corn plant and you can read the whole history of the modern world and its food supply. Corn was first cultivated from a wild grass by Mexican people around 10,000 years ago, and from there it spread north and south across the Americas. The Mexicans were the ones to steep the kernels with lye, an alkaline solution, to unlock the corn's full range of nutrients (and that distinct toasted taste of corn tortillas). That knowledge of nixtamalisation didn't travel as far as the crop did, though. Once detached from indigenous knowledge overseas, corn became an energy-rich but nutrient-poor way to eat your staple starch. Native Americans taught their invaders how to prepare it. Christopher Columbus transported it back to Europe and from there it spread to all areas of the world suitable for growing it (and some, like my back garden, emphatically not).

Corn, or maize, was the energy that powered the trade in enslaved African people during the seventeenth to nineteenth centuries. Maize first arrived on the African coast at some point during the seventeenth century, initially introduced by the Portuguese from their colonies in South America, to supply food to their trading forts. The crop was quickly adopted by African farmers impressed by its low labour requirements, its short growth period, ease of storage and transport, and its readily available energy. Maize was grown across much of the African continent by the early eighteenth century. It was a major influence on the population increase of the time – and farming corn increased the numbers of people living in landscapes accessible to slave raiders (harder to access regions were harder to raid).[58] In a cycle that became typical of the global colonial trade, the enslaved people were then transported to the Americas.

Corn is a spiritual staple as well as a biological one. Native Americans saw no distinction between the health of the earth, the health of their crops, and human physical and spiritual health. Corn is one of the 'three sisters' – a traditional farming system that uses the natural characteristics of corn, bean and squash plants to produce maximum edible yield from plots of land while naturally protecting the crops and returning nutrition to the soil. Today Indigenous Australian and American academics discuss 'molecular colonisation' – the effect of modern diet and food customs on indigenous digestive and mental well-being. Maize seeds were traditionally planted in ceremony, showing reverence for the plants and the sentient earth itself. Buffalo Bird Woman, a renowned traditional Hidatsa gardener born in 1839, said her people believed that 'the corn plants had souls, as children have souls. We cared for our corn in those days, as we would care for a child.' When spring returned, the women would welcome the corn spirits back from the south with dancing and ceremonies. The traditional relationship with food and the land was complex and profound.[59]

Corn is these days one of the most prolifically planted commercial crops, grown in sixty-nine countries; annual production is now around 800 million tonnes. As a course-ground meal it's a staple food for millions of people (polenta, grits, mealie-meal, masa). In North America, in the wide open, sunshine-fuelled plains of the Midwest and Canada, corn is *the* major commodity crop. Most North American corn is grown for animal feed and for conversion into biofuels. Instead of using all this land to fatten a luxury product like beef in intensive feed-lots in northern and southern America, however, we could be using it to produce protein that is up to ten times more efficient for human consumption, in the form of beans and pulses. Instead of converting corn into biofuel, technologists could be driving desire for less resource-hungry modes of transport than the individualist's car. But the *hidden* uses of corn are perhaps just as emblematic of the modern world's use of food crops as the visible ones. Corn is a major source of processed food additives such as high-fructose corn syrup. Industrial corn farmers are recipients of the majority of US farming subsidies, meaning corn sugar is much cheaper than sugars from beets or cane. It's the sweetness in your soft drinks and candies, as well as the source of most 'natural' fruit flavourings. It's a popular breakfast cereal and appears as both chip *and* flavouring in bags of corn snacks. It gives the home kitchen cornflour for thickening and corn oil for frying. It's tucked away in cans of pet food. From being the human fuel that powered colonialism, this one plant now fuels the modern processed-food industry.

Futures are quite literally traded on it. The international trade in corn – in the form of dried maize kernels, to be processed into meal in the Americas and Africa – is a major way of deciding a country's entitlement to food and cash. In the early 2000s, Malawi, Zambia and Zimbabwe suffered a 'maize drought' that jeopardised this staple food. The three governments called for international food aid well ahead of the harvest, anticipating (with previous experience) a delay in response. The United States aid organisation USAID shipped excess US corn to the three Southern African countries. This kept the price of US corn buoyant at home, a key strategy of capitalist economics, and often how food aid is used. South Africa meanwhile imported maize from Brazil and Argentina to sell to its neighbours, even though other, much closer, East African countries had surpluses of maize that year which they could have sold or donated to their neighbouring countries. But instead of the profit from the grain sales staying in the region, that cash had effectively gone to the United States, and directly to wealthy South Africa.

During the maize drought, the Southern African Regional

MODERN

Poverty Network voiced a 'very legitimate suspicion over the goals pursued by political elites in upholding control on trade, production, distribution and pricing of maize'.*[60] As well as distorting the African maize market, USAID and the World Food Programme also put pressure on the Zambian government to take genetically modified (GM) corn. At that particular point, the people of Zambia were actually far from starvation. And Zambia's export market for fresh produce – including corn – relies on Europe, where GM produce is popularly rejected. Once GM crops have established themselves in the soil, farmers lose their GM-free certification. USAID also support the development of biotechnologies worldwide, including in Southern Africa, where several local research projects are supported by the institution. One alternative would have been to offer hulled corn – which can't grow if it hits the soil, because it's already been milled for human consumption.

Corn is a potent symbol of how one crop literally creates the structures of trade relationships, food cultures and land use all over the world. In choosing whether or not to use land to grow corn, what to do with the harvest once we have it, and how to buy and sell it, governments, landowners, farmers and cooks make decisions about how we value human beings at home and abroad. The staple bowls of starchy porridge, the bags of branded corn snacks, the biofuel, cattle feed, vegetable oil, food additives and summer suppers – they all come from one single blade of grass. Through that grass, you are connected to 10,000 years of human generations and landscapes from the

---

* Mousseau, Fred, 'Roles of and Alternatives to Food Aid in Southern Africa: A Report to Oxfam', 2004, at: <https://sarpn.org/documents/d0000998/P1121-Roles_and_alternatives_to_food_aid_Mousseau_2004.pdf>

Americas to Africa to northern Europe, all looped together like a daisy chain.

CREAMED CORN

6 corn cobs, still in their leaves, ideally from a farm or garden near you
100g butter, or around half a block
salt (around half a teaspoon)
1 spoonful of lemon juice, from half a juicy lemon
1 spoonful crème fraîche (a good blob)

Peel the corn cobs of leaves. Remove all the hairy, fibrous corn 'silk', as any remaining threads will invariably get stuck in your teeth later.

Take a tray or a large plate. Hold the stem end of the cob like a handle, and have the other end of the cob resting on the tray. Run a sharp knife all the way from the stem of the cob to the tip, aiming to cut the corn kernels into the tray. You want to avoid the fibrous base of the kernels, so aim to cut off only the top half (the bulbous juicy 'heads') of the kernels. Turn the cob a little every time you cut off a strip.

Next, using the planer side of a box grater, grate the emptied cobs onto the tray. Now you're gathering all the starchy juice that's hiding in the fibrous base of the kernels that will make the 'cream' in your creamed corn. (Save the cobs for corn cob custard [below].)

Over a medium heat, melt the butter in a large, wide pan. When it's foaming, tip the contents of the tray into the pan, all the starchy juice *and* the kernels. Stir in a little of the salt. Put the lid on the pan, and cook for 4–5 minutes. Then lift the lid and stir. The corn should be changing from the opaque cream colour to brighter, poppy yellow. Your aim here is to lose the starchy feel of the uncooked corn in your mouth, while still having a bit of moisture left in the pan to make the creamed corn, well, creamy. There should be no browning. If there is, turn down the heat. Add a little water at a time, and stir, stir, stir. Cook gently for another 10–15 minutes, adding a splash of water if it starts to look oily or dry, until the corn kernels are tender and the juice is thickened and creamy, not mealy. Taste. It'll be delicious. Add a little more salt if it needs it, a squeeze of lemon juice, and if you like, a large spoonful of crème fraîche (I like).

In August and September, this is an Inver kitchen staple. It's a great base for soup – just add some chicken or vegetable stock, and blend as much as you like. It's great with savoury, garlicky pork sausages; with a roasted chicken; or with cooked haricot or coco beans, confit yellow tomatoes and chanterelle (girolle) mushrooms. Grated hard cheese is delicious over the top, as is fermented chilli. We use Corra Linn, a sweet, nutty ewe's-milk cheese from the Errington family in Lanarkshire.

CORN COB CUSTARD

5 empty corn cobs, leftover from making creamed corn
1 full corn cob, with kernels cut and grated off, as for making creamed corn
50g butter

250ml double cream
250ml milk
15g + 85g sugar
5 large/100g egg yolks
a pinch of salt

Heat oven to 180°C. Cut all 6 emptied corn cobs into 2"/5cm pieces, dot with the butter and roast in the preheated oven for 30–45 minutes, turning the pieces every 5 minutes, until they're uniformly browned all over.

In a large saucepan, combine the cream, milk and 15g sugar with the roasted corn cobs. Cover the surface with a cartouche (a circle of baking paper). Bring to a simmer, and cook very gently for 15 minutes, stirring occasionally. Turn off heat, and infuse the mix at room temperature for at least 2 hours. Tip the warm corn cream into a colander, and squeeze the cob pieces one by one to remove all the cream. Return the cream to a clean pan, add the corn kernels and gratings from your whole cob, and begin to heat it.

Meanwhile, whisk the yolks with 85g sugar in a kitchen mixer till at the 'ribbon' stage. This means light and thickened, so that the ribbons of whisked egg hold their form for a second before sinking into the mix. When the cream is almost boiling, but not actually spilling over the sides of the pan (it's a line as fine as a split second), pour one-third of the hot cream over the yolks in the bowl, whisking constantly, then stir in the rest. Return the eggy corn cream to the cleaned pan and cook over a low heat, stirring, for about 10 minutes till thickened and coating the back of a wooden spoon (or registering 84°C on a probe thermometer).

> Note the cream still has the corn kernels in it, so it kind of looks like it's curdled from the start. Just stir constantly, and watch carefully as the viscosity and temperature steadily increase.
>
> Have a fine sieve waiting over a bowl, and when the custard has thickened, strain it immediately. Push down on the kernels with the back of a ladle or large spoon to extract all the cream. Add the pinch of salt.
>
> There's now a couple of options. To make it into an ice cream, chill the corn custard, and churn according to the instructions on your ice-cream machine.
>
> For a baked custard, like a crème brûlée, have the oven heated to 100°C. Pour 100g, or a sixth of the mixture, of the custard into each of six oven-proof cups or ramekins. Half-fill a bain marie or roasting tin with hot water, and sit the cups of custard in it. Cover the whole lot with tin foil (or a lid if the tin has it) and bake for 45–60 minutes till the custard is just set. Remove from the hot water, then chill the custards in the fridge.
>
> We serve these with a granita made from wild blaeberries, or sometimes an elderberry sorbet – any dark, early autumn fruit is good. As is a biscuit.

THE RISE OF NORMALITY

Antonio Gramsci was a Sardinian economist, hunchbacked and barely five feet tall. Writing in the 1920s and 1930s, just before the Second World War, Gramsci argued that powerful groups in modern societies maintain their dominance through *ideas*, not violence.[61] Governments, big food corporations and the moneyed class shape a culture using schools, advertising, religion, media, arts and entertainment (in which category I'd include restaurants). I'd also add food-buying and -selling decisions, which affect the desirability, availability and accessibility of certain kinds of foods over others. Together this creates a 'common sense' – a way of viewing the world which is internalised and reproduced, knowingly or not, till it becomes the only 'normal' (food) culture imaginable.*

Gramsci counselled that to make change to a culture, you must first know yourself 'as a product of the historical process to date which has deposited in you an infinity of traces, without leaving an inventory'.[62] He believed that culture must shift first, *before* replacing the big structures of an economy or politics, that people who want things to change should create a new set of values and beliefs, tell new stories about the world. It seems to me that this puts the power to change the world in ordinary people's hands. We all, after all, create our own 'normal' together.

Scotland, at the end of 500 years of modernity, is a small nation connected through our tables and trade to the furthest-flung people and landscapes on the planet. It is *connection* that has defined who we are and what we eat in modernity, not separatism.

This is not history. Colonialism, enslavement, the erroneous idea that humans are somehow apart from and above nature: the persistence of these 'enlightened' ways of thinking is evident in the escalating urgency of the climate and biodiversity crises, and in the inequitable split of pounds and power in Britain

---

* Gramsci called this 'cultural hegemony'.

and across the planet. These problems jostle daily for a place in our headlines, fridges and on our dinner plates. They are the ingredient lists of our historic recipes, the headers on the supermarket aisles, the treats and staples we ingest and digest multiple times daily. Enclosures didn't end with the Middle Ages. Who gets to access what is very much a current affair. Rights are continually negotiated. Now, it's the fight to free nature from the gaping maw of capitalism before the whole planet becomes the ultimate 'enclosure'.

If it's true that 'history is written by the winners', and if capitalism appears to have won out, it's *this* value system that hands us the criteria with which to judge and understand the past. This is Gramsci's 'infinity of traces', left by history in Scottish food and Scottish cooks; the unseen assumptions that guide our food choices today. Modernity is the normality that binds us Scots to each other, and to the rest of the world.

Modernity, then, is as big as a planet. Modern Scottish food is in part a result of relationships that span the globe. But it's distinct, too – there are ways of eating and living here that are uniquely Scottish. What can I find in *Scottish* history that would tell me more about how our 'normal' came to be what it is today?

My own personal and family history is a micro-story within these national and global tales. My dad grew up in working-class, industrial Dundee in the years after the deprivations of the Second World War, the exact decades in which the big, globalised food-distribution networks were gaining momentum and bringing burger joints, supermarkets and cheap grain-fed bacon to a country used to mince and tatties, grocers, and the bacon roll as an aspirational treat. My second shot at higher education was a degree in food policy. That gave me the tools to map Dad's diet onto the British and European trade policies that have given Scots easy access to more cheap sugar and fat than we can eat without serious damage to our own health, and to the landscapes in which they are grown.

As I probe the roots of Scots' food habits specifically, it seems to me like a tiny minority of individuals are getting richer as the majority of Scots get sicker. And for all the battles in history and in the news today, it's starting to seem to me like this is the real fight of our time.

Chapter Three:
SCOTTISH / *PEOPLE*

When I'm rifling through my own short life's larder of memories, human habits and predilections appear immutable, fixed, and often without reason. In zooming outwards to view longer periods of time, I can see the patterns appearing in the warp and weft of history.

Scanning the landscape outside the Inver windows – the two castles, the Victorian landscaping, the hills, the forests and the loch – I can read the history of Scotland back through modernity. The Battle of Culloden was the last battle fought on British soil, and it was also the major historic shift in how Scots identified themselves and what was normal for modern Scots to value. Prior to Culloden, the clan system and Gaelic language captured an entirely different way of looking at the world. In fact, the rise of modern industrial values in Highland Scotland can be read as a kind of domestic colonisation. The Highland Clearances were Scotland's enclosures, a full 400 years after the other European landscapes had been privatised. New traditions were invented to replace what had been lost. In learning these new rituals of kilt, tartan, Highland games and haggis suppers, we dug in new habits and donned new identities.

Childhood food memories snag food habits that stay for life. Familiar foods all come from somewhere. The great Scots soups, the oats and oatcakes, the mince and the tatties; the soft summer berries, and vegetables (or lack of them); the Scots' love of milk, cheese and bacon rolls; the infamous haggis: each of these has an origin story, and it's in examining these stories side by side that we can see what they have in common.

And perhaps then we can ask, what really is 'Scottish' about what and how we eat?

TWO CASTLES

I love ruins. I love the sense of continuity: the endurance of the past and the unstoppable movement to the future both contained in the same stone walls. The decay, creating anew as it razes the old. Standing just outside the Inver Restaurant doorway, scanning the distant hills, you see two castles. The squat stone ruins of Old Castle Lachlan are opposite, on the other side of the little bay. Elegant white New Castle Lachlan is off to your right, set back from the shores of the loch beyond a picturesque, gentle, green sloping lawn, a luminescent contrast to the wilder bracken- and heather-covered hills. Follow the footpath through stands of birch and ash trees, with bolete and chanterelle mushrooms nestling in their roots, through a field misted with meadowsweet, and along a rocky shore where among the coastal grasses peek succulent sea greens like samphire, sea blite and arrowgrass. Standing on the little wooden bridge over the River Lachlan, you straddle a thousand or more years of history. When we arrived in Strathlachlan in 2015, we were just the latest in a long line of inhabitants of the little bay. There have been cooks here, grinding hazelnuts and barley, steaming cockles and picking the wild coastal herbs, for millennia.

There has been a castle on this rocky promontory since at least 1314, when the lands were first officially recorded as 'Castlelachlan'. Nothing remains of this older castle; the Old Castle Lachlan you can see from the restaurant windows was built in the 1400s. The castle was a fortress; the clan's strength in turbulent times. Standing on the rocks outside its walls you can see right up and down Loch Fyne. Medieval architects can't only have been building for protection, though. From the restaurant the castle is perfectly framed by the hills and the water, the view constantly changing with the scrolling clouds and rhythmic, heaving tide. At ground level were a large kitchen and storerooms: perhaps the first professional kitchen on Lachlan Bay. There was a huge hearth for spit-roasting boar and venison, steaming the crabs, baking the bannocks. Above these is a solar, the private chamber of the chief, his lady and their family, and above that a large hall. To have two grand rooms for the chief's use is unusual. Perhaps the ancient Maclachlans liked a party.

The pivot in time between the bay's old and new history is the month of April 1746. Fighting for Bonnie Prince Charlie in the Battle of Culloden, the 17th Clan Chief Lachlan died 160 miles away from home, on bleak Drumossie Moor. For Clan Lachlan's survivors it was a 53-hour walk home, with cold winds biting at their wounds and the dread of the coming retribution rising in their throats. The hour-long battle at Culloden was to be the last in the war between the Jacobite army of Charles Edward Stuart – fighting to restore the exiled James VIII, his father, to the British thrones – and the Hanoverian King George II's British government force, led by the Duke of Cumberland, George's son. It was a turning point for all of modern Scots, European and global history, not just for the inhabitants of Lachlan Bay.

Culloden was a bloodbath: the Jacobites were tired from months of campaigning, and badly outnumbered. During the short battle itself they lost around 1,250 men to the British government's 50. Immediately after the battle had concluded, General 'Butcher' Cumberland ordered that 'no quarter shall be given': along five miles of windswept moor the injured and trailing men were slaughtered. The Bonnie Prince escaped to exile in France. Over the next decades, Highland culture was systematically dismantled.

The Battle of Culloden was a clash of values. It was the last stand of an older, more holistic way of understanding place, as the clan system gave way to the new 'improvements' creeping through the land. It was a battle of different systems of social organisation, politics and economic policy, and of religious values. It was not simply a clash of the English and Scottish nations (as it's often popularly understood). For a start, the two countries had by that point been unified – politically, anyway. And nationalism, as we understand it today, had not fully coalesced in human imaginations. The opposition in values was as much between Lowland and Highland cultures, city versus countryside, Gaelic, Scots and English-speaking folk, rich versus poor, and Catholic versus Protestant. It was a battle between noble families – between those who wanted to return a Stuart king to the throne and those who supported the Hanoverian lineage aligned with the new, united 'British' government. It was a struggle between the traditional way of managing the landscape and people, acknowledging to each their own entitlement to thrive, versus the new habit of ascribing value to land and its inhabitants according to how much wealth they could accumulate for their 'owner'. There were English and Scots on both sides at the Battle of Culloden. That Culloden is commonly now evoked as a clash of Scots versus English, like a rugby match, says much about how history becomes a tool of the present. The winners get to tell the stories, and we storytellers can choose to forget as much as we remember.

It was in this period of time that the foundations for today's Scotland were laid. In 1707 both Scottish and English parliaments had passed the Acts of Union, creating for the first time the United Kingdom of Great Britain. Most ordinary Scots felt betrayed by the union with England, which had been negotiated by parliamentarians, peers and nobles on their behalf, in rooms closed to newsmen. Romantic Scots poet and working-class hero Robert Burns later referred to those politicians and their collaborators, handing over Scotland to the new English parliament, as a 'parcel of rogues . . . [Scotland] bought and sold for English gold'.[1]

One of the key terms of the Union gave wealthy investor Scots access to England's colonial markets abroad. This was fervently desired. During 1660–85, England under Charles II had been rapidly expanding its colonies overseas. Enslaved African people helped to produce profitable crops of sugar and tobacco that generated huge tax revenues for the English Crown, and by 1687 the customs comprised *one-third* of Crown revenue. King Charles had put his brother, later James II and VII, in charge of the new Royal African Company, which quickly turned from trading in gold to enslaved people. James led two wars against the Dutch to gain access to the trade, after which the RAC brought more African slaves to the Americas than any other institution in history.² James succeeded his brother as king while still governor of the RAC. It was in his family's name that the battle that dismantled Gaelic Highland culture would be fought sixty years later.

In the 1690s, Scotland had attempted to establish a colony in the Darién Gap on the Isthmus of Panama. The endeavour failed for many reasons (tropical disease, failure of trade routes, and poor planning), but one key ingredient was the withdrawal of funds by English investors under pressure from the London government.* Scotland was left teetering on bankruptcy. Wealthy Scots landowners, some of whom had invested in the Darién scheme, were also reeling from the terrible crop failures of that decade. The Panama fiasco threw yeast in the warming waters of anti-English sentiment, stirring the foment in the general population – and in the Edinburgh parliament, which passed several Acts incendiary to its relations with England.† It was these negotiations that created the legal structures of Scots–English relations we know today: Scots have their own legal system (article 19 of the Acts of Union), but we share a currency (article 16) and are represented in a London parliament

---

* England was at war with France (who were sheltering the exiled Bonnie Prince Charlie, Young Pretender to the Scots throne) and needed to keep Spain onside, and Spain had colonies in South America that would be affected by Scotland's Panama takeover.

† In 1703–4 the Edinburgh Parliament passed a series of contentious Acts, including the Act anent Peace and War declaring that no future monarch could take Britain to war without Scotland's consent; and the Wine Act and the Wool Act, permitting Scottish trade with France despite England's ongoing war.

by peers and MPs (article 22). In Sir Walter Scott's 1818 novel *The Heart of Midlothian*, Mrs Howden expresses the popular sentiment of the time: 'I dinna ken muckle about the law . . . but I ken, when we had a king, and a chancellor, and parliament-men o' our ain, we could aye peeble them wi' stanes when they werena gude bairns – Bit naebody's nails can reach the length o' Lunnon.'

For thirty-five years after Culloden, Highland culture was outlawed. Traditional Highland dress was banned, Gaelic language was forbidden and the clan chiefs were removed from their powerful seats. This was a particularly inflammatory move: the bans also applied to those clans who had fought for the British government. Many traditional tunes on the bagpipes and on fiddles, centuries in evolving, were lost for ever. From political and regal lords with hereditary power to organise their tenants and lands, the clan chiefs became the modern landowners we recognise today. Without their traditional powers, and with increasing pressure to make their estates financially successful in line with the new industrialised economy, their lands became modern capitalist resources ripe for exploitation. The Scots banking system had been recently established and now the lenders (not family, nor co-tenants of the land nor allies) were the source of credit and debt.* Money became the value system by which worth was judged, and by which security and success became possible, or not.

Culloden marked the true end of clan rule in Highland

---

* The Bank of Scotland, founded in 1695, was suspected of Jacobite sympathies, and so a rival Royal Bank of Scotland was founded in 1727 to administer the funds of government and nobles.

Scotland. The region's culture and beliefs were usurped in favour of the new, developing industrial-capitalist values, 'the essential influences that finally killed clanship', as Scottish historian Tom Devine says.[3] Culloden was 'the climax, not the beginning' of government intervention in Gaeldom.[4]

The Gaelic language, which was prevalent in south-west and Highland Scotland at the time of Culloden, captures a way of looking at the world which challenges some of the most deeply embedded assumptions of modernity, such as the property rights of capitalism and its related driver, individualism. One of the Gaelic words outlawed with the language was 'dùthchas', for which there isn't a direct translation in English. That's the terrible thing about banning languages and burning books, and why it's so effective as a means of subjugating another culture. It's not just the words we lose, but the ideas that the words express.*

Dùthchas is a social system that was imported to Scotland with the early Christian missionary Gaels from Ireland – stowed away in their language – in the first centuries AD. Modern dictionaries translate it as 'homeland', 'birth right' or 'territory'; somewhere you belong. In fact, its meaning runs broader and deeper than the English language can succinctly convey.

Although at the time there were no written texts documenting its meaning, Gaelic social customs were so strong that dùthchas was daily reinforced from sunrise to bedtime. Scholar Ryan Dziadowiec uses old proverbs, poetry and song to explore the many meanings of the word. '*Dùthchas* has always been

---

* Just 3 per cent of the world's population today, mostly indigenous peoples, speak 96 per cent of its 6,000–7,000 languages.

characterised by plurality and complexity, reflecting the complex Gàidhealtachd to which it belonged,' he writes.[5] Etymologically, it comes from the words for earth, place or land – it's a way of being 'in' and 'of' a place, and carries a sense of your actions being 'natural' or 'normal' *for that place*. Young Highland farmer Col Gordon explains that it's a kind of native title, or aboriginal right, and conveys a sense of responsibility, a two-way relationship with the land.[6] It's what was normal across much of Scotland till really very recently.

Dùthchas turns modern notions of ownership on their head. It refers to an ancient belief in land rights held not by an individual or a family but by all inhabitants of the landscape. In the lyrics to 'The Song of the Owl' by the sixteenth-century hunter-bard Dòmhnall mac Fhionnlaigh nan Dàn, the bird moves through the air, touching on tree after tree. The owl drinks from rivers and circles the mountains, its gaze glancing over land, people, and all of nature, across all time. The song is a haunting expression of the workings of an ecosystem; a visceral understanding of the unity between land, people and all living creatures. When we think like the owl, there can be no 'capital' because there is no ownership; the worth of the river, the field mouse and the barley is inherent.

Clanship was associated with land, before blood. If a family was living on the lands of the clan, they could claim allegiance to the chief and become clan members. Under the system of dùthchas, a clan chief's role was to ensure the general well-being of the clan. The chief had no right to evict or to raise rents. The mechanisms of clanship gave protection and agricultural land to the clansmen, who in return tilled the land for food, fuel and fabric and paid the chief rent, mostly in kind. In this way clanship was an economic system. It also included military service – the reciprocal duty to defend your shared rights. Wars fought under the concept of dùthchas were for your own land, not your chief's.

The daily strength of dùthchas was also what made the ordinary people vulnerable when customs began to change. As with the original common lands all over, there were no written records of land entitlement with which to defend their rights, no philosophical or legal tracts. The system depended on customary mutual agreement. During the tumult of the eighteenth and nineteenth centuries, the social order shifted.*

The Scots gentry were increasingly educated 'down south' and achieved high-ranking posts in the British Army and the London Parliament (despite widespread anti-Scots bigotry). 'The anglicisation of the Scottish nobility had begun before 1707 but had further advanced by mid-century,' writes Tom Devine.[7] Street names such as Hanover, George, Queen and Frederick in both Glasgow and Edinburgh proclaimed the loyalty of urban elites to Great Britain and the Hanoverian dynasty.[8] Highland chiefs educated alongside Lowland and English landowners were adopting a new, modern identity, which competed with their traditional role as patriarch of a people and caretaker of their lands. Social ties were loosened, and the tenants' rights drifted off with the tide.

---

* Among the first wave of emigration (to the Lowlands, as well as Canada, the United States and Australasia) was the social group of the tacksmen, those responsible for collecting the rents (tacks) and who formed the ordinary folks' first point of contact with their laird. Without this middle class, the land-workers became increasingly divided from the clan chief.

Culloden over, traditional culture, dress and language banned, the Highland chiefs reviewed their estates. Judged now in early modernity by their ability to earn capital, townships like Auchindrain, the subsistence settlement across the loch from Inver, were an inefficient use of land. 'The most potent threat came from the recognition that land was now principally to be seen as an asset and a productive resource . . . rather than a basic source of support for the rural population.'[9] Now crofting settlements were organised to be intentionally devoid of enough resources to sustain a multiplying family. Devine's estimate suggests that around 200 days' work elsewhere was needed to avoid destitution. This diverted labour into the landowner's profitable new enterprises, such as fishing, wool, or kelp processing (kelp was used in industry to make soap and glass).

Later termed the Highland Clearances, this massive shift in land and people was the widest-reaching domestic food policy carried out on Scottish soil since . . . well, ever. Self-sufficiency for the farming communities was no longer enough; now, rural Scotland had the job of feeding the expanding cities too. With the increased agricultural knowledge of the eighteenth and nineteenth centuries came a revolution in farming. Small tenant farms and townships in interior areas were cleared to make way for larger, more extensive grazing. The small black cattle were the first to arrive, already being managed extensively and in increasing numbers in Argyll, Dumbarton and Perthshire by the 1750s. Then, and in much larger numbers, came the sheep. The fate of the human community on some Highland estates was determined by the breed of sheep that the new large-scale tenant farmer chose to farm. Cheviots meant total clearance; a softer southern breed, they needed winter grazing in more sheltered pasture, which usually meant bringing them off the hill onto the township's arable plots. The hardier Blackface sheep on the other hand could stay on the hillsides all year, even lambing up there, so some of the old tenants could stay in their township homes. The rise of the 'four-footed clansmen'[10] was meteoric: stock numbers in Argyll, my home, quadrupled between 1800 and 1880. In Sutherland, the county associated with the widest and most brutal clearances, the sheep population swelled from 15,000 in 1811 to 204,000 in 1856.[11]

Sons and daughters who couldn't raise families on the limited land themselves were funnelled to the factories in the growing towns or to the expanding colonies overseas. Many families were forcibly removed from their homes, prevented from returning by walls of flames. At the same time, with their newly acquired access to English markets and colonies, some chiefs in Argyll, the central Highlands and Sutherland were establishing plantations in Jamaica, Georgia, New York and the Carolinas, and they needed labour. Folks were lured from their land at home by the promise of work.

Then, in 1846, the severe outbreak of potato blight brought famine of a much greater scale and duration than anything the Highlanders had previously experienced. The evacuation of the overcrowded crofting communities escalated. Destitute, starving, and often with little alternative but eviction, around 11,000 people took 'assisted passage' overseas, with unknown numbers paying their own fares.

The Clearances were a colonisation of the Gàidhealtachd by the new capitalist society. Even as far back as 1598, King James VI had given a group of men from Fife ownership of the Isle of Lewis, having by Act of Parliament deposed the chief of the Clan Macleod.[12] The king talked of establishing a 'colony' on

Lewis, using all necessary means to 'root out the barbarous inhabitants', but the Fife Adventurers, as they became known, didn't last long. In 1793, Sir John Sinclair, first president of the Board of Agriculture,* talked of the 'improvements' to the Highlands as being 'part of a grand project of domestic colonisation' to make the region 'a productive part of the mother country'.[13]

Around 150,000 people left the Highlands and Islands during the 'Fuadaichean nan Gàidheal' ('Eviction of the Gaels'), between the 1750s and the 1850s. At the time, there was a prejudicial attitude among some in both Scots and English society – a belief that 'ethnologically, the Celtic race is an inferior one'.[14] The Gaelic-speaking population were supposedly less hardworking than those of Anglo-Saxon stock, an association which may have given an economic rationale to a racial theory. Whatever the motive, the effect was to distribute the country's people into the Scotland we know today: populations clustered around the coasts and in the industrialised central belt (where the productive agricultural land could feed the growing cities), and in sparsely populated rural areas northwards. The Clearances' effect on diet and food culture, on landscape and wildlife, on land use and language, and on Scots identity, are what we recognise as 'normal' in modern Scotland today.

Popular opinion of the Clearances, however, began to shift, and for three decades from around the 1850s riots and revolts were routine. Early members of the Free Church publicly questioned the rights of the landlords to evict tenants without legal

---

* Forerunner to the contemporary Department for Food, Farming and Rural Affairs (Defra).

restraint. Eventually, Lord Napier's Royal Commission pressured the Gladstone government into passing the Crofters Holdings Act in 1886, giving more secure tenancy and fairer rents to small tenants, and curbing landlords' powers.[15]

In his book, *The Scottish Highland Estate*, Sutherland landowner Michael Wigan comments that 'the anguish of the cleared people had about it an awful predictability'. In an often insightful book, his condescension here prickles my neck like summer heather. Wigan's analysis of history from the privileged vantage point of the present is the most banal kind of dot-joining. His 'engine of agrarian and social change that was crossing Europe'[16] was driven by *people*, and it did not advance uncontested. The events that shaped today's Scotland were the result of decisions by individual politicians and landowners based on the politics, values, knowledge and inventions of the time. It hasn't 'always been like this' – and it didn't have to be this way.

North America, New Zealand and Australia are full of places called Perth, Dunedin, Glendale, Inverness and Ben Lomond. There's a Dumbarton Road in Hong Kong, a Tweedside and a St Andrew in Jamaica, a Blantyre in Malawi. There's a Bannockburn in Zimbabwe, and 38 of second city Bulawayo's 156 districts have Scottish names, including Glencoe, Morningside, and Kelvin East, North and West (after Glasgow's River Kelvin). Back home, on the modern Lachlan Estate, our landlord Euan, Chief of Clan Maclachlan, currently makes money from a caravan park, a hydroelectric plant, several holiday cottages, renting out the castle for holidays and weddings, forestry, sheep fields, selling off the occasional plot of land for aspiring home-builders (like Rob and me) – and leasing Inver Restaurant and its rooms to us.

The values that have colonised our imaginations destroy more than human lives. Today the normative forces at the centre of Scotland are not 'English'; the real modern battle is not 'national'. Individualist norms prevail across all of the western world and rise in the rest. I wonder what it would look like to 'decolonialise' Scots culture, bring the outside fringe voices to the inside, give them an equitable place at the table and equitable rights to land. I try to imagine a culture again guided by dùthchas that allows every entity – human or otherwise – to flourish equally.

A NEW CASTLE

Built in 1790, the New Castle is quite different to the Old. The landscaping today follows the picturesque style of the early nineteenth century. As the myth of the kilt, clan tartans and the romantic wild Highlander was being sketched out in fashionable city societies, so was the land being reshaped to meet the new tastes. The course of the River Lachlan was changed to run in a straight line on the east side of the glen, and earthworks were erected to reclaim ground from the tidal, estuarial marshes. Avenues of lime trees were planted to surround the view.

Inside Inver Restaurant, the view of the ruined castle is framed by the wall of windows. The dining-room decor still consists of our prints, paintings and books, documents of recent lives still in progress. There are also pieces of the landscape: Rob's birch-branch forest in the corner, an installation of dried grasses and seed heads hung from the roof, jars of wild flowers on the tables. Other rural Scottish hotels, guesthouses and restaurants embrace the traditional tartan carpet, sixteen-point antlered heads of stags, taxidermy of salmon and grouse.

It's in periods of great social change and political turmoil that people fabricate tradition, as if building a life raft for identity. Historian Hugh Trevor-Roper says, 'Where the old ways are alive, traditions need be neither revived nor invented.'[17] When I look at traditions within Scotland, and in ex-pat Scots culture elsewhere in the world, it's not a surprise to find that most of them date from the tumultuous eighteenth century, when Culloden put the full stop at the end of the ancient clan system. Simultaneously, it was also when we see the first signs of a nascent national consciousness, as in the country beginning to know itself as 'Scotland'.

Tradition binds a group of people who may otherwise be separated by time, by place, or perhaps by cultural references or political persuasion. Traditions become entrenched when they are easily replicable rituals. You can pull the Christmas cracker with your radical-socialist cousin from Fife or bigoted right-wing uncle from Perth (Perth, Australia, or the one in the central Scottish Highlands). With the tiny flare and fleeting scent of gunpowder you acknowledge a blood peace between you. These are habits repeatable as a tic. I've been back in Scotland for over a decade but the last time I had a Burns Supper was with Scottish friends when we lived in London. A long table in a tiny flat crammed with Scots and their new English conscripts, spearing a steaming meat pudding and knocking back drams as initiation rites. Tradition is a ritual with which you can just as easily include as exclude – now, as 200 years ago.

In the eighteenth century, Scotland was becoming a modern nation. Much of the rural population had decamped to the towns and cities. But despite the new cosmopolitan urban elite, connected to the Continent and the rest of the world through trade, academic or cultural collaboration, politics and empire, the country had a historic and divisive past. The picked scabs of old allegiances bled through thin modern fabrics and rubbing grudges rankled. The country was a mish-mash of influences: Celtic and Pictish bloodlines, Germanic Angles and Saxons, strains of Roman, Danish and French courtly genes, and Viking veins running south from the Shetland Islands and Orkney. The Scottish population badly needed a unifying identity.

But why was it the Gaelic culture in particular that was codified in these new traditions? According to Trevor-Roper, traditions are invented for three reasons: for community membership; to legitimise authority; and for the socialisation – normalisation – of beliefs or conventions of behaviour. Highland dress, language and foodstuffs were strong cultural symbols, made more potent by the recent 35-year ban. In a time where new patterns of living were being stamped into the social fabric, the storytellers – the musicians, poets and novelists, the tribe who articulate culture on the people's behalf – saw an alternative in Highland Gaelic culture.

The tartan and kilts we patriotically associate with all of Scotland today were made up relatively recently, and not by Highland Scots. 'Highlandism', meaning all of Scotland becoming synonymous with the culture of the Highlands, was cemented by Queen Victoria's love of the region. Her husband, Prince Albert, bought Balmoral Castle for her in 1852, and the celebrity couple adopted it as *the* royal holiday home. The Victorian upper and middle classes who now had pleasure time and income to dispose of could enjoy the entertainment of a Highland Games, a grouse shoot, a choreographed ceilidh, or a rousing, whisky-sloshing toast at the Burns Supper. These simplified rituals seemed to have the power to honour the Gaelic history which had so consciously been obliterated. Formalising proceedings just meant everyone knew what to expect: no one felt excluded. And, as ever, food culture followed the shifting contours of the wider national culture – which was rapidly industrialising.

In the Highlands of the eighteenth century, a long shirt, a tunic and a tweed cape, perhaps patterned but in shades of brown, was the norm.* The invention of the modern kilt is credited to an English industrialist in Glengarry called Thomas Rawlinson. After the 1715 rebellion had been quelled, the Highland forests were opened up to exploitation by industry from the south. Rawlinson was part of a network of Quaker families who owned a mesh of furnaces and forges in Lancashire and expanded northwards, where he redesigned the traditional dress in order to make it more suitable for Highlanders felling trees and working a furnace. He created the 'felie beg', the skirt now a separate garment with the pleats already conveniently sewn in. The modern kilt was bestowed on Highlanders not to preserve a traditional way of life, but to ease their transition 'out of the heather and into the factory'.[18]

Originally, there appears to have been no association of tartans with specific clans; instead, Highland tartans were produced to various designs by local weavers and any identification was purely regional.† In 1815, well after the ban was

---

* Still, in 1715, one minister reporting on the Jacobite army traversing his parish recalled that they wore a close-fitting coat of one colour to their knees – but neither 'plaid nor philibeg' (tartan nor kilt).

† Tartan itself – the coloured geometrical patterns woven into cloth – had been known in Scotland since the sixteenth century, possibly originating in Flanders.

lifted, the Highland Society of London began the naming of clan-specific tartans. Many of today's clan tartans in fact derive from a nineteenth-century hoax known as the *Vestiarium Scoticum*.* It has since been proven a forgery, but the designs are still in common use. Today what we recognise as Scotland is a handed baton of storytelling, created because it suited the shifting values of society.

We modern Scots have told ourselves stories and illustrated them: the weddings, ceilidhs and Burns Suppers strewn with birling kilts, those golf clubs and country hotels bedecked in tartan. Symbols are short cuts to meaning, but the simplification loses detail and nuance, which is where real understanding is found. Nationalism of all kinds is a distraction; many nations themselves have been made and re-made within living memory. It's worth examining the traditions we hold dear today, and deciphering the messages these traditions tell us about ourselves and each other. In understanding what void these habits fill or expand, perhaps we could find new traditions to help achieve the things we hope for. Which parts of society and landscape in Scotland today have been marginalised, and how much of this gaping chasm can be bound again by new traditions? Perhaps it's time for a new catalogue of tartans representing the 'new Scots' displaced and replaced by empire.

Our food is already ripe for the reimagining. Food has a powerful presence in tradition and ritual. Food culture *is* culture. Accepting a people's or a person's food is one of the most powerful ways we have of making them feel at home. Refusing

---

* It was composed by the 'Sobieski Stuarts', two brothers pretending to the Stuart throne, who passed it off as a reproduction of an ancient manuscript of clan tartans.

the communion of dinner is the loudest slam of a door. Life in the twenty-first century changes rapidly, aided by the internet, by social media, and by easy foreign travel. In the sea of shifting futures we cling to old traditions, those leaking life rafts. The identity we have created for ourselves using landscape, language and tartan dress gives context to our 'normal' 'Scottish' food in this modern world. But this edible identity has come from somewhere. In understanding where and how our food habits are created, we could learn how to build them differently.

'Aspiration and access,' says Dad as I swing into the passenger seat, by way of a spoiler for what's to come. It's the first day of May in the year 2023: big-sky east coast sunshine with a few scuttering white clouds. The news is full of the impending coronation of King Charles III and for the first time this weekend the population were subjected to the government's new emergency warning – a mobile-phone alert for impending climate disasters like extreme weather.

My dad and I are embarking on a driving tour of Fintry, the area to the north of Dundee where he grew up in the 1950s, in the years just after Charles's mother's coronation as Queen Elizabeth. According to Dad, aka Rodger Brunton, 'It's aw gentrified now' – many folks in Fintry own their own houses and much of the historic edge to this traditional working-class neighbourhood has been dulled. I'm getting a guided tour of his childhood, excavating his food habits in a bid to understand a certain type of Scots diet, the one the government mostly wants to see changed. Much of Dad's diet is the 'normal' that guy on the phone at Inver was referencing.

SCOTTISH / *PEOPLE*

Over his lifetime, my dad's diet has changed dramatically. I know some of the reasons for those changes, the big global tectonics shifting diet and food cultures: foreign trade and travel, immigration and technology, the rise of the behemoth supermarket. But I don't know where his diet started from, or why so many of his tenacious old habits have died so hard in the face of such radical change of personal circumstance.

Dad's food habits are typical of urbanised working-class Scots in cities like Dundee throughout the twentieth century. He has no affinity with the green vegetable, loves his fish fried, his bread white and sliced, his rolls baconed and his whisky un-iced. Other highlights of his daily repasts: bananas; black pudding; glasses of milk, cold from the fridge; cheese, of any kind. Bakeries feature heavily in the daily rounds; Dad still works as an architect and spends a good part of the week driving round Dundee and Angus visiting sites, and picking up sausage rolls and fudge-cream doughnuts. He cooks only occasionally. He and Mum have been together more or less since they were fourteen. Yet Mum cooks daily from diverse cuisines (Italian, Palestinian, Japanese). She loves fruit and vegetables, bakes wholemeal sourdough bread; prefers her eggs boiled and her rice brown; puts chia seeds and kefir yoghurt in her daily porridge. When I became a teenage vegetarian, she told me I'd have to cook for myself, 'because I'm not doing two dinners a day and your father won't eat vegetables'. She ended up eating what I'd made instead.

Today's short journey starts in Carnoustie, where my parents moved when I was almost five and my little brother, Alan, was two. We grew up in a nineteenth-century cottage hung with roses. There was a big garden with an old greenhouse sheltering an ancient grapevine, already gnarled in the early 1980s when we moved in. The greenhouse filled with tomato grow-bags, trays of seedlings covered in newspaper, and cuttings taken on holidays and coaxed into cascades from bean tins and beer cans. There was a veg bed where Mum grew lettuces, kale, radishes and sweetcorn. And a huge elm, 'the Umbrella Tree', under whose shade we hid and seeked.

Carnoustie is Scotland's number-two golf town, sometime host to the Open golf championship. It's on the Tay Estuary where the steely grey river meets the cold North Sea, that deep pit of black oil and bronze haddock. There's a long sandy beach typical of the east coast of Scotland – huge skies and a wide horizon; a gull's straight flight east would land in Denmark or Sweden. We're eight miles from Arbroath, famed for its smokies, where braces of haddock are still hot-smoked over open barrels of smouldering oak, and various branches of the family Spink lay claim to the best repute. The banners on the approach to Carnoustie declare us in 'Angus, Scotland's Birthplace': Arbroath is also famous for the Declaration of Arbroath, sealed in 1320 and popularly known as the first declaration of Scotland's independence.

This fine May morning we leave the seaside resort, golfing hotspot, fishing village, farming hub and commuter enclave behind and head west. Dundee is a small city at the mouth of the River Tay, and where I was born and lived for the first few years of my life. It's the Victorian city famed for 'jam, jute and journalism': a city given breath by the bellows of industrialism. The jam was marmalade; James Keiller and Son still produce it today. Dundee cake, a rich fruitcake featuring sugar and almonds, is indigenous to the city, even as its ingredients are not. Local adage 'twa plen bridies, an an ingin' ane ana' would get you two of the region's savoury rough-puff meat pies, and an onion one as well.

Dundee is only twelve miles from Carnoustie and soon we're back in the 1950s. Fintry was built by the Scottish Special Housing Association, like similar estates Kirkton, Beechwood, and Douglas and Angus, in response to a shortage of housing after the Second World War. Access to decent food was planned and built into life in Fintry. Food shops were within easy walking distance of its 4,000 or so residents (or their bairns, sent out with the daily shopping list). No one had fridges or freezers at home; even the shop itself had no refrigerated storage for leafy greens, milk or frozen peas. So shopping was a daily chore, which made planning simpler and waste non-existent.

The short line of shops we cruise by are in the same place they always were. Everyone shopped at the Co-op, meaning the Dundee Eastern Cooperative Society, each shop franchised to a member of the local community. It was colloquially known as the 'Sosh', and each household had its 'Sosh book' with its own number, like an early loyalty card or savings scheme whose rewards could be cashed in at Christmas for seasonal treats. News of new arrivals at the Sosh zipped round the doorsteps: 'Jeannie, the Sosh has got bananas!' And it was a special day indeed if you got one. Bananas are still the fruit Dad eats most readily; perhaps the only one he'll pick up of his own accord. He shows me round the back of the building where the old butchery windows are filled in, but still visible. There was a fish-and-chip shop, a once-a-week treat. And at the end of the row of shops was the dairy, Dundee Pasteurised Milk.

Today, in the twenty-first century, the built environment in modern towns and cities favours health-damaging consumption. It is easiest and cheapest to buy processed foods, and this is no accidental design. Increased distances between homes and shops, schools and work, encourage us to use cars or public transport rather than walking or cycling. Children get to school through a corridor full of messages which are largely unregulated: adverts for fizzy drinks, salty fatty snacks, breakfast cereals, sweets and treats. Schools have fast-food outlets within an easy lunch-break stroll. Fast-food outlets of all kinds are disproportionately clustered in low-income areas of towns. It is as if, to paraphrase Professor Tim Lang again, our daily lives have been designed to make us sick.[19]

We live in a highly individualised culture. Choice rules, and being able to eat foods high in sugar, salt and fat (HSSF) as often as you like is sold as an individual's prerogative and responsibility. Who this diet benefits is a moot point. It isn't necessarily the eater, or their family. Over two-thirds of Scottish adults are overweight, with 30 per cent obese and 4 per cent morbidly obese.[20] Even allowing for variation in body type across different ethnicities, Scotland's weight gain over the last half-century is of serious concern. The 'weight stigma' attached to obesity is 'a harmful manifestation of social inequity',[21] because weight is also correlated to income and social status. 'Culture reinforces that my private space can override the public space in which you and everyone pay for my healthcare,' Professor Lang told us students.[22] But individuals may not be aware how their choices are influenced behind the scenes.

A 'food desert' describes areas such as housing developments which have made no allowance in their design for food shops. City planners assume that the residents will drive to the larger, out-of-town supermarkets, but if you have kids and a full-time job, no car, and limited storage in your own house, the logistics of large supermarket shops can defeat you. Small corner shops rarely offer much fresh fruit and vegetables, nor the diversity of choice that would accommodate different cultural backgrounds, and often they are relatively expensive. Typically, food deserts are in poorer communities, where supermarkets have not thought it financially prudent to invest. In America, the term 'food apartheid' describes the same situation, recognising that poor neighbourhoods are disproportionately peopled by Black and brown communities.

Sitting in the car outside his old house, Dad draws me a plan, detailing the sideboards and the fireplace, the coal bunker and the close (passageway) where he practised hockey, football and the accordion. The houses themselves were modern: they had indoor toilets, coal fires; a kitchen with an electric two-ring hob and a hot plate heated from underneath by the grill. There was an electric boiler in which clothes were washed and the birthday cloutie dumplings were boiled. There was a larder with two outside vents and a cold shelf, to keep the milk or butter, but no fridge or freezer, no washing machine or tumble dryer. Very little storage space in the kitchen.

Commensality – an ability and willingness to share your table with others – has been an important marker of Scots food culture through modernity. Dad remembers a table so small that the four of them couldn't sit round it at one time. Dinner parties were clearly not on the agenda, even had the income been available to host them. Right up until the early nineteenth century it was common practice for a laird or farmer to eat his dinner with his whole staff of servants and agricultural workers, and his family. The equitably shared table was a marker of a society that shared its fortunes, more or less; and the diet of employer and worker were broadly the same. Often, rural farm-workers even slept in the same house as the farmer. The food provided was part of the exchange for labour. In the modern restaurant, 'staff tea' or 'family meal' seems a vestige of these past times, when all levels of restaurant staff – from owners and management to the newbies and trainees – sit and eat at the same table.

Food memories from childhood become a part of our sense of self. Any cuisine is not determined by the ingredients alone. The practices, equipment, etiquette and rituals of family living give the context and meaning to what is cooked, and therefore the staying power of habits once formed. The tenacious endurance of food preferences 'is partly due to the fact that they are learnt by direct experience at an early age, at home', says sociologist Jack Goody.[23] Food is an intimate emotional connection to our own identity, and binds us to family and home. Exploring Dad's memories feeds the roots of my own.

SOUP AND THE BOILING POT

When Dad was little, rationing was newly ended. Sugar, butter, cheese, margarine, bacon, meat and tea were all still rationed at the late Queen Elizabeth's coronation in 1953. Like most women at the time, Dad's mum, Moira Horne Brunton, was a full-time housewife. She had worked in the drawing office at the shipyards before marrying, which is where she met Grandad, a welder, later foreman, at the yard. Kenneth James Brunton was (like the rest of our family) somewhat diminutive, but during National Service with the Territorial Army in Egypt he'd lifted a lot of weights and taken up boxing, earning himself the nickname the Mighty Atom.

Gran cooked simple food, but it was all from scratch. The weekly menus didn't vary much but Dad never went hungry: there was always something on the table. There were many soups; always with a knap bone (the piece of the beef shin with the knuckle on it) from the butcher, 'Scotch brothy kind o' things where everything went in it': barley, carrots, onions, leeks, the fragments of meat and marrow from the bone itself. I am always pleased to hear of the Scots love of soup, something I share: Scottish meals beginning with broth, or consisting solely of a thicker soup-stew, traverse the centuries and join east coast and west, Highland and Lowland traditions. The crab and rice soup, partan bree, unites the Highland Gaelic partan (crab) with the north-east Doric bree (broth) as well as the fishing villages round the coast, tying the languages and communities like nets.

Indeed, although we have a great deal in culinary common with the rest of the British Isles, one of the most significant differences between Scottish and English food cultures is our northern love of the boiled over the roast. Roasting takes more energy: by the 1800s wood had become scarce in Scotland, and Victorian tourists Dr Johnson and Mr Boswell were already lamenting the barren landscape.[24] A slow simmer on the back of a steady fire that is also heating your home and smoking your hough was an efficient multi-task for an expensive resource. The tradition persists even now that we can flick switches and turn knobs, and given the renewed pressure on fuel for heating and cooking perhaps we are well armed for the future with our canon of fine nutritious soups.

Now, at Inver, every dinner begins with a small cup of simple, seasonal, nourishing broth. Clean, clear flavours are the perfect introduction to a menu that grows in complexity as your evening progresses. In summer, the cup might be cold, an enlivening chill for the hands, and in winter hot, warming and mollifying – your hands are in ours. At lunch there's always soup – we are renowned locally for it and have a dedicated following who assess every new addition to the canon. Soup, for me, is about clarity of flavours. A single vegetable is showcased in each one, and given the cooking technique most appropriate to get the best flavour from it. Garnishes are added to the bowl to give pops of contrasting flavours, acidity and texture. In late summer we might have a chilled courgette soup using the glut from Kate's garden. The deep green ones are peeled and the peel reserved. The rest – pale yellow and green speckled – are sliced thinly and cooked for a long time in olive oil, with a little garlic, honey and rosemary. The dark green peel is added at the end of cooking, keeping the colour vibrant. Leftover whey from yoghurt or fresh cheese-making finishes the smooth, blended soup, and the cheese or yoghurt itself is added to the bowl with herbs and puffed pumpkin seeds for texture, and perhaps a spoon of nutty green pumpkin-seed oil for depth.

MINCE (AN INSTRUCTION)

Dad remembers having mince and tatties at least once a week, always with doughballs, little wheat-flour-and-suet dumplings, bobbing in the mince. Minced beef (indeed mince of any meat) is still a pillar of the Scots kitchen. A few years ago I spent some time helping in a butcher's shop on a Perthshire farm,

SCOTTISH / *PEOPLE*

learning how better to approach a whole carcass of lamb or pork. The mince bucket was a prominent feature of the walk-in fridge, great plastic trugs full of all the trim. It's a thrifty approach to whole-animal butchery, and the stewing of mince a significant Scots cooking method. Our local butcher in Dunoon confided once that to be able to sell a whole carcass of pork, beef or lamb he turns at least half of it into mince and sausage. Even today, iterations like spaghetti bolognese, chilli con carne, burgers, meatballs, shepherd's or cottage pie, kofte or shish kebabs, rely on the churning mincer. When I was growing up we had mince on the table at least once a week too.

Mince features at Inver, a tradition that enables us to buy whole animals direct from local farms without any need for middlemen or butchers. The money stays in our community and my connection to the farmers is personal and immediate. Sometimes it's a ragu of venison – say, slow-braised with fig leaves and sweet, sticky Pedro Ximénez sherry, and served with wide chewy 'noodles' made of dried celeriac, given life again by the sharp juice of autumn apples. At other times there's a deep, aromatic bowl of bobotie served on the side of a plate of still-bloody wood-roasted beef. Or little lamb 'kebabs' grilled over the fire, glazed in smoky cultured tea and burnt honey.

THE BERRIES

The east coast of Scotland is famous for berries: strawberries, raspberries, blackcurrants and now blueberries. It's sunnier over east, with big open skies. The area of Dundee now known as Whitfield was, in the 1950s, 'all berries'; the drive from Carnoustie 'all fields'. Dad remembers being up at 6 a.m. in the school holidays to pick berries for cash.* When I was a kid in the late 1980s and early '90s I picked berries too. East Scryne Farm was a short cycle-ride from our house, and the 'one for the punnet, one for me' picking policy gave me pocket money and stained fingers.

The approach to Dundee is still 'aw berries'. Now, though, the white plastic polytunnels undulate like coasting breakers. From the later 1990s, when I left high school, until Britain's exit from Europe in 2020, the Berry Bus transported to the berry farms people from Bulgaria, Belarus, Romania, Lithuania, Latvia, Ukraine and Poland. Brexit ended freedom of movement for British people to Europe and vice versa, meaning the UK farming and restaurant industries were left devoid of their seasonal workforces. (In 2021, only 5 per cent of the country's seasonal agricultural workforce were Scottish.) Since Brexit, at least three of the asparagus farms we worked with at Inver have stopped producing the delicacy, citing a lack of seasonal pickers for their hand-harvested crops.

The modern farming business model depends on immigration. Journalist Felicity Lawrence writes of migrants 'hidden in the shadows . . . Whereas field work and packing and processing were once given to local workers with reasonable family-friendly hours . . . now it is 24/7 rolling 12-hour shifts confirmed only at short notice, theoretically for the national minimum wage . . . We have created jobs that are inhuman, and incompatible with any normal settled existence.'[25] Minimum wage is inadequately

---

* And my mum had a summer job at the Scottish Horticultural Research Institute (SHRI) at Invergowrie, set up in 1951. The Mylnefield site is now part of the James Hutton Institute, an important research facility specialising in soft-fruit genetics. They're responsible for the tayberry, a cross between a raspberry and a blackberry.

policed, and instead tax credits are offered to those on the lowest wages, which are paid for from the public purse. This means we citizens are subsidising private food and farming businesses, who should be the ones paying their workers a living wage. Addressing this doesn't necessarily mean the price of the berries in the shop must go up; it could mean less profit for big farming corporations and the supermarkets.

Every year, Gran and Mum made jam from strawberries and rasps we picked from farms near the house, potted in reappropriated jars with misfitting lids, sealed with paper and elastic bands. The jam was stored in an old peeling veneered-wood cupboard above the washing machine. The twin doors were always slightly sticky and a small cloud of fruit flies would swirl up when you yanked them open. It was normal just to spoon the bobbing blue raft of mould off the top of the jam each time you opened a jar. I still love the summer's loads of berries, filling the car boot from smaller east-coast farms and driving back to the restaurant in a car heady with strawberry. The kitchen fills with the scent. It's these jams we serve for breakfast with fresh-baked porridge bread. One of my favourite Inver desserts is not my own. 'Jam on Toast' was one-time head chef Matt's ode to his favourite snack: a bowl of zesty pine-shoot ice cream topped with strawberry and candied pine-cone 'jam', served with butter-fried, caramelised milk toast on the side.

CHILLED TOMATO AND RASPBERRY BROTH
(Makes 4 small cups)

At Inver, when tomatoes ripen in local greenhouses as the raspberries do in the fields and hedgerows, we unite the two fruits in a bright, savoury chilled broth. The earthy black pepper oil adds base notes to the aromatic tinkling of fully ripe summer fruit. (If you have time, freezing the raspberries in advance encourages them to give up all their juice.)

500g very ripe, even over-ripe, delicious tomatoes
75g ripe raspberries
5g salt
black pepper oil (recipe below)

Chop the tomatoes roughly and put them in a bowl with the raspberries and the salt. Using clean hands, squash them together. It feels like all the things you've been told not to do with food.

For a thin, clear broth, take a piece of muslin or a thin tea towel, run it under the tap, then wring it out. Line a sieve with the cloth, put the sieve over a deep bowl, and tip all the tomato-raspberry pulp into it. Twist the cloth gently to seal the bundle, and place the whole arrangement in the fridge for a few hours, or overnight.

The clear 'broth' is in the bowl. Taste it – it should have a clear, clean flavour of tomatoes followed by raspberries, with sweetness and acidity in a satisfying balance.

Keep the pulp. Cooked briefly with a little chopped garlic and olive oil, perhaps served with fresh curd cheese and soft herbs, it makes a great, chunky summer pasta sauce for large shapes like rigatoni or paccheri.

Serve the broth cold, in a chilled cup, with a spoon of the black pepper oil here.

Alternatively, for a tomato and raspberry gazpacho, add

50g of sliced red onion to the squashing-in-a-bowl stage and skip the hanging-in-muslin step. Allow it all to macerate overnight, then blend till smoothish or not smooth at all. Serve well chilled, with olive oil, or the pepper oil, and summer herbs.

BLACK PEPPER OIL

150g sunflower oil
50g black peppercorns

Loosely crush the peppercorns in a mortar and pestle, or blitz for a few seconds in a spice grinder. Heat the oil in a tall pan to 160°C, and remove it from the heat. Add the pepper to the oil; it should sizzle, but not scorch. Cover the pan and infuse for at least 2 hours in a warm place, or overnight.

Strain the oil through a piece of muslin, squeezing gently.

You can reserve the crushed peppercorns for a cacio e pepe pasta, or to make a bold pepper sauce for baked celeriac, roast mushrooms or steak.

VEGETABLES: THE VOID

Back in the 1950s, Fintry back gardens were multifunctional spaces. The two growing lads had their sports to practise, and god forbid Rodger play the box in the house *all* the time. Then there was Grandad's shed. When I knew him, this was full of woodworking kit and he made dolls' houses. (He also had a doorbell rigged up from the shed to the house so he could ring Gran when he wanted a cup of tea.) Like everyone, Grandad grew veg in the garden: potatoes, carrots . . . mostly potatoes. I wonder about anything green? Kale, lettuces . . . broccoli? But naw, none of that. Leafy greens take up a lot of space in gardens, and the salad especially can be fickle in cold climates where you can expect horizontal sleet well into April. Then, once you pick them, greens need eating straight away or put into cold storage to preserve them, something nobody had. And no one had a greenhouse; that would be 'asking for trouble'. So, 'normal' for the Bruntons was roots.

In working-class Dundee in the 1950s and '60s, allotments were key to a family's ability to feed itself. Dundee District Council rented land cheaply to her people for their sustenance. The Law Hill allotments site is the biggest in Dundee and keenly sought-after, then as now; 'I don't know a set of allotments that doesn't have a waiting list,' says Dad. It is one of the social supports, part of the common entitlement. Growing vegetables yourself also motivates you to eat them. But Grandad didn't have an allotment, just his small back garden.

It's perhaps no wonder that for my dad, green veg are an alien presence. Ethnologist and chronicler of Scots life and society, Alexander Fenton, notes that, in 1750, 'there was scarcely a vegetable in the town [of Dundee]'.[26] The habit (or lack thereof) continued through the modern centuries; *Border Magazine* observed in 1863 that 'in Scotland, the people have little taste for salads'.[27] Me, I love them: broccoli, kale, spinach, cabbage, sprouts – all of them, all ways. Raw and fresh; just-blanched and snappy green; slow-cooked with olive oil and garlic into deeply savoury, coarse mash; or bitter and charred from the grill. They are a treat, a go-to midweek supper, and a regular feature on the Inver menus. Mum sometimes grew them in our garden. But mostly they'd come from the supermarket, which by my early childhood was vastly expanding the range of vegetables we had easy access to. I cook from a broad range of cultures – a huge range of cookbooks are readily available to me, and I can afford them, but they weren't for Dad and his family. I've always used cookbooks both as an educational resource and a ticket to travel, and other countries treat these vegetables venerably. Applying the pickling and confiting, stir-frying and barbecuing of Italy, China or Mexico to the humble Scots kale and borecole reveals layers of deliciousness our traditional, simple boiling drains away. Even Dad's been known to eat the greens I cook.

I asked my mum, creative cook and keen vegetable eater, why her food habits are so different to Dad's. She grew up in the same city at the same time. She was living with her grandmother, whose only source of income was her state pension. Mum and Uncle Gordon were given free school lunches because the family's income was so low. Dad's family, on the other hand, had a full-time wage coming in from the shipyards. Mum remembers her gran's frugal domestic habits: nothing was ever wasted. There was a monthly butcher's bill, always for the cheaper cuts like mince or hough for boiling, and daily vegetable shopping in the grocer's on Clepington Road. This gran lived with us when I was growing up too, and I remember endless small rinsed yoghurt tubs of leftovers (three coins of boiled carrot, say; half a cooked potato) destined for the next soup pot.

But there were always fruit and vegetables on Mum's plate. In sunny Zimbabwe, these had come from the garden and from the folks who had come round the houses selling them (sweetcorn, avocados, passion fruit, bananas and citrus). In Dundee, the grocers sold carrots, leeks, cabbages, turnips, even frozen peas (Gran had a fridge-freezer, at least later in the 1960s). But Gran's own childhood was spent in the countryside, growing up around farms with a farmer and seed-trader as a father. The kailyard or kitchen garden was an important feature of the rural Scots home, from Orkney to the Borders, to the extent the phrase 'yer kail' became synonymous with dinner itself.

Various common phrases embedded themselves in the Scots language, showing the depths of common kale's roots: 'Cauld kale het again', referring to a tired story or sermon; 'to earn saut [salt] to your kail', meaning to make a living. All members of the brassica family were cultivated, not just the hardy 'curld kail'; cabbages and borecole too. During the eighteenth and nineteenth centuries, as rural families began to move towards the clotting central-belt cities, they lost their kailyards. Without refrigerated transport or storage, it became harder for urbanised generations to access the green stuff. Dad can't remember any generation of his dad's family who had lived anywhere other than the city. The ropes tying his family to their natural landscape had long since begun to fray.

BACON COMES FROM COWS

Dad loves cheese. A love for cultured dairy has been reinforced through generations of Scots and their recipes. For my dad, it's also about being able to afford the things he once couldn't. Being able to buy different cheeses and eat them when he likes is a mark for him not just of pleasure, but of success, progress, self-assurance.

Dundee Pasteurised Milk (DPM) was the dairy in the same row of shops as the Co-op. The milk cart delivered silver-topped glass bottles of milk round the neighbourhood every morning. The Co-op did sell cheese, either a cheddar-type that came in a large block, cut to order and dispensed in paper wrapping, or sometimes a whole red-waxed Edam, but the Brunton household only saw it when Grandad Horne, the Co-op van driver, got the 'ends' to bring home.

Dairy has a presence in Scots cooking as long and deep as glacial Loch Ness. Dairy is a building block of much of northern European cuisine, and Scots food in particular would be in tatters without it. Globally, around 70 per cent of people can't digest lactose beyond childhood,* but more than nine out of ten people of northern European heritage can.[28] Before farming wages were paid in money, milk or buttermilk was used as part of the exchange (along with oatmeal), a tradition that persisted into the early nineteenth century.

Through the Middle Ages and well into the twentieth century, cheese would have been the major protein for ordinary people (alongside the milk itself). Cheese-making was an important part of the local economy and identity of the Highlands and Islands: fresh milk didn't keep, and cheeses helped extend the plenty through the year. In 1553, lands in Islay, Gigha and Kintyre (all Argyll) were required to pay thirty stones of cheese per annum in rent. Cheeses were celebratory items, to gift or enjoy: the 'birthing kebbock' was presented to the new family on the birth of a baby. A unique Roxburgh

---

* Lactose is the main carbohydrate – sugar – in milk. World Population Review, 'Lactose Intolerance By Country 2024', at: <https://worldpopulationreview.com/country-rankings/lactose-intolerance-by-country>

practice involved wrapping cheeses in hemp sacking, and burying them to ripen; they were known as 'ronner', 'rollipoke' or 'roudge'. Fresh-curd crowdie cheese is still made: I buy the crowdie from Connage Highland Dairy, in Ardersier, near Inverness.

Cow's milk seeps into so many Scots recipes, and not just the milk, but the whey, cream, buttermilk and curds. Its prevalence is documented in the various languages of Scotland, the proliferation of words for milk and its products: strubba (coagulated, whipped milk; Shetland), hung-milk (soft cheese made from milk curdled in the summer heat and hung in cloth; Shetland); the buttermilk (blàthach in Gaelic) was called bleddick (in Shetland) or blatho (in Orkney). Gyola and druttle differentiated between whey in which the curds had floated versus sunk (Shetland – the words here may have a Norse origin). Clocks was produced by boiling milk for hours till it became thick and brown, like Norwegian brown cheese. Bland was the whey left from these processes of curd-making, sometimes further fermented to a sparkling drink, or mixed with water for fishermen to take to sea. Lapper was milk soured for butter-making, croods or crowdie were the curds set with rennet and salted. Whey or milk was whisked with a froh-stick or loinid to a froth, and eaten from the pan with spoons (called oon or omhan in the Western Isles, but the practice was widespread). As was the fresh bowl of cold milk sitting beside your cup of scalding oat porridge, spoon dipped from the one into the other. That practice lives on. My young nephews, Hamish and Fergus, copy their gran with a teacup of milk beside each of their small porridge bowls.

The cow in the Inver cottager's care I imagine was a Highland cow, one of the shaggy, mop-headed, brick-reddish stocky beasts that steadily graze Scotland's scrubby hills. Now mostly kept for their excellent meat, they were traditionally a dual-purpose breed and a couple of Highland cows would have provided a family or small community with their rich, nutritious milk for cheese and butter. Reddish-brown hairs have been found in samples of bog butter (buried in the peat bogs to preserve it) dating back to the second and third centuries BC. Large herbivores like Highland cattle have been a keystone species in our ecosystem since prehistory – part of this landscape since the days of wild aurochs. These semi-wild cows feed nutrients back into the hillsides. The beasts graze selectively, creating wet hollows, breaking up ground vegetation and aiding the dispersal of tree seeds, in doing so shaping woodlands and helping to sustain an ecosystem, all within the land's own limits. Since at least the Neolithic age, native breeds of cattle similar to Highlanders have been a key tool for transforming rough marginal land into edible sustenance. People used the milk for as long as the cow was able to give it, which meant the animal itself was a renewable resource (rather than only growing cattle for the meat). In addition, you'd have its dung to fertilise the rigs and dreils of domesticated land.

At Inver today, we buy Highland beef from nearby Glen Fyne, or from Auchentullich Farm on Loch Lomond where they're crossed with that other ancient breed, the Shorthorn. Highland cattle are raised alone, effectively wild, on the uninhabited island Inchmarnock, off the nearby Isle of Bute. Farmer Ian couldn't get us any for the restaurant last year because his boat was broken. Animals like these make the most use of the landscape round here, good for the whole ecosystem as well as for the human animals within it.

Dairying as an industry, rather than part of a self-supplying house or holding, was developed in the Lowlands, where fertile land was in easier reach of the rivers and thus transport to and from the cities and their ready market for perishable milk. By the 1660s Ayrshire was already famous for Dunlop, the hard cloth-bound cow's-milk cheese still produced today. Near industrial hotspot Glasgow, the area was by the late eighteenth century a centre of Scottish dairying, and the Ayrshire cow became Scotland's prime dairy animal. Dairies or farms within a two- to three-mile radius of a town would supply the population with fresh milk brought round the streets on a horse and cart. Because fresh milk was perishable and refrigerators were centuries away, buttermilk was also popular: already fermented, it was naturally inoculated with 'keeping' properties, and housewives used it for drinking and baking.* The microbes would've also kept the industrialised gut ecosystem healthier.

HATTIT KIT

Traditionally, hattit kit was made by milking a cow into a pail of fresh buttermilk left from a previous milking. This recipe has been adapted to omit the cow. The acidity in the buttermilk curdles the fresh raw milk into a soft curd cheese. Think of it like a light, fresh cheesecake. At Inver, we serve it with sugar-fermented forced pink rhubarb, a raw rhubarb sorbet and white chocolate-coated beremeal crumble.

---

* The lactic acid found in buttermilk and yoghurt whey tenderises wheat proteins to make the best scones. In Inver's scone days, we used these butter by-products in the same way.

> You can make your own buttermilk by adding a small amount of cultured buttermilk or cheese whey to fresh milk and leaving it somewhere warm overnight, say in a hay-banked byre in June; just give yourself a couple of days. Alternatively you can buy it from a supermarket or a cheesemonger.

THE HAT

500g good buttermilk
1½ litres whole fresh farm milk
2g rennet

Put the buttermilk and milk into a pan and heat slowly till it reaches blood temperature (37°C). Switch off the heat and move the pan to wherever you will leave it overnight. It should be a warm place, around 22–24°C.

Measure the rennet into a small container and add 20g or four teaspoons of cool water. Sir the rennet into the milk using a gentle up-and-down motion with the spoon. Incorporate evenly but don't over mix. Cover the pan with a cloth secured with an elastic band, and leave undisturbed for 6–8 hours or overnight. The rennet should set the milk and separate it into soft curds and yellow-ish whey, while the buttermilk sours the fresh.

Line a colander with muslin or a damp tea-towel, and gently spoon the curds into the cloth. Allow it to hang for a few hours in the fridge until the curds are just firm, like soft cheese. You should have around 1kg of soft curds and a litre of whey.

You can add a little salt to the curds and eat them like crowdie. Keep the whey to start a new batch of buttermilk, or to make sourcakes, or maybe stir into blaanda bread* or whip into frothy oon. If you're Scottish you certainly don't throw it down the sink.

TO MAKE THE HATTIT KIT
(Serves 4)

250g soft milk curds
50g sugar
pinch of flaky sea salt
250g whipping cream
around 200g, or 1 punnet, Scottish soft fruit like fresh strawberries or raspberries
4 spoonfuls of jam of the same
4 of something crunchy and biscuity, like shortbread

Whisk the curds with the sugar and salt, making them smooth and loose (if they are too firm, add a spoon of the whey back in). In another bowl, whip the cream to soft peaks. Fold the cream gently and evenly into the curds.
 Spoon the mixture into sundae glasses, with the fruit and the jam and the biscuit.

---

* Unleavened oat and barley bread, made with milk and butter.

SCOTTISH / *PEOPLE*

As industrialisation kicked in, the whey left from cheese-making gave rise to another modern Scots dietary classic: the bacon roll. In the 1880s, a large commercial creamery was set up near Stranraer capable of handling the milk of 2,000 cows. Attached to the dairy was a herd of 500 pigs. The by-products of cheese- and butter-making, buttermilk and whey, are almost 50 per cent of the original milk. As small farms and households had learned to do in previous millennia, the Stranraer dairy fed the whey to the pigs, turning it into another delicious edible product: pork. With no refrigeration, most pork meat at this time was preserved by salting and sold as ham or bacon. The now-famous Ayrshire bacon industry had begun.

Over the First World War until 1920, the Ministry of Food took control of around 800 British dairies to maintain the staple source of liquid protein and keep the population healthy enough for the war effort. The principle of government intervention in milk was set, and the Scottish Milk Marketing Board appeared in 1933. The regional MMBs were 'producers' organisations', working on behalf of the farmers. The Milk Acts of 1934 and 1936 set a retail price for milk, and inevitably there followed more and more surplus as more and more farmers took to dairying and its stable prices. Drinking milk was encouraged 'for the health of the nation' (and the health of its farming sector, to whom the MMBs were diverting the public's money). The MMBs set up creameries to produce butter and cheese, as well as cream, whey products, milk powder and flavoured milk drinks, speeding the decline of home or smaller-scale production. By the 1960s and '70s refrigeration was becoming more common, and now young Rodger could enjoy his cold glass of milk.

BETWEEN TWO WATERS

PORK COMES FROM THE AMAZON

The 'Sosh' sold bacon in thick slices cut to order off a big piece of salted belly or pork loin and brought home wrapped in paper, but the Brunton family saw little of it. The increased imports of cheaper Danish bacon in the 1960s was when Dad's bacon-roll habit really took off. Like bananas and cold milk, bacon was a treat to be savoured. With Dad's rising income and the country's dropping bacon prices, this treat could reward the most flippant of achievements. Like the old adage says, though, there's no such thing as a free lunch.*

Bacon came to rule our breakfast and supper tables through Scotland's love of dairy, and because of an easy access to salt. Pigs were a great way to turn whey, with table and field scraps, into delicious salty bacon, mealie puddings (white puddings) and ham houghs for the soup pot. Even the fat was traditionally rendered, salted and peppered, and stored to spread on oatcakes.

The Scots' diet has always had a heavy presence of salt. Alexander Fenton remarked that the importance of salt to earlier Scots was 'almost beyond our conception'.[29] There's a history of salt pans around the long and winding coasts of Scotland, mapped at least from the sixteenth century, with many still on the go today (for example, Blackthorn Salt in Ayr, or the Isle of Skye Sea Salt Co.). Salted fish and meat were commonplace, to eat, to store and to trade; to see us through cold winters and long journeys. Now, salt is one of the many dietary demons the health authorities would see purged; it's

---

* Cheap bacon rolls externalise their costs, and too many of them racks up a big bill in healthcare and environmental clean-up to the tax-paying citizens, essentially subsidising the cheap meat industry.

associated with raised blood pressure, heart disease and stroke. A diet containing lots of processed foods (including cheese and bacon) is also likely to be far too high in salt.

Domesticated pigs appeared in Scotland at the beginning of the Neolithic period. Joints of pork have been found at Bronze Age burial sites in East Lothian, Aberdeenshire and Kinross-shire, though pig bones are less common in archaeological sites than those of other animals, suggesting they were not then such a prominent part of the diet. The Pictish King Uurad, who ruled from AD 839 to 842, is shown shooting a boar with an arrow on the ninth-century Drosten Stone. By early medieval times, hunting 'noble' boar and deer had become a regular pastime of royalty and leaders. Boars were hunted to extinction probably by the thirteenth century, but by this time pigs had long been domesticated, and were grazed in royal forests as part of the common rights. In the eighteenth century, Shetland and Orkney still had wild breeds of pig – 'ugly and high backed with coarse bristles' – though a hundred years later, breeds perhaps more like the contemporary Tamworth had appeared: 'black or red coloured and middle sized'.[30]

These days, traditional breeds of pig trough around the country's smallholdings, gardens and organic farms. Inver delights in cooking Large Black from organic Ardyne Farm near Dunoon, or occasionally from Newmiln Farm in Perthshire. Now Ian at Scalpsie Farm on the Isle of Bute is raising Mangalitsas alongside his Herdwick sheep and Highland cattle. We buy whole animals and use the whole carcass. We salt our hams and leave them to dry, stuff sausages, hang salamis, pour liquid blood puddings into casings and – my favourite of all – make mealie puddings from oats, pork fat and rinds, and lots of black pepper. I was delighted to find historic mention of 'flead' (leaf lard, soft spreadable fat that lines the inside of the pig's belly) in the Pitlochry area of Perthshire. We too use flead to make a light, savoury short or puff pastry. Pigs' trotters make a great soup stock or a thickener for the jelly used to set the potted heid. The chimney at Inver has those iron hooks inside it, for hanging pans or hams, or both together.

During the period in which we were building our 'national' identity in the nineteenth century, more of the stuff we ingested was being imported than in any other country. By the turn of the twentieth century, we Scots depended on Australasia and America for beef and lamb, Denmark for that bacon and butter, Canada and the US for yet more bacon and fresh pork. At the same time, Ayrshire bacon was on sale in Lyon, Paris, Malta, Cape Town, Beirut and Tunis. Yet Danish bacon became the twentieth-century norm in Britain. The Danish government's marketing board had made belonging to it mandatory: the Danish factories were co-operatives owned by thousands of farmers who were compulsory members, and benefited from the subsidised facilities and infrastructure. Meanwhile, British bacon factories had no contracts with the farmers, were operating to only 50 per cent capacity, marketing and curing standards were variable, and the price and availability of British bacon suffered. Still today, our 'free' daily food choices are shaped by government decision-making, and our continued reliance on food from overseas makes us vulnerable.[31]

Modern pork became normal in Britain because it used waste, the traditional combination of whey and 'swill' (human food waste), an efficient, circular use of resources. Swill-feeding was outlawed after the BSE crisis of the 1980s and '90s. Now, the UK wastes more than a third of its food: if global food waste was a country, it would be the third-largest emitter of CO_2

after the US and China.[32] Instead of diverting some of this to pigs, the UK imports on average 3 million tonnes of soy for animal feed each year. Brazil accounts for a third of global soy production, including in regions of high biodiversity such as the Amazon, the Cerrado and the Gran Chaco rainforest. Today, almost 80 per cent of the land used for farming worldwide is used for animals, and *a third* of that global area is used to grow their feed.

One company, Cargill, is the UK's largest importer of soy and the third-largest meat processor worldwide. Cargill is America's largest privately held, family-owned company, with 21 billionaires in its ranks and annual revenues of $177 billion.[33] It is also the third-largest greenhouse gas emitter of all global livestock companies.[34] In 2022, Cargill was one of the 'Deforestation Dozen': twelve soy traders who control 89 per cent of soy exports from the Paraguayan and Argentinian Gran Chaco rainforest,[35] getting rich on public goods.*

Another multinational food giant is the Brazilian company JBS, the world's largest meat producer. Its UK subsidiaries, Moy Park and Pilgrim's Pride (previously Tulip), have about 30 per cent of the UK market share for chicken and pork, and supply most major UK supermarkets and all the most familiar fast-food chains.† JBS is so big, it's estimated to produce around half the annual carbon emissions of fossil-fuel giants such as ExxonMobil, Shell and BP.[36]

Pigs and chickens fed with imported Amazonian soy

---

*   Cargill's joint venture with UK poultry giant Faccenda Foods processes 4.5 million of the 20 million chickens handled in the UK each week, and is Tesco's primary fresh chicken supplier.

†   Moy Park supplies Burger King, KFC, McDonald's, Nando's and Pizza Hut, while Tulip received a supplier award from McDonald's in 2017.

contribute to deforestation and climate collapse; they are also a 'nutrient loss'. A Dutch Landrace pig, the typical pink industrial pig, needs 2.8kg of feed to put on 1kg in weight. If instead that 2.8kg comprises waste or is foraged by the pig itself in woodland, this could be a useful transformation. Feeding UK pigs and chickens partly on UK-grown pulses and legumes would avoid some deforestation, but we'd have to eat as much as 80 per cent less pork and chicken. 'It would mean that small- and medium-scale pig, poultry and legume farmers could actually make up a larger market share of the sector, and build resilient and thriving farming businesses which focus on the production of higher quality and more ethically produced meat,' says one recent report.[37] And it would address the UK food-waste problem, which the inimitable Professor Tim Lang calls 'a cultural act of planetary stupidity'.[38]

Bacon rolls became part of the Scottish breakfast because Scottish pig producers used waste from expanding dairy and cheese production. An occasional treat food became more widely available and accessible with industrialised production and strategic imports from Denmark. Nowadays, eating less meat (or none at all) and more UK-grown beans and pulses, as Scotland used to, would mean wealth was spread more equitably, with indigenous lands, global commons and biodiversity protected; lower greenhouse-gas emissions; and a healthier and much cheaper diet available for all. My dad, however, still sees bacon rolls as both a dietary essential and a special treat. It's one of the few foods he's happy cooking and he always brings out the breakfast bacon when I'm home for a rare visit. It's hard to refuse.

At Inver, I'm wondering how much longer we can feature pork on our menu, knowing what I do now. Ian's Mangalitsa pigs are almost wild, foraging in woodland, their diet supplemented with discarded fruit and veg from the farm's vegetable plot. The meat is full-flavoured and delicious, though it takes careful ageing, curing and cooking to overcome the natural bite of muscles used to hard work. A restaurant menu that reflects animals' roles in a functioning ecosystem could only very occasionally serve a meat like this. Of course, we use every part. Crispy fried pig's head and tail make it to the specials board. Savoury, pâté-like rillette (a French technique for cooking belly and shoulder in their own delicious fat) is served for breakfast. Every dinner plate will feature different cuts: sausage, belly, kidney, as well as loin chops cooked over coals. Our menus offer only one meat course in eight or nine servings. And yet. How much rainforest is it okay to eat?

OATS

Traditionally, the Scots staple grain was oats. Orcadian writer and feminist pioneer Floss Marian McNeill described oats as 'the flower of our Scottish soil ... Scottish oatmeal has been transmuted through centuries into Scottish brains and brawn.'[39] Alexander Fenton lists bread as one of his five 'major elements of the Scottish diet', but he doesn't mean wheat bread: until well into the twentieth century, 'breid' meant oatcakes; the moniker denoting its centrality to the meal. Scotland is 'A Land o' Cakes'.*

I'm slightly obsessed with oats. Till really very recently oatmeal, with regional variations in presentation, was a major

---

* Originally from 1659, the phrase was popularised by poet Allan Ramsay in 1728 and again by Robert Burns in 1789.

element in the daily food of nearly all social strata in Scotland. The oat persists even now, and the Scottish farming press reports 'record' harvests in recent years. Brose, porridge or sowans were for breakfast; oatcakes or bannocks for lunch, and again at suppertime. Sowans is a thick paste made by adding water to oat husks (leftover from milling) and fermenting it, then cooking the paste into a warming gruel. Swats is the thin, sour oat-water left over from the sowans-making, a refreshing and highly nutritious drink. Once I made sowans at the restaurant, and served the tangy, nutty, creamy paste with soused herring and a salad of wild herbs and flowers. Then of course there's the oats used for 'breading' fried herring; or steamed in a cloth to make a mealie dumpling or 'fitless cock'; or stuffed with pork fat and onions into a sausage casing to make a mealie pudding.

The oat, *Avena sativa*, is one of a range of edible grasses originally from Anatolia (aka the Fertile Crescent). They were introduced as a crop to Britain by the Romans around AD 600, much later than wheat. Like the turnip in the 1700s, they arrived as animal food, for the Roman horses. The oat is a much hardier grain than wheat and flourished more readily in our colder, wetter climate. The later Middle Ages saw its popularity really take off in Scotland: in the face of medieval famines and plagues, the hardy oat nudged barley off the top staple spot.

At the restaurant, 'porridge bread' goes in the breakfast baskets, with butter, jam, local cheeses, potted hot-smoked trout, or our own charcuterie. Oats are highly nutritious, and once eaten, slow to release their energy (the main soluble fibre in oats is beta-glucan, which helps slow digestion, increase satiety and suppress appetite). They are also relatively cheap, and given that the other major ingredient of porridge is water, I can imagine why many high street brands relish the presence of porridge on their menus. Fenton describes oatmeal as 'embedded in the mentality of the Scots as an identification mark'.[40] Delicious, nutritious, easy to grow here – so with very short supply chains – oats have as bright a future as they do a venerable past.

SKIRLIE
(according to one indigenous east-coaster)
(Serves 4 as a side, or perhaps one hungry harvester, as his sole sustenance in 1871)

Oats are cooked with onions and chicken fat to make skirlie (from 'skirl-in-the-pan', the sound the dry meal makes sizzling in the fat). I know it well: Mum made it regularly, often to serve with roast chicken. It's a kind of loose, free-form stuffing, sometimes with a splash of water added, sometimes, when I make it at the restaurant, a splash of good chicken stock. And always with black pepper. In Orkney, a dish called 'hoonska' seems to be a similar thing.

125g pinhead oatmeal
1 medium brown onion
50g chicken fat, harvested from the top of a stock, or
    from the pan of a roasted bird (or use butter)
½ teaspoon salt
125ml hot chicken broth or water
freshly ground black pepper

Preheat the oven to 180°C. Toast the oatmeal on a tray for 10 minutes.

Dice your onion finely. (In the restaurant we'd say brunoise it. In my mum's kitchen it's more like a scatter of jigsaw pieces.) Melt the fat in a saucepan, add the onion and salt, and cook over a low heat until translucent and warmly golden, around 10 minutes. Add the oatmeal and stir till it absorbs the fat. Stick a lid on the pan, turn off the heat and let it soften for 10 minutes or so. At this point you can legitimately stop, season and eat; this is how my mum makes it, and how my Highland gran did too.

However, I prefer the nubbly chew of a hydrated oat over the sandy texture of my childhood skirlie. So, I add the hot chicken stock. This will make the oatmeal clump immediately into a sticky mass. On a very low heat, let it cook, stirring often, until the oats absorb the liquid, the starch cooks fully and the oats dry somewhat, separating again into an open, crumbly pudding. Season enthusiastically with black pepper ground fresh from a mill, and add a little more salt if needed. It should be slightly spicy (IMHO). It will sit happily till needed, so give yourself plenty time.

Serve with chicken, or on its own, to combat the sort of Scots malaise that descends with the first of the November storms.

THE PLAIN LOAF

Back in 1950s Fintry, the Sosh bakery supplied rolls and loaves. 'Plain' was the traditional Scottish white loaf, baked in large batches in a huge iron baking box; each dome of dough touching the other, giving the characteristic 'torn' sides to the loaf, with a darkened domed crust and bottom (except for the 'enders', the loaves on the exterior of the box, which had a third crusted side). The long fermentation time of sixteen or more hours with a traditional 'barm' eschewed industrial yeasts and gave a dense, close-textured crumb. It also meant that bakers didn't have to come in overnight to work the dough, or to work on the Sabbath: Monday morning's bread could be started Saturday night. It's still popular; there's a version made by Mothers Pride (which despite the tartan packaging is from Manchester), and the 'Scottish Plain Loaf' has been given its own category in the annual Scottish Bread Championships. 'Pan loaf' was the pricier, 'posh' version, baked in individual square tins with an even, golden crust all round. Thus, 'talking pan breid' would be talking with a fancy accent, perhaps with certain aspirations to grandeur. By the 1960s, MacFarlane Lang's mass-produced Milanda bread came in big vans from Glasgow, but it was still recognisably the same plain loaf.

Wheat has been farmed in Britain since around 6000 BC. Trade in wheat between Britain and northern European countries like France and the Netherlands (which were both once connected to Britain) may predate farming by a couple of millennia.* The original Einkorn wheat itself originated in Anatolia some 10,000 years ago. So wheat and bread have had a significant presence in the British diet since the Neolithic – even in Scotland, where wheats were the main grains found

---

* There was some excitement in the archaeological community around 2015, when a stash of wheat grain was discovered in a peat bog under the English Channel, dating from around 2,000 years before evidence of farmed wheat.

at a prestigious hall in Balbridie, Aberdeenshire, dating from 4000–3500 BC. Its importance as a staple is evident from the thirteenth-century Assize of Bread and Ale, Britain's first-ever law to regulate the price and quality of wheat grain.

By the eighteenth and nineteenth centuries, being able to eat white wheat bread was a status symbol. Wheat needs sunshine to fully develop its gluten (the protein that gives bread its particular structure), and sunshine is not one of Scotland's specialities. Open-skied, drier, flat regions in the south-east, such as the Carse of Gowrie or Fife, had better success with growing wheat than the northern, western and Highland areas, where oats and pulses flourished. White bread made from wheat was sometimes given as a reward or a treat at harvest time by farmers and landowners to their labourers, cementing the social status both of the bread and of the benevolent laird, and giving the former the appealing sheen of 'special occasion food'. In the 1950s too, white bread was enjoying renewed desirability after the National Loaf of the Second World War years: this nutrient-injected, solid and unappetising wholemeal loaf was introduced by the Attlee government to make best use of Britain's existing wheat stores, without having to import more from abroad. Bread rationing ended in 1948 and the National Loaf was 'abolished' in 1956, but during the recent 2020 wheat shortage, farmer and miller Angus McDowall at Mungoswells in East Lothian ground only wholemeal flour, to make the most of his harvest and get the maximum grain to the people.

Pioneering baker and grain zealot Andrew Whitley was the original leaven in the UK's contemporary sourdough bread movement. Returning from his production post with the BBC's Russian Service, Andrew opened the organic Village Bakery in Cumbria in 1976 to make bread from grain milled at a local watermill, aiming to encourage a more self-reliant rural community. Now, as director of Bread Matters, we find Andrew championing a heritage Scots grain economy from his fields and mill on the Balcaskie Estate in Fife. The charity Scotland the Bread is tasked with bringing 'Flour to the People' using traditional Scots-grown wheat varieties rescued from global gene banks. These have poetic names such as Rouge d'Ecosse and Golden Drop, but Andrew's plans for them are not romantic; his mission is nothing less than a secure, equitable supply of our staple food without damage to the natural environment. As he explains: 'We call our wheat grain "Balcaskie Landrace", an indication of our ambitions to create an increasingly diverse population of plants that adapt to the local soils and climate.'

In 2014, the James Hutton Institute at Invergowrie tested the Scotland the Bread wheat samples and found that all these 'old' varieties have generally higher levels of nutritionally important minerals and trace elements than the types of wheat being grown commercially today. They are also better suited to growing in our wetter, colder climate and may offer a secure, nutritious food supply more resilient to the shifting global climate and geopolitics.

'Aspiration and access' *are* the most common drivers of our food choices. When Dad was growing up, white bread was desirable, and through the second half of the twentieth century it became increasingly available, thanks to tariff-free trade in global wheat (most UK wheat comes from the wide sunny plains of Uzbekistan or Canada), industrial bread factories and the supermarkets. Now, in the early decades of the twenty-first century, what's 'posh' in bread-baking is rustic-looking, naturally fermented wholemeal loaves made from grains you can name alongside their farmer. And with the proliferation of small craft bakeries, homes, community groups and restaurants choosing to bake their own, this nutritious and more environmentally benevolent loaf is increasingly more available. My dad still prefers his white sliced.

BAKERIES AND BUTTERIES

Bakeries and their goods have a venerable place in the Scots dietary canon. On our road trip down memory lane, Dad and I stop for breakfast at Rough & Fraser (Quality Bakers, Est. 1860), now on the Kinghorne Road. It's a showcase of classic Scots savoury and sweet baked goods: sausage rolls, pies, bridies, fudge-cream doughnuts, strawberry tarts, pineapple tarts, rhubarb tarts, empire biscuits, millionaire's shortbread and fruit slices (the dead-fly ones), as well as the loaves and rolls.

Growing up, we had salty-savoury butteries for breakfast as a weekend treat. Butteries, or Aberdeen rowies, are a kind of misshapen, blobby, yeasted rough-puff pastry, traditionally laminated (layered) with pork fat, butter or both (another blind spot for the teenage vegetarian). Carnoustie is at the southern limits of the rowie's heartland in the north-east, where they are traditionally eaten with more butter and that bittersweet Dundee marmalade. Rowies are a well-documented breakfast item in and around Aberdeenshire; an Angus woman quoted in Alexander Fenton's epic recounts 'a row an a cuppa tea' being a 'universal breakfast'.[41] We sometimes serve them for the picnic-basket breakfasts at Inver – I was keen to sneak in the familiar scent of bacon even though we weren't doing a fry-up. We always have lots of trimmings from our hams and sausages, which we render with butter and more pork fat to make ham butter. All our breads are naturally leavened with a rye sourdough starter. And the best laminated breakfast pastry is undoubtedly the croissant. So there we have it: a sourdough croissant laminated with rendered ham fat, rolled like a pain au chocolate, with slices of house-cured pork belly in place of the chocolate.

POTATOES, PERUVIAN SEABIRDS AND MEXICAN BEETLES

Dad remembers 'an awfy lot of potatoes'. Even when I was growing up, the October break was still 'the tattie holidays'. (Using school kids for the potato harvest during school hours ended in 1962, but the name persisted at least till the 1990s.) This is the vegetable that changed the whole modern world: after the potato's popularity was secured and countries such as Scotland, England, Holland, France and Spain could both feed their peasantry and their rapidly industrialising cities, those nations could turn their attention to economic development overseas. The potato was the dietary leg-up for the rising West.

Potatoes were the first monoculture, meaning that they were planted in large fields to the exclusion of other crops. The first nitrogen fertiliser and the first pesticides were all introduced to bolster the potato's growth, forever changing how we farm and feed ourselves. It is yet another familiar Scots ingredient for which we owe thanks to cultures, families and their historic sacrifices elsewhere.

At the time the potato was introduced, the staple grains of oats, barley and peas were ground into flour and made into a bread or stirred with hot water into a brose or a pudding. Famines were ubiquitous; all over continental Europe developing nations struggled to consistently feed their own populations.

Scotland's 'Seven Ill Years' (the failed harvests and related famine from the 1690s) were part of the tumultuous backdrop to the 1707 political union. Particularly at risk were the rural poor, who had no back-up should their grain harvest fail.

As a staple food, the potato is way more efficient than any grain. Stalks of wheat or barley can only store as much energy as their seed heads can take before they get so swollen the entire scrawny stalk falls over and rots in the wet earth. Potatoes, supported by the soil in which they grow, have no such limitations.* They will grow happily in a wider variety of soils and climates than grain; they are nutritious, spoil less readily and require no special equipment (like a grain mill) to cook and eat. Shifting the diets of 'potato country' populations (from Ireland through northern Europe and all across Russia) from grains to spuds effectively more than doubled European food stores, in terms of calories.

Credit for the agricultural innovation behind the world's first documented domesticated vegetable goes mainly to the Andean peoples, possibly as long as 10,000 years ago. The original wild potatoes were toxic, and wildly diverse. The contemporary International Potato Center in Peru has preserved almost 5,000 varieties, and still today a single Peruvian potato field will host up to twenty diverse 'landraces', a practice which allows the variety most suited to that local condition to flourish and gives security in times of pest infestation. Spaniards invading Peru brought back this novel food around the mid-sixteenth century; records document potatoes grown in and exported from Spain from the 1560s.[42] From there they spread to France

---

* The world's record-holding potato, grown in Somerset, England, in 2011, weighed 4.98kg.

and the Netherlands (then part of the Spanish Empire), and entered Britain a decade or two later. But it was another century before the plant took root in Scotland. Earliest references are in 1672 in the north-east, and 1698 in the Edinburgh area, and only at the higher social levels. But just a year later the new Lord Belhaven was encouraging his tenant farmers to plant potatoes in their gardens.

People had to be convinced of potatoes. It took campaigns from government, royalty and landowners to persuade the peasantry to plant them. Unlike any other crop of the time, potatoes are grown from pieces of other potatoes, not seeds: they are clones. They are also a member of the nightshade family and may be poisonous, thought some, or the work of devils and witches. Russian Orthodox Old Believers thought they may have been the Bible's original forbidden fruit.[43] French agronomist, pharmacist and food innovator Antoine-Augustin Parmentier (also responsible for extracting sugar from beetroots, mandatory smallpox vaccination and preserving food by refrigeration) became a tireless promoter of the potato and published *Examen chymique des pommes de terre* in 1773, extolling their nutritional virtues. Soon King Louis XVI and Queen Marie Antoinette were wearing garlands of potato flowers to their fancy-dress balls.

However, Europeans had imported potatoes without the Andean people's farming wisdom. In Scotland, as in Ireland, by the late 1700s the potato was increasingly a staple food for poor town-dwellers, Lowlanders and Highlanders alike. For subsistence communities such as Auchindrain, the coming of the potato was a blessing. However, over-reliance on the monoculture of clones made the north-west Highlands and northern islands of Scotland vulnerable to pest and disease. (Central and southern Scotland meanwhile maintained a diverse agriculture of grains, greens and turnips, as well as potatoes.) The crop had no resistance to the potato blight which hit like a mouldy tsunami in 1845 and decimated fields each year for a decade, one of the deadliest famines in history. The Scottish Highland potato famine resulted in 160,000–200,000 deaths, while in Ireland the death toll was as high as one million. Disease wreaked further damage on weakened bodies, especially in cities overcrowded by rural people fleeing the famine; typhus claimed as many lives as starvation. As Amartya Sen reminded us, however, famine is caused not solely by a lack of food but by a lack of *entitlement* to food: during the worst year of the Irish potato famine in 1847, almost 4,000 ships carried food away from Ireland.[44]

Along with the potato, Spanish conquistadors had found Peruvian guano: the nitrogen-rich, dried remains of millennia of seabird excrement, excavated from the uninhabited Chincha Islands first by Peruvians, and then by indentured Chinese people. With the power of pelican pee, European farm yields were doubled or tripled; farmers' expectations quickly shifted, and with them the whole template of industrial agriculture. American journalist and author Charles C. Mann writes that 'Industrial monoculture allowed billions of people – in Europe first, and then in much of the rest of the world – to escape poverty.'[45] But Mann also acknowledges that European peasants of the time ate *fewer* calories than societies in Africa and the Amazon, who were not farming industrial monocultures. And by this time, European peasants lacked access to the land that could have fed them more diversely.

Peruvian guano ran out in the late nineteenth century and the country went bankrupt.[46] Shortly afterwards, the chemist Fritz Haber and his colleague Carl Bosch invented the Haber–

Bosch process, for which they won joint Nobel Prizes. Using massive amounts of energy, the process pulls nitrogen from the atmosphere and turns it into artificial fertiliser suitable for farm use. Unfortunately that nitrogen is then released into the atmosphere, and so successful is this process that nitrogen levels are now double the safe limits. Fertilisers are farming's largest output of greenhouse gases, and over-use of nitrate fertilisers has been described by the UK Parliament's Environment Audit Committee as a 'time bomb'.[47]

Artificial nitrogen fertiliser (in lowland UK farming) costs £10,000–£20,000 per square kilometre, which farmers can claim from subsidies. But misapplication of fertilisers – waste – counts for a gigantic 70 per cent of all fertiliser use. I asked a local farmer if he thought that sounded accurate and he replied, 'On a good day.' When huge doses of fertiliser escape the fields and run into rivers and lochs, they cause 'algal blooms'. The algae form thick, gelatinous rafts, reducing the light in the water and killing other plant life, which decay and cause a dangerous spike in bacteria levels. Shellfish farmers in Scotland rely on clean water and must submit weekly test results to the local environmental health department; in the summer, algal blooms can mean mussels, cockles and oysters are not fit for sale. It's in the summer that people want to sit in the sun outside our restaurant, supping cold wine and slurping briny oysters. The cost of clean-up by water companies means more money comes out of the consumer's pocket (that's everyone) in the form of water bills. That's a double public spend on something that doesn't need to happen at all. Collecting all our food waste and turning it into compost could replace fertiliser use *2.7 times* while also enhancing ecosystems *and* reducing water clean-up costs.[48] This has got to be one of the first ports of call for food-land system change.

Then, in the early 1860s, one black-and-orange beetle kick-started an industry now worth more than $60 billion.[49] The Colorado potato beetle, *Leptinotarsa decemlineata*, followed colonisers and their animals northwards from Mexico and, deprived of its usual diet of Mexican buffalo-bur, devastated potato crops from the Missouri River to the Atlantic coast. Because American growers planted just a few varieties of a single species, pests like the beetle and the blight had a narrower range of natural defences to overcome. Desperate farmers tried everything, till one reportedly threw green paint at a field – and it worked. The compound in the paint was 'Paris Green', a pigment made from copper and arsenic. Chemists isolated the compound . . . and the modern pesticide industry began. Farmers now run like hamsters on the 'toxic treadmill', trapped in a vicious cycle of pesticide use as the evolving 'pests' increase resistance and immunity to each new chemical. The global 'crop protection chemicals' market is set to hit over $80 billion by 2028. Yet in 2009 potato blight managed to wipe out the potato *and* tomato crops on the east coast of the US . . . again.[50]

Now, only half of all potatoes bought in Britain are actually consumed.[51] Intensive fertiliser has been responsible for raising living standards worldwide, but we have dramatically overshot the mark. It's worth repeating: the UK wastes a phenomenal amount of food, 156kg per person per year, worth £20 *billion*.[52] Its associated 20 tonnes of greenhouse gas emissions include potent methane, which is produced when food rots in anaerobic conditions, meaning in landfill.[53] The 'Buy One Get One Free' salad bag we throw away jettisons all the labour, land, water, transport, plastic packaging and environmental damage that went into producing it. Rich countries – like Scotland – waste up to a third of all food produced, 'because it is so cheap,

SCOTTISH / *PEOPLE*

the culture is so lax, and recycling and reuse systems are either underfunded or disparate'.[54] Lower-income countries waste much less, because the food is valuable. It's hard to take seriously claims that there are too many people for the planet to feed, when waste on this scale is systemic.

We're a small restaurant in modern Scotland, so potatoes feature in multiple spots on the menu. One afternoon I arrive in the restaurant kitchen to find our sous chef, Nicola, animated by the price of potatoes, which has just doubled from one order to the next. A brief internet search tells me that this potato shortage was forecasted at the end of the previous year, due to a combination of drought in Europe (meaning a lack of 'seed' potato stock here), soaring electricity costs (one Aberdeenshire potato farmer reports a 500 per cent increase in his farm energy bills) and the speculative costs of artificial fertiliser and fuel for transport spiking due to the invasion of Ukraine. Added to a lack of farm labour due to Brexit, this meant farmers were disinclined to plant potatoes for 2023. The supermarkets are refusing to compensate in increased payment, and their shelves are showing more and more hungry gaps. Farmers are warning of more vegetable shortages to come.

POTATO BROTH
(Serves 4–6 as a soup, more as a sauce)

Our potato broth is made by roasting slices of flavourful waxy potatoes in foaming cultured butter, and steeping whole local milk with leftover baked potato skins. It tastes like the best baked potato with cottage cheese, a staple from my vegetarian teenage years. The broth sometimes sauces pillow-light potato dumplings, made from the baked potato flesh, alongside the Gigha halibut's springtime roe (delicate sacks of the fish's sweet, mild eggs. Buying them helps to put a price on the whole length of the fish's lifecycle, for our neighbours the halibut farmers). Served with sweet, poppy, just-podded peas and soft herbs, the plate makes edible a moment in the year and everything that matters to me.

50g good butter + 100g for finishing
150g Russet Burbank or similar, good-flavoured potato, thinly sliced (don't peel them!)
350ml good chicken stock
500ml potato milk (recipe below)

Melt the butter in a wide pan, and add a little salt and the sliced potato. Cook over a medium heat, stirring frequently to avoid too much sticking (if a little sticking and browning happens, no bad thing; the next step will take care of it).

When the potato slices are translucent and a gentle gold, perhaps with patches of deeper brown, cover them with the stock, bring it all to a simmer and cook gently for 10 minutes. Turn the heat off and allow the potatoes to infuse the stock for an hour.

Strain through a sieve, reserving the broth and the sliced potato. Put all the broth and around half the potato in a blender and blend till very smooth. (The remaining potato is very good fried for breakfast or in an omelette. Or, if you just want to make a heartier potato soup, add all the potato to the blender. It will be thicker, but very potatoey.) Return broth to a clean pan.

Add the potato milk. Simmer, and with a hand-held blender or a strong whisking arm, add the 100g of butter and check the seasoning; you'll probably want more salt.

It should be the consistency of double cream or thin soup. Serve hot, and if you'd like it to be light and bubbly, use the blender or whisk to froth it up a little before pouring into bowls.

POTATO MILK

250g leftover baked-potato skins, with good colour all over, cold
500ml whole milk

Combine the skins and milk, and leave in the fridge for at least 24 hours. A couple of days is best. You can also freeze the milk with the potato skins in and then defrost it, which encourages more potato flavour to leach out into the milk.

Strain through a sieve, squeezing the skins to wring it all out. The potato skins have given all they can and you can probably discard them now.

NEEPS LIKE SUGAR

In Scotland, the 'neeps' of the popular triumvirate 'haggis, neeps and tatties' refers to the Swedish turnip: a large root vegetable whose flesh is yellow in colour and most commonly served 'bashit', that is mashed, with liberal intrusions of black pepper and butter. Etymologically, neep comes from the Middle English 'nepe', meaning turnip, itself originally from the Latin *napus*, the same. At the time of the Swedish turnip's introduction to Scotland in the late eighteenth century, smaller varieties were already commonly grown in gardens here, and had been since at least the 1400s, including yellow varieties. Some were so sweet that street cries calling children to come and get their turnips ('Whae'll buy neeps? – neeps like sucre! whae'll buy neeps?') may once have been as enticing as the ice-cream van's chimes. As late as 1776, a plate of small turnips was served at dessert in the fancy houses of Edinburgh.

The Swedish turnip (*Brassica napus*, var. *napobrassica*) was first documented in the seventeenth century. It is not simply a variety of turnip, but a complicated hybrid of a turnip and cabbage, novel even in Sweden at the time.* Scottish agriculture at that point was not flourishing; conditions were hard and the tradition of leaving the beds fallow in rotation every three years meant both farmers and livestock struggled to survive the winters. The swede was a dense store of carbohydrate – a fantastic crop to sustain cattle, sheep and ultimately people. The Scots found it delicious straight off, and in the contemporary spirit of scientific improvement, turnips were eagerly planted. Its introduction brought Scottish agriculture out of the medieval and into the modern era, but the subsequent enthusiastic, large-scale turnip-planting also displaced farmers and contributed to the Lowland Clearances. Ironic, then (or rather fitting?), that poet and social commentator Robert Burns is now celebrated by a vegetable that so changed Scotland's social structure.

---

* A Korean-Japanese biologist by the name of Woo Jang-choon came up with a theory, The Triangle of U, in 1935, to explain the hybridity, but it seems that the original unity was serendipitous.

SCOTTISH / *PEOPLE*

Neeps are as delicious as they are cheap and easy to grow here. They benefit from long, slow roasting, where all the dense sugars that keep sheep alive over harsh winters can caramelise. Burnt just a tiny bit, or charred on a wood fire, they are lent smoke and bitterness to counter the root's long-stored sweetness. They're also good raw, shredded in a wintery sort of salad with pear and toasted walnuts, dressed with fresh ginger juice, perry vinegar and walnut oil. Scots embraced the neep on its arrival, and so do we in the Inver kitchen.

HAGGIS AND THE HOLY TRINITY

With neeps and tatties, haggis is possibly the dish most synonymous with Scotland's cuisine today. For the uninitiated, haggis is an item of charcuterie, a sheep's stomach stuffed with its 'pluck', incorporating the 'lights' (lungs), liver and heart, mixed with oatmeal, onions and spices. Haggis appears in the first published British recipe books, and is mentioned by poet William Dunbar in the early 1500s, so we can verify its continuous history on dining tables of at least 500 years.[55] The name may come from the Old French 'hacheiz', or from the Old English 'haggen', both 'to hack or chop'; or from the Norse 'höggva', meaning 'to hew, strike or smite'. As its etymology tells us, haggis is not originally Scottish. Its persistence on modern tourist menus seems to come from that place of 'other', where non-Scots marvel at the novelty, the traveller's ritual of overcoming disgust at another country's food habits, to prove something about themselves. Scots' familiarity and acceptance of haggis is kind of a club membership, sealed with the tartan and the whisky toast.

Food historian Catherine Brown made headlines with her myth-busting in 2009, when she revealed to the Scots public that older haggis recipes exist in English publications than they do in Scottish versions.[56] The first documented Scottish recipe for haggis appears in a 1712 collection of over 300 recipes in a leather-bound volume originally belonging to Martha Lockhart, aka Lady Castlehill, and now kept in Glasgow's Mitchell Library. This recipe is much different to the contemporary haggis: there is no oatmeal, and it includes cream and eggs, as well as currants and 'sweet herbs'. Mrs Susanna MacIver's recipe from 1773 is much more recognisable, though she differentiates between 'A Good Scotch Haggies' (using beef offal) and 'A Lamb's Haggies', which seems to be a more delicate affair using eggs, flour and milk, rather than oats or breadcrumbs. The recipe I use is from (the English) Fergus Henderson's *Nose to Tail Eating*, in which Fergus bats back the haggis to the Scots.

Prior to both Lady Castlehill and Mrs MacIver, there were several recipes published in English cookbooks from the sixteenth and seventeenth centuries. But significantly there *were* no cookbooks published in Scotland till the early eighteenth century, so any used before that would have been English. The cookery traditions of the two neighbouring countries are not entirely distinct.

Today haggis is an industrially produced, processed food – it's rare to find it homemade or even made in small batches at an independent butcher's. Each of its components too are processed: the oats dried and cut, the spices dried and crushed. The classic haggis seasonings, black pepper and allspice (and in earlier versions, nutmeg, cloves, cinnamon and mace), are not grown in Scotland. Black pepper thrives in hot, humid, tropical climates, and is originally from the Western Ghats, a range of mountains in Kerala on the south-west coast of India. Poet and academic Dr Anna Sulan Masing recently produced an episode of her podcast *Taste of Place* tracing the origins of pepper (and in which I appear, spooning black pepper oil into a cup of neep broth). Anna explains that it was the British love of pepper and other exotic spices that eventually gave rise to the British East India Company: the private company instructed by King James I to 'turn a profit' if they wanted to keep their royal charter, triggering the twin loaded barrels of colonial exploitation and capitalism. The ubiquity of pepper in modern kitchens, barely registered on café tables and thrown thoughtlessly into soup pots, stands in stark contrast to the perilous journey the little dried fruit of *Piper nigrum* took to get here and the sacrifices made by far-off families to ensure its safe passage. Perhaps the perfect metaphor for the modern migrant.

Allspice (*Pimenta dioica*, aka Jamaica pepper) is originally from Jamaica in the West Indies. The tree is a member of the myrtle family and can grow to thirty feet tall. It was given its enduring English name in 1621 by a Dr Diego Alvarez Chanca, the doctor on board Columbus's second voyage to the 'New' World. He called it 'allspice' due to its heady scent of clove, cinnamon, pepper and nutmeg. At the other end of the trade routes, allspice appears in Swedish lutefisk and Finnish Karelian hotpot, Portuguese stews and American baking. And it is a familiar flavour in northern European pickles and charcuterie – such as Scottish haggis, potted hough and Shetland's reestit mutton.

Modern Scots' nostalgia for an imagined past obscures much that it would be helpful to remember as we travel to an uncertain future. Our most famous national dish includes ingredients from Peru, Sweden, the Middle East, India and the West Indies, and the recipe itself is shared with our most popular sporting foe. It hardly seems to matter, though, if two small bordering northern European countries share a recipe book when their ingredients connect them so intimately to so many of the furthest, most disparate food cultures on the planet (and do so through a shared history of violence and exploitation). Robert Burns claimed the 'great chieftain o' the puddin' race' for the Scots when he wrote his ode to it. Once a year on Burns Night, dressed in our tartanry, and following a tight script of graces, toasts and addresses, we delightedly spear our annual haggis, spewing it forth over its neeps and tatties, in honour of a struggling farmer and social campaigner who himself bought a ticket to work on a Jamaican sugar plantation (though he stayed in the end).[57]

We've made haggis at Inver, from the pluck and offal of the whole Herdwick sheep we buy from Bute, or the Blackface that still nibble the Loch Lomond hills. Sometimes it's included as one of the many cuts of the whole beast served at dinner. We've done haggis, neeps and tatties too, the turnips thin chewy ribbons roasted in butter and the potatoes a crisp fried shell enclosing the buttery mash, with a proper lamb-bone sauce.

The Scots values that haggis truly encloses in its paunched entrails is a respect for the whole animal and an abhorrence of waste. There's a strong Scots tradition of whole-animal cookery, such as the fantastically named dishes 'ceann-cropaig' (cod's head stuffed with its own liver and oatmeal) and 'powsowdie' (a sheep's head broth), or liver-muggie (fish stomach stuffed with liver or fish fat). Sausages (sasis, sawster or sausis) feature from the sixteenth century, and specific delicacies like rodykyns, the fourth stomach of a ruminant, were bought for the royal households of James IV and V.[58] A dish of entrails stuffed with offal and humble oats, seasoned with exotic spices that show a broad, inclusive palate and economy, and served with vegetables introduced as animal feed, is now a common cause of celebration across *all* strata of society. Oh, and it's totally delicious, and a well-balanced plate of flavour and intriguing texture. This is a national identity I can get behind.

'SCOTTISH'

I've rummaged through the family attic and found the stories we tell each other about how the 'I' coalesces in the midst of a community. I've uncovered shared values: I abhor waste, and I can trace this through my family into antiquity. My brother and I have both inherited the love of growing and cooking. I eat what my parents eat: I recognise the marmalade, the butteries, the porridge and the mince. I know the features of our shared landscapes. These are my foods, my identity. I understand where my dad's food habits come from and why they are so entrenched. I can look with some perspective at mine, and understand what I too will not willingly give up, and why food is so important to people who have lost their home and other tethers of their identity. Through my mother's loss I find gaps I want to fill, understanding that I hunger to have. I am alive right now, and I feel acutely the role that food has had in shaping the world in which we live, and what role it can have in solving the communal problems that we face together. In this I see a role for myself in this chaotic, marvellous world.

I've explored the furthest human history of this scrap of ancient rock, and I can see things that resonate still with how I choose to cook and eat today. There are ways of living on this landscape which persist in the kitchen at Inver; in the emphasis we choose to give the wild landscape, preference for traditional breeds of sheep and cattle, the presence on the menu of the shellfish and coastal herbs, foraged berries and wild mushrooms in the autumn, more vegetables than meat. The use of grains like oats, beremeal and barley, and traditional varieties of wheat; ground hazelnuts and peasemeal; and the flavour of meat grilled over wood fire resonate through time. The language we use has a conscious continuity: flat barley breads are still bannocks, even if the barley was inoculated with the mould spore *Aspergillus oryzae* that hails from Japan. The Inver menus sometimes feature brose, sowans, whipkull, partan bree and hatted kit.

My love of good dairy – rich mellowing butter and the enlivening lactic tang of yoghurt and buttermilk – feels justified by history, even as its future may be insecure. I love rolling layers of butter into pastry and whisking it into sauces, scooping thick yoghurt or crème fraîche onto rich plates of chocolate pudding or roasted lamb, and making simple cheeses and marinades from leftover whey. At Inver we use every part of an animal, fish, and plant, and I love wringing all the extra flavour and texture out of the bones, the head and the offal, or the skins, the seeds, the stem and the flower. I value skills and craft and the meditative joy of their repetitive practice. Through their practice I find myself at home in this historic landscape. However, were I lactose intolerant (as an increasing number of our guests tell us they are) or vegan (nearest big city, Glasgow, is often featured in lists of best vegan cities), I could easily loop together a different past that venerates the landscape's great tradition of grains, berries, seaweeds, tatties and kailyards.

Scots' willingness to share a table is a part of our national identity I can celebrate. I too find joy in transforming humble ingredients into something delicious to commemorate life's occasions. Our ability to turn scraps, leftovers and animal food into nutritious delicacies is a test of real skill and craft that makes me truly proud. Our traditional understanding of the human place in a landscape, expressed by dùthchas, is prescient and will travel with me now through kitchens at home and at work.

After the tour of Fintry, my dad and I drive to my brother's house to see him and my two young nephews. It's spring and the family are all in the garden: the boys are poking at frogspawn in a pond and the older, Hamish (aged four), asks to plant some seeds. We prod holes in compost and tuck in the blanched white squash seeds, leave them in the greenhouse that their dad made out of recycled windows, and wood that fell down in a winter storm. As we do I see my hands beside my brother's, furrowed with dirt like when we dug for snails as kids. The grooves are deeper now, and there are more of them. It is through these hands that his sons will learn the skills they'll need to inhabit this world, too.

Chapter Four:
SCOTTISH / *LAND*

'The land is only as wild as we are wild,' says ethnologist Alexander Fenton.[1]

It's also true vice versa: human beings are part of nature, and nature has taught and shaped us just as we have shaped the natural world. Early humankind's very DNA was coded by our interactions with the 'natural' environment, and the post-industrial separation from nature is increasingly linked to poor mental as well as physical health. Even the existence in our language of the word 'nature' is problematic, because it suggests to us that humankind is somehow distinguishable from nature, that 'human nature' doesn't follow the same rules as the other animals. Contemporary Scot, forager and mycologist Monica Wilde lived for a year on an entirely wild diet and wrote a book about it, *The Wilderness Cure*. Monica notes that in Scots Gaelic the word for the science of physics is eòlas-nàdair, literally 'knowledge of nature'. With intriguing ambiguity, eòlas also sometimes means 'lore', or 'spell'.[2]

Cooking, baking, fish-filleting and meat-butchery, cheese-making, brewing, wine-making, malting, distilling, gardening, foraging, tending, rearing, fishing, hunting, farming: these are the skills that teach us to know nature, to know the world in

SCOTTISH / *LAND*

all its dimensions and to feel, fingertips first, for our place in it. Food, after all, is our most intimate way of encountering the non-human world. Anthropologist Tim Ingold writes, 'Knowledge of the world is gained by moving about in it, exploring it, attending to it, ever alert to the signs by which it is revealed. Learning to see, then, is a matter . . . of acquiring the skills for direct perceptual *engagement* with its constituents, human and non-human, animate and inanimate.'[3] We need *all* of our senses to even get close to understanding the complexity of nature and our place in it. Knives and pots, fishing nets and spades, forks and spoons – they are navigation instruments for our paths around nature.

Using these tools to explore Scottish natural landscapes can help understand further what it means to eat 'Scottish' food. Iconic wild Scots plants and fungi (like sourocks, slokan, blaeberries and brambles, chanterelles and penny buns) and animals (deer, salmon, shellfish and game birds), and newer modern produce like farmed halibut, all need us to manage the landscapes that benefit them and, ultimately, us. But what values guide this landscape management? Which of them are identifiably 'Scottish', and which serve a future that would see all of nature equitably represented?

Bounding the shore of Loch Fyne, along with the two grand castles – repositories for one strand of history – there's also the cottage, Inver. For the former inhabitants of this cottage on Lachlan Bay, there were whelks, periwinkles and limpets on the shoreline, and spoots – razor clams – squatting in the sand, identifiable by the small curls of sand they exude as they burrow down. Mussels and cockles are likely to have fed the humans on Scottish coasts since at least the Mesolithic, the last age of the hunter-gatherer, and perhaps since people first watched the gulls and wading birds knocking them from rocks. From their boat, the tenants of the cottage between two waters would have dropped creels for crabs, lobsters and langoustines. Now, every weekend we receive a delivery of crabs and langoustines pulled up in creels by Mary, who was once the local high school PE teacher. She brings us scallops too, dived for one at a time by her brother. There are still cockles and mussels in the bay. Dondering on the tideline you can find their empty shells, ravaged by the gulls and wading birds. We know the cottage's tenants paid some of their rent in fish, and that fishing was an industry on the loch, especially for herring. Until the 1990s, kippers were smoked and traded on Loch Fyne, and there were mackerel, pollack and haddock. Our neighbour Robin and his family take their boat out in the summer and will bring us occasional buckets of mackerel, trading them for fresh loaves or drinks at the bar. There are rarely cod and we have only ever had three herring. Gina Maclachlan, the clan chief's sister, was in for dinner that night and we served them lightly soused, with a mayonnaise made of roasted beef fat and fried oatmeal, in a nod to their traditional preparations.

We serve mussels at Inver, too, though these are farmed, grown on ropes hanging from floats in the moving tide and cleaning the water as they go. We have raked the sand for cockles, shushing them in buckets of water to sluice out the sand before steaming them open over bonfires on the beach. Tender little nuggets, a perfect balance of sweet and brine. Sometimes cockles are one of the first bites of a dinner at Inver: lightly cooked, served in their shells and set in their own cooking juices cut with fresh, grassy lime juice, tasting of smoky fires and open sea.

It's commonly assumed that, worldwide, there was a sequence of human development, from hunter-gatherer man at humankind's appearance two or more million years ago, to early agriculturist and food producer 11,000–10,000 years ago. But 'the change is perhaps little more than one of emphasis . . . There is no easy definition of wild . . . As far as the planet is concerned, even the most remote and earliest human communities must have disturbed the ground in some way.'[4] Through millennia of observation, early humankind discerned patterns in spring's green shoots, summer flowers and the fruit of autumn, watched how birds and mammals raised their young through the year's scrolling seasons. Nature taught mankind how to farm. While farming increases the overall quantity of food available, however, those food stuffs are all largely the same. Even after settled agricultural communities became the norm, wild edibles would have supplemented and varied the diet, and learning to cook allowed humankind to vary the flavours and ingredients (and therefore energy and nutrients) of a potentially monotonous diet.

Walking along the green-steeped summer paths around Inver is like browsing a fresh produce market. In among the grasses there is sheep sorrel and common sorrel, and wood sorrel in the trees. Not far away we find the edible seaweeds: dulse, sea spaghetti, kelps and sloke. In the hedgerows, repeated like an incantation: golden saxifrage, vetch, wild camomile and carrot, bitter yarrow, nettles and goosefoot, meadowsweet, red clover and pignuts. In the spring, wild garlic on all the banks of all the burns. There's elderberries, crab apples, rosehips and sloes, and in the autumn, everywhere, there are brambles. On the shore back at Lachlan Bay, we find all the edible coastal greens: marsh samphire, sea blite, arrowgrass, sea plantain, sea aster, scurvy grass, sea campion.

And there are hazel trees. Hazelnuts were one of the first Neolithic sources of protein. They were a valued resource; they could be transported and therefore traded, and before grain was common they were possibly used as flour. Burnt hazelnuts have been found in great quantities in archaeological sites in Peeblesshire dating from 3650–2900 BC, and on Islay (not far from Inver) from about 6500 BC. Burning the nuts may have made them easier to shell, and perhaps learning to process wild hazelnuts in this way taught Neolithic mankind to handle hard cereal grains.

The modern Inver Restaurant larder shares these same ingredients. We use hazelnuts in the kitchen a lot; fresh hazelnut milk split with burnt garlic oil makes a rich savoury sauce for light fish and poultry. Our hazelnut and beremeal shortbreads combine ground nut meal with the Neolithic six-row barley, bere, indigenous to Scotland.

HAZELNUT AND BEREMEAL SHORTBREAD
Makes approximately 20 biscuits

These shortbreads combine the toasted nut meal with beremeal. Bere is indigenous to Scotland and is still grown in Orkney and milled there at Barony Mill. It has a nutty, toasty flavour, and is low in gluten, meaning it's great for keeping shortbread biscuits 'short' – delicate and crumbly (the dough is also good for crumbles).

150g beremeal
125g plain flour
100g ground hazelnuts
250g unsalted butter, at room temperature
250g caster sugar

Preheat the oven to 150°C (fan).

Mix the hazelnut meal and flours. In a stand mixer, cream the sugar and butter together until pale. Add the flour and hazelnut mix gradually, scraping down the sides of the bowl occasionally, until evenly incorporated. Don't over-mix, or you'll work the gluten in the flours and your biscuits will be tough, not 'short'. Wrap the dough in baking paper and chill in the fridge for 30 minutes or so.

Work with the dough while it is cool but pliable. Lightly dust a work surface with flour. Roll the dough into a sheet 1cm thick, and either cut triangles with a knife, or stamp out circles (or dinosaur shapes!) with a cookie-cutter. Lift the biscuits carefully onto paper-lined, flat baking trays. Leave a space in between each; the biscuits will spread a little.

Bake till the biscuits are a pale golden colour all over. They will take 35–40 minutes, but check them after 20 minutes, turning the tray if your oven isn't even (ours isn't). The shortbread should feel firm in the middle but remain pale throughout.

Towards the end of cooking, use a small sieve or tea

> strainer to dust the biscuits with caster sugar. Return the tray to the oven for 2–5 more minutes (this will encourage the sugar to stick).
>
> Cool the shortbreads on the baking tray till they firm up, then transfer to a cooling rack to cool completely. Decorate with a few crushed or grated hazelnuts.

Of course, in the Inver kitchen we have electric gadgets and plastic packets and produce from far-off lands. We have memories from foreign holidays and images from social media, glossy cookbooks and magazines to help us decide what to cook. And I know that the land around here in the vicinity of the bay has itself changed radically in the last few centuries. But there have always been changes, the new ideas garnishing the old, till the new is the old too. The continuity in using the products of the nearby land is to me liberating. Bending down to pick the sourocks and slokan, knowing that this has always happened here, I am not a modern individual but a link in a human chain, bound through place to time. With the perspective of millennia, enduring actions like collecting and sharing food are given permanence, while others of less significance are shown their fleeting place.

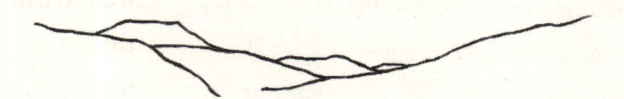

Tracking the history of game animals in Scotland is reading the changing relationship that humans have had to the landscape and its other inhabitants, and the relationship that animals and landscape have to each other. Forestry, farming and game management have a knock-on effect on the rest of the ecosystem. Nothing at all happens in isolation. Being able to read the land is essential to understanding its place in our culture and future.

The Scottish Highlands are not easily cultivated. The introduction of commercial flocks of sheep in the eighteenth century gave new economic value to this land, with a source of food as these animals converted the grasses and shrubs we cannot digest into densely nutritious meat, plus valuable wool. But sheep are not as benevolent a presence in this landscape as the traditional Highland cattle. They give little back to the soil, and their 'incessant nibbling' does not perform the cattle's role in shaping the ecosystems. The heavy stock density post-Clearances soon depleted the fertile soil, the market for mutton shrank, and sheep-farming started to decline. The land needed a different use, and game-shooting seemed to have an answer.

Game are wild animals shot or trapped for human food. The history of game animals in Britain is at least as long as the history of human presence here, around 10,000 years. Red and roe deer were already present in the Mesolithic period, and there's evidence of human beings enjoying them embedded in our language and landscape.* The wild boar may have been hunted to extinction before the thirteenth century, but salt venison shows up in courtly records from at least the fourteenth. Our relationship to wild animals now, in the twenty-first century, has changed beyond recognition.

The British Game Act of 1773 set laws that are still in use today. This was three decades after Culloden, the Highland Clearances were under way, and game shooting was a new

---

* For example, the place name Elrick comes from 'eilear', meaning a deer-trap enclosure.

currency in land management. By 1811 there were six preserved deer forests in Scotland,* and by 1842 there were forty; by the 1880s, 4,500 stags were being shot in the Highlands each year and the annual 'grouse bag' was estimated at around half a million birds. These massive cash injections to the Highland economy are estimated to have been worth £250,000 and £500,000 respectively,[5] and sporting returns to the estates overtook sheep graziers' rents. The late-nineteenth-century collapse of wool prices and the invention of refrigerated transport to import New Zealand, Australian and Argentinian lamb further hammered Highland sheep-farming. Shifts in the world economy again had a transformative effect on the Highlands, which were still dependent on a tenuous use of marginal land. Today, land reformer Andy Wightman reckons the 340 sporting estates in the Highlands and Islands represent a third of the total privately owned land in Scotland, and over half of privately owned land in the Highlands and Islands themselves.[6]

Winston Churchill is our local gamekeeper, supplying venison and pheasants to Inver Restaurant. Winston's father was himself a gamekeeper in Essex in 1951 when he named his new baby son. As Winston remembers it, Mr Churchill senior's job was equal parts ecologist, ornithologist and sportsman. Hedgerows provided shelter and food for the birds and rodents, so keeping them and the surrounding fields healthy and in balance was the focus of his daily chores. His wages were paid by a syndicate of farmers keen to manage the population of pheasants on their farms. Too many wild pheasants, and the farms' wheat crop would be destroyed. But the sales from three or four

---

* Atholl, Blackmount, Glenartney, Glen Fiddich, Invercauld and Mar.

modest shoots per year meant that the keeper's wage was paid, there was some extra cash for the farm households and an occasional pheasant for the farmer's wife to roast on Sundays. There was no pheasant for the Churchill pot; the small family knew their place and the price that a brace of pheasant would fetch for their employers. Rabbits and pigeon were home staples instead.

Winston left school at fifteen to become an apprentice to his father. By then, the family were living on a private forest estate, controlling wild populations of pheasants and partridge and some brown hare. The Churchills were content, appreciative of the sense of continuity which landscape timescales brought to family life. By Winston's teenage years in the late 1960s, modern industrial farming ways were taking hold. Fields were getting bigger and hedgerows and woods were shrinking. Chemical fertilisers and pesticides were stealthily bleeding through the worm-ways and spider nests, the bee holes, seed-heads and root-stocks of the game birds' larder. Autumn game-shooting was becoming a popular pastime, and affordable to the post-war middle classes. The wild stock of pheasants was now supplemented for the lucrative shoots by birds hatched and raised on specialist farms and released in the late summer to fatten on brambles and rowan berries. At this point, remembers Winston, it was maybe one bird in every three that started off life as a chick in a hatchery. But the recreational shoots were still modest affairs and the job was still the one that Winston remembered from his childhood in Essex lanes. The dark clouds of uncountable thousands of birds, raised in barns big enough for trucks to drive through, were yet to come.

The pheasant is not native: it was introduced to Britain from Asia, probably by the Romans, and already popularised as an object of sport and dinner in the eleventh century. A millennia later, in the 1980s, Winston had become disillusioned. Farming methods were no longer supportive of healthy wild game stocks. But most jarringly, the expectations of the people on the shoot had changed. A group of these men in Barbours and tailored tweed would once be content with a day's haul of 80 birds. Now, they wanted 150 or 200 pheasants to shoot in a single day! Estate owners could charge by the kill, and demanded that the keepers maintained stocks of 3,000 or more birds; more than the land could naturally support. More and more pheasants were being hatched indoors, fed on pellets in barns and released as poults (young birds) to fatten for the autumn guns. Virtually all the pheasants eaten in Scotland and Britain are now raised this way.

Scotland's native woodlands were once said to be so vast that a red squirrel could travel the 300 miles from Lockerbie in the south to Lochinver in the north-west without once touching the ground. It took several thousand years for half of Scotland's tree cover to disappear. It's taken the last 1,500 years to almost finish it off, those trees building the Navy's ships, and fuelling furnaces and factories at home. Now native woodland covers just 4 per cent of the country's land.

In the 1980s, a new landscape management experiment was escalating on Scottish hillsides. North American sitka spruce is a fast-growing tree, well-conditioned to the harsh climate. The Economic Forestry Group (EFG), a coalition of regional forestry syndicates, was planting sitka forests in Argyll intended for commercial logging forty years later. As I write, these trees are being harvested outside my windows, destined for timber yards, paper mills and furniture factories; their bark potentially producing pharmaceuticals, liquid bio-fuels and adhesives. They leave behind stubbled, bald hillsides. Spruce plantation investors in the 1980s were encouraged by huge tax incentives that flowed like popped champagne through private and celebrity bank accounts; icons of 1980s popular culture Terry Wogan and Steve Davis were investing in trees for tax breaks. On a 1927 Ordnance Survey map of our local area there is one tiny fingernail of green. That's the first Forestry Commission industrial spruce plantation. Now, that same map is all dark sitka green.

Planting trees sounds like an ecologically benign move. But, warns Sutherland estate owner Michael Wigan, 'a policy to plant up the Highlands with conifers is effectively a once-and-for-all decision... Recreating heather moorland or flow ground from the jumbled landscape of tree stumps and wagon tracks is out of the question.'[7] So much of Scottish land was dedicated to commercial forestry, the Forestry Commission (now Forestry and Land Scotland) set up an HQ in Edinburgh. As Wigan says, 'forestry itself is neither a good or a bad thing; it is a matter of where trees are planted; at what cost to other land uses; what species of tree is planted'; as well as considerations of what the eventual products are for. 'Horrendous mistakes' have been made in planting the block monocultures of spruce in Argyll; 'mistakes which people today are obliged to live with.'[8]

Just like monocropping on arable or horticultural farms, one species of tree or plant alone can't produce all the many ecosystems needed for a diverse population of insects, birds and small mammals to cohabit and thrive, keeping each other's populations in check by the time-honoured natural limits of predator and prey, grasses and grazer. If just one species could exploit the environment in a sitka forest they could escalate unchallenged by natural competition. And in Scottish spruce plantations, that species is deer.

Back when Winston arrived in Scotland in 1983 there were relatively few deer. Deer don't like to cohabit with sheep (they graze in a similar manner and so compete for food), and in the centuries following the Highland Clearances the hills around Argyll had been managed as a series of sheep farms. When in the late 1970s and '80s companies like EFG cleared hills of sheep to grow spruce, they created the perfect environment for deer.

First, roe deer populations exploded. Roe deer are very small, and territorial, moving in pairs or small family groups. The young spruce plantations offered shelter and easy grasses to graze. The trees were all around the same age, because they had all been planted within the ten-year period in which tax benefits had been dangled by a resource-hungry government. When the dense spruce trees matured and closed the canopy, the vegetation on the forest floor couldn't survive in the sudden gloom, and the roe's larder was quickly depleted. Starving, stressed animals can't reproduce easily. The roe population collapsed.

The other native Scottish deer, the red, are large animals, not restricted to territory. They move over broad distances in supportive herds, able to use the spruce forest as shelter during the day and to roam upwards above the treeline to find food at night. With numbers no longer kept in check by a booming roe population, the red deer population multiplied. More spruce farms are planted continuously in Argyll, as elsewhere in 'wild' Highland Scotland, but the entrenched population of red deer keeps roe numbers relatively low.

Sitka spruce saplings are resilient. Browsed by hungry deer, the trees throw up side branches away from the nibbled tips, year after year until the tree is too tall for the deer to eat spring's

SCOTTISH / *LAND*

new shoots. But for vulnerable young native hardwoods like oak, ash, rowan and holly, deer are catastrophic. In order for Scotland's native hardwood trees to strew seed and grow to maturity, bringing all the ecosystem and environmental benefits of a diverse woodland, deer density must be no more than 2–5 deer per 100 hectares. Winston's annual deer cull suggests the population is up to ten times as many as a young forest can handle. Deer have become a 'landscape-scale suppressor' of ecological processes in the Highlands, exacerbating the damage caused by intensive sheep-grazing.

Game sale dynamics are different now too. In 1989 the Iron Curtain came down and western European venison dealers who had been buying from Scotland turned to Eastern European deer forests. The price of deer carcasses plummeted to as little as 77p per kilo. Winston had to add value to his own carcasses, become his own dealer; he borrowed money to start his venison business with no butchery training, no money to recruit staff, and no customers. The outbreak of BSE helped him as public distrust of farmed meat swivelled shoppers' heads to wild alternatives. Venison is a healthy meat, with more protein, vitamins and minerals than most farmed beef, and less fat. However, only 65 per cent of UK demand for venison is met with homegrown meat; the rest is imported from countries like New Zealand and Poland. Now Winston Churchill Venison is a familiar label in local shops' chill cabinets, and their venison burgers and pheasant sausages feed Argyll's Highland games, beer festivals and weddings.

Another man-made control for the deer population – the law – limits the number of deer Winston can shoot at different times of the year. Young deer and their mothers are off-limits in the spring to protect the next generation. But in a natural, 'wild', relationship of predator and prey, those vulnerable mothers and young would be easy targets for predators, and their deaths would be one means of keeping a balanced population. Winston and his colleagues simply can't shoot enough deer to keep numbers at a level that would allow old woodland to renew and bring the rest of the Highlands' biodiversity back with it. The last wolf was killed by 1750, lynx and bears were extinct in the UK by medieval times, and raptor populations (buzzards, hawks and eagles) have been decimated. There are currently no significant predators left for the deer population except man, and we have tied our own hands.

I relish venison season at Inver. It might be the only moment in the year I allow myself to feel satisfied with my role as an apex predator. There's venison available all year really (females, males, red and roe are shot at different times) but the autumn red stag shoot coincides with the elderberries, brambles and mushrooms that often end up sharing the plate. My favourite accompaniment to venison is a green peppercorn sauce and 'turnip cake' – a terrine of thinly sliced yellow turnip, cooked slowly overnight with brown butter till everything collapses and the sugars run. Pressed till cold, it's sliced and roasted in hot butter, so that all the many edges scorch and burn. The turnip, the deer and the peppercorns are a story of Scottish landscapes over time and place.

Glen Esk is one of the five Angus Glens. They're an hour's drive from where I grew up, and we came here often to walk in the summer. The pale blue air above the gentle open glen stretches to the Montrose Basin and the North Sea on one side, and to Balmoral Castle, Royal Deeside and the Cairngorms on the other. The names of the big families here were the names of our sports teams in high school: Lord Dalhousie (red), Lord Ramsay (yellow), Lord Maule (green), Lord Guthrie (blue). Returning today, I peer back through binoculars across time, finally joining the dots across three decades.

The week before the 'Glorious Twelfth' of August, the start of grouse-shooting season, I have come to meet Colin Lanyon, head gamekeeper at the Gannochy Estate. The estate manages grouse moors as part of a sporting portfolio that also includes deer and salmon. Unlike the pheasant and partridge, red grouse is a native wild game bird, never raised in captivity. Instead, the grouse's landscape is managed to benefit the bird over other inhabitants of the hills. The bird is another edible symbol of the wonders of Scotland's wild landscape, as rich in meaning as its dark purple flesh is in blood.

I tell him that I'm writing a book about food culture and land use in Scotland and all the things that has meant throughout the last 500 years. Colin nods, and says, 'So many problems, and man's at the root of them all.' It's what I've come to understand about gamekeepers, stalkers and ghillies; these men who tend wild landscapes (and they are mostly men, though there are now fifteen qualified female gamekeepers in Scotland too). They're acutely aware of the issues facing the natural environment – and of modern life's views of them, the keepers, too.

It is hard to view Scottish estates like Gannochy with objectivity. Land-ownership in modern Scotland stirs bunkered emotions from trenches on all sides of the country's social divides. From twelfth-century forest law to the legacy of the Clearances, the landscape of the Highlands is contoured with shifting values. Hunting game was a way for common folk to subsist from shared resources for millennia, but now it lavishes rich folks' tables as more of the commons have come under private control. There's an inverse snobbery that gives much fuel to contemporary anti-shoot fire. 'They think we're all toffs,' says Colin.

As well as travellers, musicians, poets and novelists, cookery writers contributed to the ideal of the Highlands as a sporting paradise. Recipes track the significance of the grouse to Scots food and culture. 'But, oh! My dear North, what grouse-soup at Dalnacardoch! You smell it on the homeward hill, as if exhaling from the heather,' wrote Victorian writer John Wilson in one of the seventy-one dialogues in *Noctes Ambrosianae*.* More recently, two recipes for grouse are to be found in *Lady Maclean's Cookbook* (1966), penned in Strachur, a few miles from Inver, and containing the spoils of a well-travelled life: the author's husband, Sir Fitzroy Maclean, was reputedly the inspiration for Ian Fleming's character James Bond. One of them is for 'Devilled Grouse'† and comes from a Lady Ogilvy of Cortachy Castle, Kirriemuir, in the grouse heartland of Angus. A few years later, in Catherine Brown's *Scottish Cookery* (1985) and *A Year in a Scots Kitchen* (2013), there's a list of 'Other Scottish Game' and their seasons, but only grouse and pheasant have actual recipes. Grouse persists.

'I thought you lot loved that kind of thing,' says Colin. He

---

* These vignettes between rich imaginary Scots characters were set in Edinburgh's Ambrose Tavern and published in *Blackwood's* magazine from 1822 to 1835. Wilson was an advocate, author and literary critic, and professor of moral philosophy at Edinburgh University from 1820 to 1851.

† Ingredients including Patna-brand rice, curry powder, Bovril, and a tin of Campbell's consommé.

means chefs. The 'kind of thing' is the romantic storytelling that commonly dresses the grouse on restaurant tables. And he's right – I do love to tell meaningful stories about the connections between the food we serve and the land and people that have produced it. Stories transform fodder into dinner. But I find grouse difficult.

For at least at the last century, the bird has not been a symbol of the kind of egalitarian food access that saw commoners taking game for their own pot. These days it's found on expensive restaurant menus from Edinburgh to London. Grouse is one of the three courses on Tom Kitchin's £115 'a la carte' menu at his eponymous Edinburgh restaurant, with celeriac, blaeberries and 'Spean Bridge girolles'.[9] To buy from a butcher, it's £10 a bird (the small birds would typically feed one person, a lot of money for a dinner at home). I asked an Edinburgh butcher where they'd come from. He first said 'the fridge', and then after shouting into the back for more information, 'the Pentlands' (a range of hills not far from the city). As to which estate, well, 'We can't disclose that information.'[10] Strange for a food so representative of landscape that its origins be kept secret. When consumed in a city, a plate of grouse may feel to the urbanite like a connection to a different time and place. When eaten in a country house, cooked by someone else after a bracing day's shooting on the autumn hills, perhaps it really is a meaningful connection to the here and now.

The Victorian hunting estates were not only cleared of people. After the sale of the estate of Glengarry in 1840, cash prizes for local gamekeepers provided the incentive to clear the new purchase of 'vermin'. In three years, the *Inverness Courier* reported, 4,000 heads of vermin were cleared from the land, including 108 wildcats, 48 otters, 246 pine martens, 106 polecats, 27 white-tailed eagles, 18 osprey, 98 peregrine falcons, 462 kestrels and 109 different owls. 'The effort and man-power that went into this grand-scale obliteration is stupefying to imagine,' says Michael Wigan.[11] By 1912, there were more than 200 such sporting estates covering 3.6 million acres, all with their vermin management programmes.

Birds of prey are now protected by law,[12] but the Scottish government acknowledges that 'raptor persecution is a serious problem in some parts of Scotland, particularly in areas linked to driven grouse shooting'.[13] In 2020 there was a well-publicised poisoning of an endangered white-tailed eagle in Aberdeenshire (near Balmoral), and government websites note the 'suspicious' disappearance of satellite-tagged golden eagles in and around grouse moors. I ask Colin about it. On his estate there is no illegal shooting of birds of prey, of course, and he refers to those who do it as 'bad eggs', saying it's been a while since he heard of any incident. In November 2023, however, Nature Scotland, conservation groups and Scottish citizens were distressed at the disappearance of a golden eagle called Merrick, who had been thriving in southern Scotland since her translocation from an Angus estate in 2022. Police Scotland are treating the bird's disappearance as suspicious.[14]

Colin has been at Gannochy for twenty-six years. It was once part of the Earl of Dalhousie's estate, in the days when that laird could ride from the foothills of the Cairngorms to Edinburgh without ever leaving his own land. In 1983, Derald Ruttenberg, an American industrialist, bought the estate and invested in it. 'As is the way with benevolent landowners, the tenants and staff trusted the man in the big house and invested their money and lives accordingly, without the safety of long-term leases,' explained one reporter.[15] In 2003, Gannochy's

16,585 acres was bought by a property company called Edinmore Investments, broken up and sold in forty-two lots for a profit of several million pounds. When Edinmore split up the estate, tenant farmers and glen inhabitants without the security of long-term leases faced eviction.* I ask Colin where he lives. He points beyond an adjacent hill; he lives in a house that belongs to the estate. What will happen to the house when he retires? He keeps his eyes on the horizon and says, 'I suppose we'll see.'

We take the 4x4 up to the top of a hill. First, Colin wants to talk about the heather. One of the most contentious issues about grouse-moor management is the routine burning of patches of heather. It's what gives grouse moors that distinctive mottled army-camouflage appearance: strips of burnt heather and the different stages of regrowth. Public perception of 'muirburn' is scathing: fire is destructive, right? 'Heather is the heart of the hill ecology,' says Michael Wigan. Moor managers burn the heather because the grouse like to eat the soft nutritious tips of new growth, and the burning potentially increases the food supply on the moor 'ten-fold'.[16] This type of burning does not harm the peat: these fires are 'cool burn', meaning shallow, only burning the top layer of heather, and done when the ground is still damp, not summer's tinder-dry. The managed burn actually helps prevent wildfires because it splits the land into strips, so a big fire can't take hold and blaze through the ancient peat below.[17] However, critics of the practice point out

---

* Edinmore are part of Caledonian Investments, the property portfolio of the uber-wealthy Cayzer family, whose riches started with Sir Charles Cayzer's 1878 'Clan Line' steamers, the world's largest cargo line, which shipped to and from India.

that 'muirburn is a hindrance to tree regeneration on Scotland's upland heaths. Carried out annually to "improve" heather condition and structure for the benefit of red grouse, muirburn effectively kills most regenerating tree seedlings.'[18] One report from Leeds University, which studies moorland in the north of England, suggests that the water table is lowered by excessive muirburn, meaning that the surface of the peat is more prone to drying out and experiences greater temperature variability, in turn affecting the plant life and dependent creatures, and releasing stored carbon.[19]

Burning vegetation is a land management technique with deep roots. It was used by Native Americans on the land now known as California for the same reasons as on the Highland hillsides: increasing food supply for wild game and for humans. Intentional burning increased the abundance of edible tubers, greens, fruits, seeds and mushrooms.[20] Burning also limited wildfire, increased materials used for cordage and basketry, removed dead material and promoted growth by recycling nutrients, and helped maintain specific plant communities, thus increasing or protecting biodiversity. Indeed, this burning was a crucial part of making the American landscape so incredibly fertile and lush at the point of the Europeans' arrival.

In August 2023, the West Kelowna wildfires devastated an area the size of Greece in British Columbia, Canada, where some of my close family live – ten times as many acres as the last record-breaking wildfires, in 2021. The 2023 fires consumed almost 200 buildings and upended the lives of about 35,000 evacuees. By contrast, a 50-acre fire-resistant zone starved the 2021 wildfires, keeping it to the forest floor, where it was easier to manage, and allowing firefighters to suppress it before it got too close to houses. Ntityix Development, a forestry company owned by Westbank First Nations people, drew on indigenous forest-management techniques to create the burn zone. The company has burned ground cover and debris, thinned the forest by removing smaller trees and removed lower branches so the fire has no 'ladder' to climb to the canopies, at a cost of $100,000 a year. Dave Gill, the non-indigenous general manager of forestry at Ntityix, has said the First Nations elders and his indigenous co-workers have changed how he thinks about the forest. 'We're leaving the trees that have the most timber value behind. This is trying to just instil a different paradigm in the way that you look at the forest, not just putting dollar signs on trees.'[21]

Back on the Glen Esk hill, Colin is crouching, his hands combing the springy new growth: there's ling heather, bell heather, cowberries (lingonberries), *so* many ripe blaeberries, the odd bob of cotton grass and papery violet-blue harebells, the iconic Scottish bluebell. I spot birds-foot trefoil, and a tiny harvestman spider clambers like a space-walker over the shrubbery. A curlew starts and skims the hill a ways away. Curlew are 'near threatened' according to the International Union for Conservation of Nature (IUCN), and their UK populations are declining. Some Scottish grouse moors are showing nesting success. Colin may be managing the hill for grouse, but it also benefits the curlew and lapwing, wading birds who live mostly on the nearby Montrose Basin, a well-known bird reserve, and nest on the mixed heather moorland. The smaller birds – meadow pipits, ring ouzels, wheatears and skylarks – enjoy the delicate heather tips and mixed forage-and-shelter of the grouse moor, too. They also benefit from the legal 'predator management' of carrion crows, stoats and weasels. Red kites roost in older mixed woodland in the glen and hunt on the exposed hills.

I ask Colin about the 'medicated grit' that keepers put down for grouse – that's a pesticide, right? He explains that grouse are prone to strongylosis, caused by the nematode worm *Trichostrongylus tenuis* in their gut, which they spread in their droppings.* Grouse eat grit naturally; it helps them digest their food. The keepers leave the medicated grit in small stone containers around the hillsides, and the grouse will supplement their natural foraging with it. The quantity in these containers is tiny – a scant man's handful. I think of the massive quantity of fertiliser and pesticides drenching some 'conventional' farms, where up to 70 per cent of the nitrogen runs off into watercourses, damaging birdlife and the rest of the aquatic ecosystem, and I think that this restrained use of medicated grit is not the first concern for food-land system change.

Then there's the tick. The tick, the deer, the grouse and the sheep form a kind of new taxonomy of Scottish hillsides. *Ixodes ricinus* are tiny, spider-like creatures that suck the blood of animals, including humans. Colin mentions a time, maybe the 1980s, when spotting a tick on a deer was an event worth mentioning. Now ticks infest the Scottish countryside, and they carry disease: Lyme's disease in particular can affect humans, but ticks are also terrible for the mountain hare, grouse and other birds, as young chicks and leverets infested

---

* Grouse populations cycle accordingly: when conditions are right and worm count is low, they proliferate, thus increasing the presence of the worm, which weakens or kills the grouse. The grouse population therefore crashes, bringing the worm count down with it.

with ticks can be overcome. Deer and sheep both carry ticks. The warmer, wetter summers and massive boom in deer populations mean an explosion in tick populations too. The hills at Gannochy are managed for this: on one side of the glen the deer were removed for two years to try to reduce the tick population, allowing the grouse and other birds to flourish. Sheep are kept mainly to the fields or the other side of the glen for the same reason, and used as 'tick mops': twice a year the animals are doused in insecticides, which marauding ticks then ingest.

So because of a forestry policy that encouraged monoculture spruce farms, intensive sheep-farming that overgrazed much of the hills, and because humans had previously decimated populations of predators like raptors and carnivorous mammals, the pests that co-exist with the sheep and deer are overrunning landscapes and affecting the species we *do* want to flourish. This says to me that land managers and policy-makers would do well to consider the whole enmeshed natural eco*system*, rather than target individual species for specific financial gain.

'Invermark, now that's a beautiful estate,' says Colin, gesturing westwards, his awe momentarily bared by the wind. 'What do you mean by beautiful?' I ask. There's a flitting gust between us. I wonder if he will answer at all, but he does: 'Well, I suppose I'm thinking of it from the deer's point of view. It has altitude and the corries, old woodland for shelter, the river and Loch Lee for the fishing. And the forestry and sheep. A good mix.' Not all the deer's point of view, then – he's looking as a man who has many roles: a steward of wild animals and their landscape with a business head that understands what it takes to make the land's sums add up in the modern world. The sheep mean that the estate was eligible for the Single Farm Payment, an EU subsidy for farmers now set to be revised. Colin mentions the tracks across the hills, put in by the estate so that vehicles can transport stalkers and guns (not everyone who pays for a week's stalking up Scottish hills has the physique and fitness to walk them). 'Some people say they're ugly, scars – but folks walking the glen get to use them too.' Twenty years ago there were reports of owls caught in a crow trap and a destroyed peregrine falcon nest on Invermark Estate, but there's been nothing since,[22] which I'm hoping gives credence to Colin's claim that minds are changing about the significance of ecology – locally at least.

We peer through Colin's binoculars, tracking the river along the long glen to the grand house, Invermark Lodge, a Victorian hunting lodge built in Aberdeen granite. It's banked beyond in the dark shade of sitka spruce, with scribbles of older native woodland around the building itself and a neat, glowing-green lawn. My mother worked at Invermark in her student summers, changing the beds and serving breakfast to holidaying families. In my childhood we came back to walk the glen, then eat warm scones and ogle the taxidermy in the little café. Owls, grouse, capercaillie and ptarmigan, a golden eagle, all in their own dioramas, staring for ever into a middle distance. I will return to the café later this afternoon for a bowl of soup, and find some of the collection of stuffed birds still there, displayed together in a glass cabinet alongside a selection of sporting guns. Two stuffed foxes patrol the top of the case. 'In the 1850s the glen was a busy place with 860 people living here,' says the infographic at the entrance. 'We are all historians. We live always in the present but the past is forever with us . . . The past helps to tell us who we are. Today there are just over 100 people living in the glen. Now climate change forces us to re-evaluate the way we live . . . perhaps we can learn something [from the past] which might enrich our lives and the lives of the future.'

Critically, the actual shoot at Gannochy Estate is not a 'driven' shoot but happens 'over pointers'. English pointers are dogs bred to 'point' with their muzzle to indicate the location of the birds. At Gannochy, small groups of 'guns', typically four or five at a time, will go out onto the 3,000 acres of grouse moor and bring back perhaps eight brace (pairs) of grouse in a day, three days a week, for the nine weeks in the season. This 'walk-up' shooting can be a more selective activity and target specific birds. By contrast, the evolution of the breech-loading shotgun in the latter half of the nineteenth century escalated the practice of 'driven' game.[23] This refers to grouse beating, where lines of usually local folks walk through the heather and flush the grouse from where they shelter on the ground, driving them towards a line of guns hiding behind 'butts', or shelters. For this, a grouse population has to be plentiful; the guns will be able to shoot a large number of birds, sometimes 200 brace or more, in a day. At Gannochy in 2024, hire of the lodge (which sleeps a maximum of eight) for a week's shooting costs upwards of £12,750, to include ten brace of grouse, two stags, salmon fishing, plus pigeon- and rabbit-shooting.* The guests' expectations are high. It is under this kind of pressure that some grouse-moor keepers illegally shoot and poison eagles and owls, trap and snare the foxes, stoats and weasels.

---

* In the brochure for 2024, the ghillie cost £700 extra, and the (mandatory) cook a further £2,200, not including the cost of the food.

In the other direction, towards the hazy white-blue of the sea, Colin points to a hillside marked for different land management. Aviva, the giant insurance company and investment-fund manager, has bought all 22,000 acres of the adjacent Glen Dye Estate for £30 million as part of a 'carbon capture' scheme – meaning planting native and commercial forests, restoring and protecting peatland, with the aim of capturing atmospheric carbon dioxide and sequestering it in the soil.[24] Colin also mentions another carbon-capture scheme in Speyside, Kinrara Estate near Aviemore, which was bought by self-styled Scottish 'punk' brewers BrewDog for £8.8 million, using some public money. The scheme is causing controversy: BrewDog have erected large deer fences to protect young tree growth.[25] However, the fences also exclude mountain hares and will interrupt animal migration, diverting the deer population to swell numbers on nearby estates, as well as restricting public access even in the face of Scotland's 'Right to Roam'. The company's decision to hire 'contract keepers' is also not popular. A better way, suggest the online commentators, may have been to establish a permanent staff, knowledgeable and connected enough to cooperate with adjacent land managers, and who would be invested long-term in the land. 'Carbon capture' sounds benevolent, but it doesn't answer the dangling questions about equitable land-ownership and meaningful public access to nature. And by default, schemes like these are themselves food policies.

Just as in the nineteenth century, investing in Scottish land is still a way of cleaning capital and conscience. Next to the food sector, fast fashion is one of the biggest contributors to climate collapse and environmental degradation.[26] Danish billionaire

Anders Holch Povlsen is owner of international clothing chain Bestseller and the biggest single shareholder in online fashion retailer ASOS. He's also Scotland's wealthiest man and its biggest landowner. His Wildland estates are managed 'as a 200-year vision of landscape-scale conservation . . . we work to let nature heal, grow and thrive', says the website. Wildland run old estate houses as upscale hospitality businesses with restaurants, using game and other produce from their estates. They are very successful at achieving conservation targets. Glen Feshie Estate in the Cairngorms is, according to land-rights campaigner Andy Wightman, an exemplar of what can be achieved through natural regeneration of native woodland in a relatively short space of time. Since 2004, red deer numbers there have been dramatically reduced, and the natural regeneration of Scots pine, juniper and silver birch is developing across the estate.[27]

Perhaps there's at least a sense of justice in the diversion of private gains to the eventual public good (and restoring ecology and mitigating climate collapse certainly does that). As they are currently managed, Highland estates take a lot of cash to upkeep. Maintaining an estate for shooting requires year-round salaries for gamekeepers, book-keepers, office staff; equipment, vehicles and farm machinery; dog kennels, maintenance of buildings, roads, woods and fences; sometimes visitor centres and other public facilities. Shooting seasons are short and venison and game-bird prices are not high enough. Sheep-farming and forestry work economically only due to massive public subsidy. It takes a rich landowner to manage land this way.

On the way out of the glen I stop for a cup of tea with Lesley, her mum, Sheena, and her dad, Euan.* Lesley has worked many summers as a grouse beater. She reckons the day rates haven't increased since she first started as a young student; beaters are still on £75 a day after tax, starting at 8 a.m. and working till at least 5 p.m., sometimes as late as 7 p.m. Food and temporary accommodation is included – though staying elsewhere doesn't mean a pay bump.† Euan still works on one of the nearby estates as a loader, meaning he carries each customer's two guns, and loads one while the guest shoots the other. On Euan's estate the loaders are only guaranteed pay for the three 'friends and family' weeks at the start of a season, at a rate of £100 per day after tax. Other shooting parties wanting the services of a loader are requested to tip: letting agents suggest £70 per day, though it's not obligatory. Euan obviously enjoys the work – the camaraderie with men he has known most of his life, the banter with the guests and the time out on the hills.

Grouse-shooting for me sits on a balance that threatens to tip with every straw. Again, it comes down to values other than the merely financial. What is all this land *for*? Currently grouse moors and deer 'forests' are managed to allow a few select species to flourish, one of them being mankind. The moors are 'playgrounds' – sports fields – for the extreme minority who can afford their services. Ramblers and bird-spotters and picnickers can use the land too, for free – in Scotland, anyway – and their respective pastimes are given value by the way the land is managed for shooting. But in a country that imports half of its food supply,[28] what exactly do we want to happen

---

* Names changed for diplomacy.
† The Scottish Living Wage at the point of this conversation was £10.90 per hour.

with the 98 per cent of Scotland that is not urban?[29] How *do* people and landscape get to interact in a way that lets us connect with, value and protect nature, when so much of that land is privately owned and must cover at least the costs of upkeep, if not make a profit for its owner?

From a purely environmental point of view, grouse-moor management done well, such as with low-intensity, walk-up shoots, sensitive muirburn with compensatory native woodland planting, and strictly restrained predator control, *could* be a way of giving financial value to a large swathe of landscape, allowing estates to 'wash their own faces', keeping some now-traditional roles alive, providing some skilled employment in rural areas and helping to manage a landscape that can have other benefits than just to the grouse. In the early 1990s, Michael Wigan mused that 'the time may come when environmental benefits may be written in to cost equations of comparative land uses, which would be of manifest benefit to the sporting case'.[30]

Grouse can be delicious. If you consider killing animals for food acceptable at all, then animals allowed to live their own lives and forage their own diets without the need for (say) imported Amazonian soy,[31] are inarguably a far higher-welfare, lower-impact, healthier source of meat than industrially farmed beef, pork or chicken. But grouse-moor managers and the incentives that guide them still prioritise human profit over the needs of the hills, their woods and their wildlife. Until all grouse moors are managed with equitable consideration for *all* their potential inhabitants, grouse will remain as rare on the Inver tables as its place should be in a vast Highland ecosystem.

SALMON

It's the river that gets me. As almost an after-thought on Colin's tour of the glen, we swing open a locked gate and the 4x4 lurches through. Colin and the Gannochy Estate are famous for 'the Macnab': the *Field* magazine reports annually on this and other estates' success at the challenge, when guests aim to stalk a deer, shoot a brace of grouse and catch a salmon all in the same day.* It's a bright morning and there's a glare on the pale sandstones on the riverbank, rounded and smooth like the ostrich eggs of Victorian curiosity cabinets. The current is at a brisk trot, a steady shushing canter tripping over rock. I know how that water feels, tastes: a whispered secret on a wet neck; a vanishing scent of metal. On a spot just like this we once picnicked with friends and suddenly my mind is a still – a peopled photograph from another summer day.

For millennia, the Scottish springtime was full of silver light as rivers pulsed dense with fish returning to spawn in their birth pools. Today, wild salmon in Scotland's rivers are in crisis.[32] In December 2023 the IUCN reclassified the main UK Atlantic salmon populations as 'endangered'.[33] Salmon have been historically important as a source of food, but equally so as a badge of Scots culture. They're featured on the coats of arms of Glasgow, of the Royal Burgh of Peebles, and of Clan Donald. In Gaelic stories, the 'ceasg' is a mermaid, with the body of a beautiful woman and the tail of a salmon. In Celtic

---

* Silver, Madeleine, 'Meet the *Field*'s 2021 Macnabbers', 20 January 2021, at: <https://www.thefield.co.uk/macnab-challenge/the-field-macnab-challenge-2021-46631> The endeavour is named after John Buchan's 1925 novel *John Macnab*, the story of three gentleman poachers trying to shake off the ennui of a privileged life.

legend, it's the 'salmon of wisdom', and the spots on its belly are the red hazelnuts on the Tree of Knowledge which the fish ate as they fell into the sacred wells of Tír na n'Óg, the Land of Youth. One modern clan member observes, 'What our ancestors recognised as Wisdom and Knowledge are in modern language identified as essential Omega 3 fatty acids, high quality protein . . . vitamin A, vitamin D, vitamin B6, vitamin B and vitamin E, which are all essential to maintain peak brain function and health.'[34]

Salmon are migratory fish: they are born in freshwater rivers, where they stay for the first few years of their lives, and travel to the sea for one to four years before returning to the very same river to spawn. Written in the mid-1980s, Annette Hope's *A Caledonian Feast* was already noting that wild salmon were seriously endangered by illegal trapping, particularly by the use of dynamite and two-mile-long gill nets used in the estuaries. Hope speculated that 'the answer may lie in fish farming . . . a boom industry',[35] describing small family businesses that conformed to high standards in order to qualify for aid from the Highlands and Islands Development Board. In 1986 there were 100 such small companies on 210 sites, producing about 10,000 tonnes of salmon worth around £42 million. In 2021, there were 12 much larger companies farming 213 sites (only 12 certified organic), producing 205,393 tonnes of salmon and employing 1,495 people. The industry is now worth £760 million to the Scottish economy, concentrated in the five remote, rural, salmon-producing regions, which include my home, Argyll.[36] In 1970, only about 4 per cent of all the sea fish consumed around the world was farmed. Today, it is over 50 per cent, and farming is predicted to account for two-thirds of the fish we eat by 2030.[37] Salmon is one of the top two major farmed species. Salmon-farming is no longer about allowing small family farms to diversify with a wee pond at the foot of their burn. 'Boom' it did.

The reasons for the salmon's decline are legion and together form an uneasy collage of a sickening marine landscape. On the west coast particularly, salmon farms are implicated in wild fish decline due to both the excessive populations of sea lice and the excessive use of pesticides in the intensively stocked cages. Salmon are highly vulnerable to lice, which infest the young fish and can kill them. Nine tonnes of antibiotics were used in UK salmon farms in 2021, a 168 per cent increase on 2017. 'Chemicals such as formaldehyde and hydroperoxide are used to tackle lice. Lice are crustaceans, so there is collateral damage to other crustaceans,' says Don Staniford of anti-salmon-farm campaign Scamon Scotland.[38] This affects the human food supply through the country's shellfish industry (lobsters, crabs and langoustines are all crustaceans), and the supply of krill, much smaller crustaceans, which are a significant part of the wild salmon's diet.

Wild salmon flesh is naturally pink because of the krill, which contain a red pigment called astaxanthin. It's also this diet that makes them a healthy, omega-rich protein. Farmed salmon eat fish feed at a 'feed conversion ratio' of approximately 1.25:1, meaning a salmon needs to eat 1.25kg of feed to produce 1kg of flesh.[39] Feed for carnivorous fish like salmon is made from wild-caught fish, sometimes from offcuts from other fish-processing industries, which would make the salmon flesh an unappetising grey. So farmed salmon colour is decided by a chart called the SalmoFan, which indicates how much 'Carophyll' pink astaxanthin a farmer should feed his fish for his desired pinkness. There's also the issue of fish oils; salmon and trout feeds require a lot of oil to produce the familiar texture, flavour and nutritional make-up. Salmon would usually get this from eating small fish themselves, but instead it's extracted from the sardine and anchovy catches during fish-meal processing. Fish-feed producers like BioMar are running out of fish oil before they run out of the meal itself.

Meanwhile, weaker farm salmon escape and breed with the wild fish, further debilitating the wild population. (In one 2017 incident alone, 20,000 farm salmon escaped their sea tanks.[40]) Colin also mentions overfishing out at sea. Salmon spend at least one to two years of their young lives at sea and rely on healthy wild fish stocks to eat. But the young smolts themselves are often caught in the nets. With fewer other fish to eat, dolphins and seals at the river mouths are also feeding more intensely on the young salmon. Colin reckons that only 1 in every 100 smolts is returning to their river to spawn, when once it would have been around 25 per cent.[41]

Once back on the home stretch, the fish struggle too. Rising temperatures due to climate change have put neatly synchronised nature out of whack: the insect larvae that newly hatched salmon feed on may already be grown and gone. Rivers are polluted, by industry, and by fertiliser and pesticide run-off from adjacent farms. Salmon like the shelter of trees on the riverbanks, which also encourage diverse bird and insect life; some farms have torn out their trees and hedgerows to make fields bigger. Saprolegnia is a water mould that affects salmon eggs, and can weaken young fish and cause unsightly cotton-wool-like blotches on older fish. It's been linked to fish stressors like low water flow, prolonged cold spring temperatures, barriers to migrations (such as dams), or stressors out at sea.[42]

When I visit, it's just after a day of heavy rain and Colin is keenly noting the rise in water level. Everything is connected.

There's been some help for the wild salmon. In 2016, the Scottish government imposed a three-year ban on river-mouth salmon netting, which catches the fish as they move between sea and river. It was extended indefinitely in 2019, when the Esk District Salmon Fishery Board purchased the last salmon-netting station at the Nab on the North Esk. It was the end of a centuries-old tradition, and to the benefit of the anglers; the Esk salmon and trout fishery is estimated to be worth around £2 million to the local economy, including indirect cash going to local hotels and other tourism businesses in the area.[43] On most Scottish rivers, 'catch and release' is now the law – there simply aren't enough wild salmon for humans to enjoy any more.

The Scottish Association for Marine Science estimates that the annual haul of 200,000 tonnes of farmed salmon emit waste equivalent to that of half the population of Scotland.[44] Fish that otherwise would swim several thousand miles during their migration are kept in densely stocked 'feed-lot' cages. Death-rates for farmed fish are grotesque: 25 per cent of the 65 million salmon in farms around Scotland's west coast die each year, bodies dumped in the dunes of remote beaches, such as at the Whiteshore Cockles site in North Uist. Photographer and anti-salmon-farm campaigner Corin Smith posts photos on his Instagram of giant burial pits – mass graves – full of thousands of diseased, malformed fish.[45]

Mowi Scotland, formerly Marine Harvest McConnell, is one of the major fish-farming companies in Scotland, its name stamped in marine blue on the white (non-recyclable) poly-boxes dyked at many fishing ports, small harbours and fish-shop back doors around the west coast and islands. It's part of a Norwegian company that has 25–30 per cent of the global salmon and trout market (remembering that the Competition Commission considers anything over 25 per cent to be an anti-competitive monopoly share),[46] and operations in Norway, Scotland, Ireland, the Faroe Islands and Chile. In Scotland, the company operate twenty-five farms, four freshwater farms, two processing plants, and a harvest station in Mallaig. In January 2017, *Private Eye* reported that Mowi was responsible for depositing the majority of an estimated 400kg of the insecticide azamethiphos into Scottish waters to control lice in its salmon.[47] In 2022, Mowi's turnover was 4.9 *billion* euros; it's listed on the Oslo Stock Exchange with shares also traded in the US.[48] It is using the 'blue commons' (the waters to which all people have rights to access and use) to generate private wealth, and is doing so by creating 'collateral damage' – externalities which are not adequately accounted for in the price of the salmon or any dues paid by Mowi.[49] At the same time the company is trading on Scotland's romantic name and the depictions of our beautiful seascapes on its packaging, both of which it is jeopardising. Scottish citizens pay the healthcare and environmental clean-up costs.

Farmed salmon is now a supermarket chill-cabinet staple. But what's it *for*? The National Diet and Nutrition Survey shows that everyone in the UK, including on vegetarian and vegan diets, eats *more* than the recommended daily amount of protein.[50] Essential amino acids omega-3 and omega-6 can also come from healthful, sustainable mussels, mackerel, sprats and sardines; or from eating a diverse range of nuts, seeds, beans and pulses.

Rural employment is often cited as justification for allowing practices to continue that are detrimental to the commons. As of the 2019 census, rural Scotland accounts for 17 per cent of the total population. The 1,500 people employed by the salmon farms are 0.161 per cent of rural dwellers. I'm also interested in the *quality* of that employment and the level of pay those workers get. Quality of employment affects the quality of life a whole community experiences, their relationships with each other, their place and their self-identity. Are salmon-farm wages a fair share of the profit they generate? Are those jobs engaging and meaningful, and are the employees well protected? I've lived on the west coast on and off since my early twenties and I know that many of those jobs are poorly paid and unpleasant. They're also dangerous. One recent tragedy saw fish-farm manager Clive Hendry drown after being crushed between a workboat and barge. The subsequent investigation found health and safety failings in the company's procedures.[51]

Do we really need to be eating a severely degraded version of a beautiful animal, the supply of which is also jeopardising the wild original and its habitat, when there are so few obvious benefits to people and their communities? The Norwegian government has recently introduced a 'ground-rent tax' for the larger salmon farms of 25 per cent.[52] (Now that's commons sense.)

Bren Smith, Canadian former industrial fisherman turned 'regenerative ocean farmer', is scathing of salmon-farming, where he also worked for a while. He questions why, with thousands of species to choose from, we're farming those that clearly don't respond well to captivity and industrial production. Then he answers his own question: we're growing what people wanted to eat based on the wild fisheries. 'Just because we've successfully hunted salmon and tuna in the wild for hundreds of years doesn't necessarily mean that those are the species we should grow . . . Instead, we need to approach the ocean as a unique agricultural space, and ask: What do you want us to grow?'[53] And this, for me, is it: this is how you 'decolonise' food supply, and put the voice of nature centre-stage.

Through no heated haze of romantic imagination can farmed salmon be considered an expression of an unspoilt 'natural' landscape, nor an icon worthy of a family crest. I don't serve it in the restaurant. The association with the loch and hills outside the dining-room windows would feel a lie. Every year there are fewer and fewer wild 'fin' fish I'm happy to serve. We are always overjoyed when the mackerel appear in the loch in the summer, and till then we revel in the umami-rich shellfish and seaweeds that have been part of Scottish coastal diets for millennia.

If we want to eat fish at all, then it's likely that aquaculture is going to have to play some role. Wild fisheries have been brutalised for profit. Bren Smith's memoir-manifesto *Eat Like a Fish* talks vividly of his time as a fisherman at the highest point of the 'industrialisation of the oceans'. Says Bren: 'We ripped up entire ecosystems with our trawls . . . one of the most destructive forms of food production on the planet . . . Those of us working in the high seas in those years were mere cogs in the grinding wheels of industrialization. We lived and died at sea.'[54]

Technology developed for the Second World War is now used to hunt the last fish in the oceans with military accuracy. Underwater radar and pinpoint echolocation arm massive floating factory ships kitted with enormous on-board freezers so they can stay at sea for months at a time. Bren describes 'the global conglomerates that run 450-foot, six-thousand-horsepower trawlers with four-thousand-ton capacity and leave swathes of dead bycatch behind every haul... the tickler chains and rockhoppers dragging along the ocean floor, leaving deserts of destruction'.[55] It's no wonder the Grand Banks cod fishery off Newfoundland collapsed in 1992. When the cod ran out, the Canadian government closed the fishery and 35,000 men lost their jobs overnight.

This isn't a question of poor fishermen just trying to feed their families and keep local coastal tradition alive. In 2018 an investigation revealed that in Scotland just five families, all featured on the *Sunday Times* Rich List, hold or control 45 per cent of Scotland's fishing quota.[56] In addition, more than half (thirteen) of the top twenty-five UK quota holders have directors, shareholders or vessel partners who were convicted of offences in Scotland's £63m 'black fish' scam – a huge, sophisticated fraud that saw trawlermen and fish processors working together to evade quota limits. Fish factories used underground pipes, secret weighing machines and extra conveyor belts to land 170,000 tonnes of over-quota fish over several years.[57] 'Day boats', on the other hand – meaning boats that return to shore each day with the sort of catch that one man or a small crew can achieve in that time – are selective, and catch precisely what their quota allows, each fish individually assessed, processed or returned. These small-scale coastal fishermen, who operate 80 per cent of Scottish boats, have just 1 per cent of quotas *between them*.

Our neighbours the Barge family live on top of a hill at the end of a steep, careering driveway that takes you past their pretty Jersey cows, lowered peat-water eyes reflecting long black eyelashes, and a long view over the grey loch and its distant, misty hillsides. Fiona runs the small farm and makes cheese from the cows' milk, which we serve in the breakfast baskets at Inver. Alastair is the man behind the Gigha Halibut farm and its hatchery, Otter Ferry Seafish at Largiemore, just at the foot of their driveway.

Gigha halibut has been on the Inver menus since we opened. Learning to cook with all its many parts has been a labour of love and craft. It's been a joy to cook with, and an early connection for us newcomers to the people here, and to our shared landscape. Alastair's dad set up a small salmon farm on the Largie burn in 1968, at the time when salmon-farming seemed like a good way to support rural livelihoods. But by the late 1980s, with big-bucks investment, the salmon industry had economies of scale that were rapidly turning an expensive, occasional-treat fish into an everyday, cheap supermarket commodity. The smaller family operation couldn't compete, and investor Booker McConnell wanted to transfer the whole operation to the Hebrides. The Barges refused. The family tried a few alternatives for their tanks, such as lobster (which ate each other in the confinement) and turbot (which didn't grow quickly enough) and cod (which was wasteful; a lot of a cod's weight goes into its head, which has little market value). But halibut ticked all the boxes.

Halibut-farming requires a different mindset entirely to salmon. Halibut responds to compassionate husbandry, not mass production. Its growth is, says Alastair, 'more like an oak tree than a sitka spruce'. It takes time, that most expensive of commodities. It's a long-term ethical investment with a ten-year horizon for returns, and the road to that return is 'bumpy'; fish-farming is not for the faint-hearted. Gigha doesn't make a return on its investments, certainly not enough to attract big business; little beyond what Alastair needs to survive on his small farm with his family.

In 1991, the Barges and a couple of industry collaborators caught their original brood stock in waters off Iceland and started breeding at several potential hatcheries, including Otter Ferry. It was more difficult than they had originally thought. The others gave up. The early stage of rearing halibut is, Alastair says, 'tricky'; a marine-water environment is a bacterial and viral soup, in contrast to clean water coming straight from a spring, which has had no chance of contamination, let alone a whole ecosystem breeding in it. The seawater can be UV-treated and filtered but can't be completely purified, and the tiny halibut larvae, much smaller than salmon eggs, are vulnerable to micro-organism attack. Otter Ferry Seafish filter the seawater and add probiotics to naturally counter the populations of pathogenic bacteria, essentially mobilising a microbiological army to protect the larvae. The 'slime' coating the exterior of the fish is another protective feature that naturally repels sea lice and other destructive pests, meaning there's no need for chemical pesticides to be flushed through the tanks.

Gigha halibut scores high on sustainability tick-lists. Wild Atlantic halibut populations are critically endangered, and the fish is listed by the Marine Conservation Society as a flame-red number 5 in their sustainability chart, meaning it should be avoided at all costs. The halibut is the oldest and slowest-growing of all the flat fish. As Alastair says, choosing wild Atlantic halibut for dinner is a bit like eating pandas.

The Atlantic halibut's 'feed conversion rate' is more like 1.5kg of feed to 1kg of whole fish, but the feed itself is less impactful on wild fish populations. The Gigha halibut feed includes cereals, and fish-meal made from fish-processing industry trimmings, thus in part recycling waste. It takes much less fish oil to produce a feed appropriate for halibut. In essence, it's turning fish that people don't want to eat into desirable, edible product. Of course the question remains whether we'd just be better learning to eat more sardines instead – or indeed, sticking to lentils.

Gigha is a tiny Inner Hebridean island with the characteristic soft white-sand coastlines, turquoise seas and breezy floral machair landscape. The Gigha Halibut tanks are on land and are fed by seawater pumped in continual motion from the pristine sea, metres away. Shoals of grey mullet cluster round the exit pipes, feeding on the nutrients being cycled through the water. There's potentially a social boon to the story too; the community bought out their landlord around five years before Gigha Halibut arrived, so the residents own their own island. The halibut farm employs four full-time and three part-time staff, in a population of 163 (down from its peak of 614 in 1792, but rising again now). The energy fuelling the pump is renewable, coming from the island's wind turbines; Gigha is a net contributor of energy to the grid, and this profit stays on the island too.

Asked about the future, Alastair wonders about 'other Gighas'. Scanning a map of Scotland, you'd have to find sites where there was potential for renewable power. Perhaps it would work well somewhere that would struggle to connect its renewable supply to the national grid. Instead, that power could circulate locally and provide an income, via a halibut farm, for a remote community. It would be another way of using the landscape itself to transform one resource into sustenance for its inhabitants, akin to using native breeds of cows to convert the hillside grasses that we can't eat into beef and milk.

Alastair's words are given poignancy now: despite all his efforts, during the writing of this book he announced that

Gigha Halibut will cease production. Rising sea temperatures around Gigha are causing problems. It's a shallow-water site so the water pumped round the tanks is relatively warm, and these deep-water northern Atlantic fish need real cold. The exorbitant cost of electricity (UK fuel prices quadrupled in 2022) means they could not afford to chill the water themselves. The search for 'other Gighas' – colder and deeper sites to continue the halibut project – has become more urgent.

Alastair describes halibut-farming as 'a drug' – you do a little of it just to try it out, then you keep doing it even when you shouldn't because it makes you feel good. It's predominantly a lifestyle choice. It 'attracts nice people' who are in it for the skills and craft of the job, and who can take pride in knowing that they are contributing to a business run by good people and producing a good thing. Through serendipity and entrepreneurship, Scotland was able to offer another premium ingredient that is a product of both its landscape and its people. Thinking optimistically, what role could a product like Gigha halibut have in Scottish food culture of the future? Could it be a source of national pride and identity, like salmon once was, despite its small-scale production and high price point?

But then, salmon was originally an occasional treat, unless you lived near the river and could catch it yourself. And think of langoustines and lobsters, slow-grown organic beef and lamb, or the grouse shoots at estates like Balmoral. These have all shaped Scots food culture and identity over the millennia, despite not having a daily presence on the table. They're mostly still special-occasion restaurant treats. The produce with the highest commercial value – the roasts, the chops, the sifted wheat for white bread; the seafood platters and the glories of the twelfth of August – have historically been sold or traded. The people who raised and harvested them crafted their own meals with the milk, the cods' heads, the sheep's bones or the whelks. There is value in these skills too, and in the parts of the plants and animals that don't command a market premium. Bringing back the skills and knowledge we need to make the most of our home-grown produce is perhaps the strongest stand for equality and empowerment that we can make.

Since the beginning at Inver, we've served the head and tail of the Gigha halibut as well as fillets, made sauces from the bones, dried and fried the skin to a crisp, and we have taught ourselves various things to do with the rendered fat from the frilly bits. An iconic specials board regular is the whole grilled Gigha halibut head, with red sausage and green onions. The huge head itself has a fantastic selection of treats on it, from the dense collar (the top of the fillet) to the tender nugget of flesh behind the cheek, the gelatinous skin and the springy eyeball. The green onions are the tops of spring or new onions, often discarded, but delicious from the charcoal grill. The 'red sausage' is our take on the Calabrian speciality nduja, a soft, spreadable fermented spicy sausage, first made in the Inver kitchen by an Australian chef called Blair with dried chillies we brought back from a holiday in Mexico. It uses up all the pieces of fat and scraps from any local pig we've been working with. Melted with a little water, the sausage sauces the whole grilled fish head, and provides contrast and seasoning for all textural meat. In China and in southern Europe, the fish head is reserved for the most honoured guest at the table. At Inver, you are all our honoured guests.

The words 'normal' and 'modern' are now so heavily loaded they're in danger of falling through the page.

History, personal and national, writes my menus. I'm Scottish – and the foods that build my identity in the kitchen are recognisably 'Scottish' too. I'm living in modernity. And I'm a cook. But this skeleton identity is shared by many, many people in the country today. We're not all unified in our notions of what it means to cook normal, modern, Scottish food. It's the features of my own personal landscape, as well as our shared national, global and familial landscapes, that contour the food on the Inver plates.

But there's more still I can't quite explain: how do all the other facts of modern life guide my hands as I twist the juicer and rock the knife? I'm a woman, and I know gender issues are played out in kitchens at home and work. Meanwhile the guidebooks and awarding bodies, media and PR, jostle to tell the stories that make modern food culture what it is, and are often the ones shouting the loudest. Food culture exists in a much wider cultural context, influenced by movements in arts and literature as well as science and economics. How do these storytellers shape modern food, and influence the cooks themselves? Who gets to define or dictate the kind of food I cook?

Is there a way of reconciling our reason with our senses, and to make room in modern Scottish food for *all* its contributors?

Chapter Five:
A MODERN SCOTTISH COOK

Who gets to decide the criteria for 'excellence' for different kinds of food and cooking? What assumptions simmer under notions of 'normal', like the rising steam that swells a dumpling dough?

I'm a woman and an equal partner in our small restaurant business. Women are 50.6 per cent of the UK population, half the human inhabitants of this landscape. It's impossible for me to talk about modern, contemporary cooking in any kitchen without asking what role women have in all this. If colonisation was about asserting the supremacy of the white male, then *de*colonising also includes recentring the voices, experiences and presence of women, of all colours.

'Authenticity' is a slippery notion, hard for cooks to traverse. Who gets to decide what's 'authentic'? Unless it's the individual cook herself, demanding 'authenticity' – the constrained re-creation of a time and place always just out of reach – perpetuates the colonialist's judgemental stance. Allowing roots to be a start, not the end, to creativity makes room for infinite possibility.

To cook well uses *all* the senses. The last half-millennia has demoted taste, touch and smell and disconnected us from all the interactions with the world that those senses enable. A world in which sight and hearing are prioritised is an unbalanced one, today increasingly mediated by two-dimensional screens. Acknowledging the input of all our senses reunites us with the world at the end of our fingertips and gives us a way of more fully connecting with each other and ourselves.

So who is it that is entitled to define 'modern Scottish food', in and out of the restaurant world, and which influences on the Scots larder are given credit on the normal, modern plate? How do I find my own criteria for success, in a rulebook written by others, for people not like me?

There's a simple dichotomy implicit in western gender associations with cooking: 'Men work in professional kitchens; women work in home kitchens.' Even quite recently, I've been asked to comment on 'women's growing gastronomical influence, after years of having their culinary ability confined to the home'.[1] It's frustrating. Women have cooked professionally for as long as food has been served outwith the home. Women have cooked in restaurants of all kinds for at least two documented millennia – from medieval taverns to ancient Chinese market stalls. More recently, they've cooked in schools and prisons, workplace canteens; in bakeries, cafés and bistros, and in multi-starred fine-dining empires. It's mainly in that latter world of formal 'fine dining' that they have been under-represented. So the question itself shows the importance that a particular kind of male-centred cooking has been given by some people, over all other forms of cooking. But fine dining is a style of food, not itself a quality mark. Excellence is reached by many routes.

A MODERN SCOTTISH COOK

Even within fine-dining restaurants, which are a relatively new convention of the last 200 years, there have always been women cooking – just not as many as men. Scotland in particular has a history of women leading successful professional kitchens: until her retirement in 2001, the Norwegian Gunn Eriksen held two Michelin stars as chef and co-proprietor at Altnaharrie Inn on Loch Broom (the only chef in Scotland with two Michelin stars in the 1990s). Shirley Spear started the Three Chimneys on Skye back in the 1970s, and Hilary Brown cooked at La Poitinière at Gullane through the 1980s. These days, the majority of Glasgow's most prominent contemporary kitchens are run by women: Rosie Healey at Gloriosa, Julie Lin at Julie's Kopitiam and now Ga Ga, Aysha Abulhawa at Sunny Acre, Ranjit Kaur at the eponymous Ranjit's Kitchen, Lorna McNee at Cail Bruich, and Anna Luntley (with her partner Sam) at bakery Two Eight Seven. Only one of these – Lorna – has a Michelin star.

When tyre manufacturers the Michelin brothers first published their hallowed touring guide in 1900, women in the UK still didn't have the vote.* The *Michelin Guide* established criteria for lodgings, garages and restaurants, the judgements written by men for the men who would be driving the car and paying the bill. These days, those proudly unchanged criteria act like a feedback loop: chefs and restaurateurs value the guides, giving the guides and awards credibility; thus they cook to the qualities the guides promote. Awards and guidebooks largely serve to reinforce the status quo, not to challenge it. At some point, though, if change is to happen

---

* It was 1928, less than a century ago, when the Representation of the People (Equal Franchise) Act gave all women in Britain the vote on the same terms as men.

– which as history tells us, it always does – someone has to think differently.

'A woman's place is in the kitchen.' Used by a male speaker this phrase is restrictive, presumptuous and clearly derogatory. It evokes the opening decades of the twentieth century, when the woman's role in a certain kind of post-industrial society was increasingly strained. Women were joining the workforce in part, but were also required to keep the home fires lit, the home larder stocked, the home laundry washed, the home socks mended, the homework done, the children bathed and the dinner on the table. The phrase says nothing about how these jobs were valued, either by the husbands or the women themselves, or by the wider capitalist economy to which they contributed without reward. From our vantage point only a century later, the kitchen (as a metaphor for domestic duty) looks like a trap from which women did well to escape.

'A woman's space is in the kitchen.' In her book *Voices in the Kitchen*, Dr Meredith Abarca distinguishes between North American and Mexican discussions of the feminist movement. In Abarca's lived experience, the women in her rural Mexican childhood used cooking as liberation and as creative expression. Time spent in their kitchens was empowering. In the kitchen, they could reclaim a space for themselves, carve out time and create their own agency. They used the senses as their library. In a kitchen, there is a world of knowledge to be had, five parallel worlds to explore. These women did not share the western–North American vocabulary around feminist 'liberation' from the stove. 'Labour-saving' kitchen gadgets and disposable plastic cups and wrappings are sold through the promise of 'freedom', the liberation of time, but what if you don't want to be freed? (And what are you freed to 'spend' this time on?) In her 1963 classic *The Feminine Mystique*, Betty Friedan looked at what household technologies had done for women and concluded that they had just created more demands. 'Even with all the new labor-saving appliances, the modern American housewife probably spends more time on housework than her grandmother.'[2] Instead, in spending time using your senses, practising a craft, and gifting the crafted platefuls to a family and a community, you gain a sense of self-worth and the rewards inherent in these activities themselves. (What, indeed, if capitalism is the biggest cage of all, asks Abarca?)

Perhaps the next tectonic shift in cuisine isn't about what's new on the plate, but in the rising awareness of how it got there; a movement about kitchen culture, in particular a feminisation of the kitchen. Kitchens are a prism for all the influences the world throws at us, the cooks; for the ingredients we choose to put in the fridge and onto the shelves. Whether or not we are conscious of these forces is up to us.

The Office of National Statistics data shows that fewer than one in five chefs in UK restaurant kitchens are women.[3] Feminisation of the kitchen might mean that I'd like to see more women in kitchens. I certainly enjoy working in an atmosphere of mutual support and respect, a united team operating towards a common goal rather than a collection of individuals jostling for their own position. Building a good team is about seeking balance, gathering personalities and skill sets that complement each other. In reality it probably means that you'd have a mix of men and women. And in order for every kitchen to benefit from that, then yes, the industry as a whole needs to attract more women.

I started cooking professionally in the late 1990s, in a seafood restaurant near Kyle of Lochalsh, on Scotland's west coast. At that time there were even fewer women in restaurant kitchens than there are now. In fact, cooking as a profession wasn't really on the radar for the university-educated middling classes (even if they had just ditched university and decamped to the western wilds of Scotland). In 1998 Jamie Oliver had just got naked and there was no internet for the masses, never mind social media; if you wanted to know good restaurants to work or eat in, you went to a book shop and bought the *Michelin Guide*. After a year or two cooking in Scotland I moved to London, where I spent the next decade, the first six years of which were spent in fine-dining, Michelin-starred kitchens, with one dreamy year in rural south-west France. The female chefs then were mostly in the pastry sections. I can remember only one or two other girls in the main kitchens in all that time, some of which had brigades of twelve or eighteen chefs. In France there was one other, Delphine, making two of us in a team of ten.

Looking back, being one of very few young women in a team of men didn't bother me at all. I grew up with a younger brother, and many of my best friends at school were guys. I had no problem in batting back the banter and had very little sense at the time of being disadvantaged for any reason. Kitchens are hard physical work, and I am very small, but I was there out of my own volition. I'd walked into a game and asked to play, and I was learning the rules. In fact, feeling a bit different might even have been part of the appeal of the job.

In 2010 American journalist Charlotte Druckman wrote a piece provocatively entitled 'Why Are There No Great Women Chefs?' in which she described a recent experiment on 'gender confusion in the restaurant kitchen'.[4] A panel was asked to guess which of two cooks – a male and a female – had prepared each version of six different dishes, based solely on how the dishes looked and tasted. The panellists, as predicted, could not successfully differentiate the two cooks' work. But the more interesting question that arose was why had the panellists assumed that certain flavours and garnishes were feminine or masculine? That edible flowers were an indication of one gender, and precisely stacked layers another? The conclusion of the experiment was that men and women don't really cook differently, but we judge their food in different ways. When a cook's gender is known, we can even use different vocabulary to describe the same dish; a ragu can be 'bold . . . intense' or 'comforting', depending on who's stirring the pot. On TV, cooking shows featuring women style their chef protagonists differently to programmes featuring men.* The point is, it's not women chefs or their food who aren't great, it's the socially constructed value system which is failing to encapsulate all the diverse ways in which people can achieve greatness. I'd broaden that to include all the inspectors and commentators who visit restaurants these days, and perhaps even the guests themselves – their own expectations influence what they think they find on the plate.

---

* Think cheeky chappy, one-of-the-lads Jamie Oliver, or raging bull Gordon Ramsay, versus sauté seductress Nigella, or matronly Delia.

Writer and intellectual Simone de Beauvoir wrote the seminal feminist tract *The Second Sex* in 1949. Women are 'second' because we have been historically defined in relation to men. The Bible may have popularised it in western thought, what with the Adam's spare rib story. Aristotle had women as 'afflicted with a natural defectiveness'. Thomas Aquinas was more explicit; woman to him was simply 'imperfect man'. It was de Beauvoir who first articulated the 'sex–gender distinction', meaning the difference between the biological sex we are born into and society's immediate swaddling of our infant selves in the norms and stereotypes that frantically construct our gender. It seems in the intervening seven decades that not much has changed.

The gender qualifier ('Best *Female* Chef') simply perpetuates what the Bible started. We're thrown a bone, the spare rib, to keep us gnawing away; to keep us apart. What about all the other variations in gender? Where's the award for excellence by transgender, non-binary, genderqueer, agender, pangender or two-spirit chefs? If they really want to recognise what non-male-identifying chefs do, then the bloggers and commentators, list-builders and award-givers should expand their criteria to encapsulate it; level the playing field. If not, then perhaps it's the list and awards themselves that need the qualifier if we are to accept them as legitimate. Perhaps '50 Best Male-led Restaurants'? 'The Michelin Man-Star'?

Back in 2014 one well-known fine-dining chef was asked publicly why there were not more women in top catering positions. He replied, 'A lot of that fire in a chef's belly you need [in a kitchen], because you need them to force themselves to be ready for dinner service . . . That's probably why there [are] not so many female chefs.' He went on to say, 'To go to the extreme where some kitchens go to – where it's very uncomfortable, where at some point there is perhaps violence, where it perhaps feels threatening – that is taken away a lot by having girls in the kitchen.'

I'm leaving that chef nameless because he's not alone. One 2018 report, which included fifty-four in-depth, face-to-face interviews with male and female Michelin-starred chefs in Great Britain and Ireland, concluded that 'Banter, Bollockings and Beatings' were part of the 'occupational socialisation' of chefs in Michelin-starred fine-dining kitchens. Gender segregation was a persistent problem, and the bullying was 'deeply embedded' in the culture and in the induction of new chefs.[5] The report recommended a course of action to eradicate this phenomenon involving human resource professionals, hospitality managers – and the *Michelin Guide* itself.

COLLECTING EQUALS

In the Inver kitchen I'm fond of saying we're a heterarchy, a collection of equals. Our business benefits from a 50 per cent female workforce. The kitchen roles are organised according to experience, but we are all dependent on each other to get the job done well. The head chef is paid more than the commis chef because more of her time is spent working; although they do the same hours on the rota, much of the junior chef's time is spent learning. The head chef's also got a ten-year career invested in her every move, which deserves recompense. There is relatively little difference between the rate of pay of the juniors, the managers, and us, the business owners. It varies, because Rob's and my pay depends on the profit the business makes; everyone else's pay is secure. The risk is all ours, we work more hours in the week, and for the first five years we often took home less than the dish-washer. But usually it's somewhere around a ratio of 1:2 between the most junior salary and Rob's and my annual take-home pay.

Current McDonald's CEO Chris Kempczinski meanwhile makes almost 1,000 times the annual salary of its median worker. 'The millions of dedicated McFamily members' would have to 'create delicious feel-good moments' for 1,000 years to make what he does in one. Even for CEOs, this is extreme. Typical CEO compensation is more like 200-300 times the median worker's pay, up from a modest 20:1 in 1965 (while worker compensation has risen only 12 per cent in the same period).[6] Mandatory, restricted salary ratios are one tool to promote social equality and ensure that a capitalist's profit cannot exploit worker well-being. The economy would suffer no harm if the money generated by a business was spread more equitably.[7]

Feminising kitchens is about more than just a head count. Change is about what's going on inside those heads too. As in the experiment about gendered food presentation, it would be as inaccurate to claim certain ways of thinking and doing only for womankind as it would be constrictive to the individual woman and exclusionary to the spectrum of other genders. Men can of course be psychologically and emotionally enlightened, value the information of the senses, and be in control of their own anger and stress. There's no gender restriction on understanding the importance of group participation in fostering creativity or in motivating a whole team. But there's history here; an implicit coding of certain forms of knowledge and behaviour which have been claimed by men in kitchens for men in kitchens. And society has colluded to save the rest for women.

I have eyes in the back of my head. Or up my nose, in my ears, in each of the tips of my fingers. I know who's left the tub of shallots half-filled with the lid ajar in the big fridge without seeing the culprit; I can tell the diced shallots are burning in their sizzling butter before I stride across the kitchen and smell the browning milk solids, taste the scorched sugars. Some of this is simple intellect at work: I have an intimate knowledge of the many components of the menu, what needs done at what time by whom, how many kilos of shallots arrived this morning, and who would have put them in what tub. Some of it, however, is knowledge delivered by my senses, singing in harmony; a chorus of betrayal of the negligent cook in question. I hear the way the fridge door slams and know which person uses that kind of force in her daily rounds. Standing at the far side of the kitchen I can hear how hot a pan is by listening to the noise of the moisture in a vegetable escaping the hot fat. It's the first sense to kick in, way before I can see inside the pan. Sloppy gentle puttering, and the onions are on their way to an evanescent translucence, before an elegant gold allium sweetness sets in. A frantic rattle, like panicked mice scrabbling at the sides of the pan, rising steeply to a seething hiss, and from ten metres away I know the pan is too hot. Then it's smell, the sweet warm scent of alliums caramelising in a sour, cheesy reek of cultured butter, freed compounds diacetyl and butanoic acid snaking over the cold steel workbenches and slinking up my nose. Only when I'm standing over the pan, calling the cook's name, can I see the layer of darkened sticky vegetal sugars on its base, and catch the meandering heatwaves, flirtatious shimmer belying the torn depth of heat's ragged claws. I don't need to taste the shallots to know they are too far gone, that the black bitterness has devoured the sweet. This is a lesson I have learned before.

In 1891, the twenty-one-year-old prodigy Edith Cannon's sensual, tactile approach to cheese-making was documented by a male researcher, Dr F. J. Lloyd, using his new instruments of measurement for acidity, temperature and bacteria. Edith's 'ability to produce first class cheese day in day out simply by responding to the information provided by her senses was akin to the prodigal skill of a genius like Mozart'.[8] Meanwhile, the scientist who spent long days in successive years observing her and documenting the minutiae of her methods – from the name of the field where the cows grazed to the chemical conditions within the curds – could still at the end of his report not decipher every variable that might affect the outcomes of a day's cheddar-making in the same way as could Edith, whose instruments were personal and biological. Still, it is Lloyd's recorded work that has endured to inform the global cheese-making industry today, not Edith's testament to the senses – information which would have been equally as teachable or transferable. Authors, scientists and cheese aficionados Bronwen and Francis Percival question why it was that a flawed scientific approach was the one that history latched on to when Edith's tests – the rennet cup and the cheese iron – were more accurate and could capture the many facets of cheese-making.

Lloyd's approach is a misappropriation of 'scientific progress'. His methods have contributed to building a modern cheese-making industry which misunderstands the role of the microbe in food safety. Instead of fulfilling its potential as a perfect expression of local microbial, social and physical landscapes, modern cheese is a perfect metaphor for much that is wrong with modern food-production systems. Milk from multiple dairies is trucked many miles from its source to the cheese-making plant, and then heat-treated to destroy potential pathogens introduced during the long industrial supply chain, annihilating its native, healthy microbial community at the same time. Then the microbial cultures necessary to turn the milk into cheese – now impossible for a cheese-maker to create themselves – are reintroduced from a laboratory-produced packet. This cheese may be microbiologically 'safe', but there are already safety mechanisms in place in traditional cheese-making processes, not least of which is high welfare for healthy cows. With this new, controlled 'scientific' approach, things can still go wrong, but we have lost the connection between land, producers and cheese-eaters. The power to make the cheese itself is now partly in food-tech companies' hands. Meanwhile governments lament the effects of an uninterested public disconnected from its food supply, and 'Big Dairy' companies accumulate profit that might instead have been distributed more equitably throughout a range of small producers.

Since Plato in ancient Greece, there has been a tradition for western philosophers to categorise the five senses into a binary opposition, pitching 'higher' senses (interpreted as objective and distal: sight and hearing) and 'lower' bodily senses (taste, smell, touch) against each other. The western philosopher's love of the higher 'intellectual' faculties comes with 'an implicit gendering: the bodily senses are feminine, and the intellectual are masculine. The 'higher' can be experienced without actual physical contact, and are the ones principally required for scientific proof and discursive expression. The 'lower' express bodily experience. Thoughts are powerful. Society ends up prioritising some activities over others. Jobs become hierarchical. Office work, at computers, using sight and hearing, is important. Cooking is not. When cooking is for men, it's in the high-end, fancy, fine-dining sphere. The food itself has to be valuable: read expensive, labour-intense and rigidly controlled. It must require sacrifice and endurance to produce; every day, every service, must be a battle. A desire to cook for a living because it satisfies all the senses and the intellect is, to some, not enough.

This binary distinction is of course only a tradition, a concept. All the evidence of all the senses continually feeds into our brains and it is in their synthesis that we get not only our impression of the world but our connection to it. 'That information is not in the mind but in the world,' says anthropologist Tim Ingold.[9] During the transformations that we call cooking, growing, tending, harvesting, we learn to translate the world into the human mind and body.

I wonder sometimes why philosophers have not traditionally spent more time examining food, the most common and pervasive of human experiences. It couldn't be that they want to preserve their distance from the common sensual experience? Dr Abarca, Professor of Food Studies and Literature at the University of Texas, writes, 'some philosophers speculate . . . if cooking had received more attention from the time philosophies of human nature were beginning to develop, the distinction between theory (mind) and practices (body) might not have taken root'.[10] Living in a world that prioritises one way of experiencing life over another has serious implications for individuals' mental health and well-being. Some of your experience – some of you – will always feel deprioritised. And some of the things society pressures you to care about are perplexing, because they don't seem to matter at all.

Men can't cook well without using all their senses either, of course. In Ferran Adrià's modernist El Bulli, full of cutting-edge kit and reappropriated industrial food enhancers, and for five years named the world's best restaurant, it was his team of human cooks – actually, the team of unpaid *stagières* – that Ferran described as his greatest 'technology'.[11] Kitchens are perhaps the last bastions of a sensual epistemology, repositories of bodily wisdom able to redress the balance of modern life in this Cartesian hurricane that is the modern world. There is no kind of food you can cook well without relying on the information conveyed by all your senses. Is an influx of women to professional kitchens a movement of empowerment, returning them to an epistemological milieu where they have historically and conceptually been given authority? Perhaps the rise of cooking as a respectable profession is indicative of a surge of interest in other ways of knowing the world, no matter your gender.

One day in the late 1970s, chef Kenny Shopsin of New York's seminal Shopsin's General Store added to his 900-item menu the 'postmodern pancake': a pancake composed of pieces of other pancakes.[12]

It was during the latter few decades of the twentieth century that something called postmodernism happened. It might be over now. 'A work can become modern only if it is first postmodern. Postmodernism thus understood is not modernism at its end but in the nascent state, and this state is constant,' said French sociologist and cultural theorist Jean-Francois Lyotard.[13] So . . . to be cooking modern Scottish food, I must be cooking postmodern food, because postmodern is the newest of the new, so in order to be modern I must embrace postmodernity. Right . . . ?

Where the epoch of modernity had till then been characterised by a search for reason, stability and grand truths, applicable to all people everywhere, postmodernists saw fragmentation, scepticism and a consumer society full of stuff we didn't need. Humankind had been over-sated, over-stuffed with things; all expression had been forced out of our blankly staring eyes (see: Jeff Koons). Artists like Salvador Dalí went as far as to call out original thought; everything, said Dalí, had been said or done before. It was his role as an artist to mix and match to create something not new but representative of society at that moment (a pancake of other pancakes). The meta-narrative, the grand story of humankind, was an illusion. Postmodernists sought to replace overarching theories with the micro-narrative.

Truth and experience became localised. Stories were about yourself first, and only ever partially true. Grand narratives need other people to collude, value and verify them, yet the world was fragmented and so was human thought.* Lyotard and friends supplanted scientific knowledge (amassed by deduction and experiment) with 'narrative knowledge' (the kind of truth we find by telling ourselves stories). There is truth in story-telling, even if the people and events do not exist outside the

---

* Lyotard went so far as to call into question whether anything could be known by all, or ever be completely true, thus dismantling all Descartes' hard reasoning.

bound book. There is a human experience that we can grasp and understand; an emotional intelligence that can be passed on and recognised outside the bounds of our own heads. Lyotard didn't think that scientific and narrative knowledge were at odds with each other, or that one had to be supreme, but that they were equivalent. This is a permissive way of thinking that can make space for traditional cosmologies. In avoiding nostalgia for what exists in the three physical dimensions, say subscribers to postmodernist thought, we find truth.

Postmodernism seemed to indicate the beginnings of a shift from overarching, Euro-centric paradigms of the world to something more subtle, which allowed for more inclusivity. Detractors of postmodernism feel that the opposite has happened. One critique comes from Dr B. Charles Henry, who explains that denying that there is a universal experience of objective truth means that those with the power to define local truth can perpetuate and abuse their own power.[14] The underdog, the people with less access to power, do not have a secure stance from which to challenge wrong. Says Daryl B. Harris, writing in the *Journal of Black Studies* in 2005, 'at its core, postmodernism is yet another way of expressing the individualistic ethos of the European'.[15]

Fragmentary social philosophy did not in the end make room for tolerance. Scepticism and irony are emotions of privilege. To use them, you need to be secure enough in your own social position to criticise it.* Postmodernism was over-comfortable

---

* The killing of George Floyd by a US police officer in 2020 caused reverberations around the planet, reminding the world that power in American and European society is still not yet equally divided among all men and all women. People of colour are still systematically disadvantaged; 'food apartheid', coupled with a lack of universal healthcare, means they suffer inequalities in health and longevity. A

white guys speaking to themselves. For the peoples that white European and American social structures disadvantage, it was additionally debilitating. This itself is enlightening: even the theories of unity do not work for all.

In the first years of running my own kitchen, I wondered if I was indeed a postmodern cook, taking fragments of other people's cuisines and reassembling them on a plate – a collage of different cultures. You can see how a trend like 'fusion cuisine' might relate to postmodern ways of viewing the world. You cherry-pick flavours, methods and ingredients at will from around the world and unite them on a plate. 'Pacific Rim Fusion' was a thing for a while, in the 1990s and early 2000s, with New Zealand chef Peter Gordon's Sugar Club being one of the successful examples. (I did work experience at the Sugar Club when I first moved to London in 2000. I deseeded so many chillies that my hands were visibly red and throbbing, and at the behest of a concerned chef de partie spent the evening observing service with my hands in a pot of cold camomile tea.) Sydney's Tetsuya Wakuda melded his native Japanese with French techniques, and ingredients like ocean trout and foie gras. I spent a year and a half at Mju, his outpost in a Knightsbridge hotel, making chawanmushis with foie gras and learning the names for shiso, sancho, goma and enoki. When I was cooking at the Greenhouse, the Mayfair temple of luxury fine dining, the French head chef Antonin Bonnet

---

strong cultural identity is a platform on which you can stand in solidarity and feel confident about your place, and your rights.

was married to a Korean woman, and kimchi and doenjang became normal kitchen ingredients.

Then fusion fell out of fashion, derided as 'confusion' cooking in clumsy cooks' hands. Culinary mash-ups of distinct culinary traditions presented 'the worst of both worlds', with fumbling opportunist chefs open to accusations of cultural appropriation. The concept of fusion as the melding and transcending of cultural boundaries through food is not new nor a trend, though, it's what has always happened as food cultures have absorbed influence and morphed through history. The spirit and skill behind the cooking is perhaps the defining authority.

Earlier this year I sat on a judging panel for the 'Cateys', industry magazine the *Caterer*'s annual 'Menu of the Year' awards (which Inver won in 2019). The panel members had a conversation about the inclusion of influences from different cultures. One restaurant in the north of England whose menu featured 'Moroccan barbecue', dukkah, pomegranate, corn salsa and jerk flavours alongside French staples like crème brûlée and beurre blanc, and mostly English seasonal produce, was derided for having too many flavours and disparate influences. To the panel, the menu didn't feel coherent. Another restaurant, situated in London, had a menu featuring pistou, soubise, ancho chilli, tahini, rayu, mole and 'merguez ragu'. This, however, was excused by one panel member because 'that's just how Londoners eat these days': you pass so many places from around the world as you walk down the street, and eat in so many of them through a normal week, of course you would absorb these influences. Except there are many restaurants operated by cooks and restaurateurs from different cultures all over the north of England and in Scotland too, and have been for at least a century. How come it's permitted that the London guy absorb these influences, but they mustn't permeate kitchens further north? Who exactly is entitled to define or dictate another person's culinary influence?

I remember it from when it was my own: the Londoner's feeling of centrality, the judgement meted to the rest of the country, which always comes up lacking simply because it's not London. Unchecked, it's the sort of thinking that could colonise an entire planet. 'Taste is local,' says writer Jonathan Nunn, creator of the food newsletter *Vittles*. 'It is not centralised nor gate-kept by a few people, but constantly made and remade by tongues; in friendly discussions, mock outrage, arguments with your mum, in the pub, in ice cream parlours, on sofas, in the backs of Ubers.'[16] I had to unlearn the bias of living in a global capital city, as I learned to live somewhere that celebrated (Scottish) food critic Marina O'Loughlin once called the 'not-London'.

'I think in the UK we have a very narrow window for what we call authentic food – it's like the window has become so narrow that it has become colonial! You get people saying, that's not authentic enough for me . . . And, actually, these dishes are here because of colonialism!'

One sunny summer morning in Glasgow, I'm having one of those friendly discussions with Julie Lin, a self-described 'cook, rather than a chef – maybe that ties into my cultural heritage'. Julie is Malaysian-Scottish. At thirty-two, she's already got an appearance on *Masterchef*, a food blog ('Breakfast at Julie's'), a street-food stall and a popular bricks-and-mortar restaurant called Julie's Kopitiam under her satin sash. Now she's cook and co-proprietor at Ga Ga, a 'Malaysian-inspired diner' in the city. Julie was born in Glasgow: her dad is Scottish 'through and through' and her mum is Nyonya, the Malaysian-Chinese community descended from a wave of Chinese immigrants to Malacca, the port town in Malaysia that was a crucial trading post between East Asia and the Middle East. Malaysia was a British colony from 1824 till 1963, and a Dutch colony before that, and a Portuguese colony before that, such was its strategic importance in the global trade of spices.

Julie's mum came to Britain in the 1970s, at eighteen, to study nursing at Leeds University. She got a job in Glasgow, where she met Julie's dad in the city's iconic Ubiquitous Chip pub. Julie remembers taking food for granted when she was a kid: her mum was always cooking, Malaysian home comforts like char siu fan and new dishes like lasagne and carbonara. It all seemed so effortless, the young Julie thought the flavour just came from nowhere. It was only when she tried to recreate the carbonara – just with some cream, maybe fried bacon, and the boiled pasta – and was confused as to why it didn't taste like anything, that she started seriously learning to cook herself. Her deep love of her mum's Malaysian food seems to have worked like a forcefield; as a child, her school lunchbox was the one with the strange smells, full of Malaysian noodles and spices, but she didn't care.

The family returned to Malaysia for four weeks every summer and stayed with Ahma, her grandma. Julie's mum had thirteen brothers and sisters, and Ahma cooked for them all. Food always had to be delicious, that was the non-negotiable, but functional too. It's this aesthetic that Julie identifies with now. She learned to cook by watching her mum and Ahma. No one cooked from recipes, it was all done by the senses: feel this one, listen for this, smell that, taste it now. In Malaysia there's a term for it – 'agak agak' – meaning 'a shoogle of this, a dash of that – you season till the ghosts of your ancestors whisper that it's correct'. Julie herself likes to teach using these methods; 'They are reflective of how I feel; my kitchen isn't divided and hierarchical. I want everyone in my kitchen to know how to do something so they can lean on each other.' The fear of cooking dissipates when you learn to trust your senses, you're empowered to respond to ingredients and circumstances, whether at home or in a professional kitchen.

Julie's mission right now is to be able to call her food 'authentic' without feeling displaced from anywhere – from either Scotland or Malaysia. I ask if that's a change to the food, or to her mindset. 'To my mindset . . . Probably me growing up a wee bit. I'm feeling more comfortable with who I am. I no longer pull in every ingredient from Malaysia and bring it to the restaurant, I'll use a bit more from what's around me, to be more respectful to where I am. I might use wild garlic if that's available.'

Julie mentions a conversation she had with a white male chef who runs multiple Asian restaurants in London. His focus is on replicating as exactly as possible the food he has found in Indonesia, Thailand and Vietnam, using Asian herbs and plants he has brought back and is able to propagate himself on his family farm. He told Julie that he didn't find her food authentic enough.

I find slavish copying of cuisine rather curious. It sounds a bit like eating a museum piece: an exact replica preserved in the cabinet of a menu. It's a strange word, 'authenticity'. What is deemed 'authentic' shifts constantly, and needs qualification with a time as well as place and person. The chef is transplanting a cuisine exactly as it's found in an entirely different location, climate and culture. It feels to me like clinging to that life raft of 'tradition', as all around swells and crashes. It takes security and confidence to let go the ropes. As multiple-Michelin-starred chef and anthropologist Andrew Wong puts it, 'The innovation of today can sometimes really be the authenticity of the future.'[17]

Julie says that sesame prawn toast will always be on the Ga Ga menu from a sense of respect to Chinese immigrants. 'The prawn with ginger is a typical prawn ball, but if you put it on toast it's familiar to people here.' That British-Chinese restaurant-menu staple helped immigrants to survive in a new culture, to make a living in order to feed their families. It is 'authentic' not to the whole of China and its millennia-old food culture, but specifically to British-Chinese communities in the twentieth century. But its creation encapsulates the resilience of this immigrant community. In using ingredients from around her, Julie cooks with feet in two countries, but they are both on secure ground. She's not cooking on behalf of all Malaysia, or Scotland; just as herself.

Julie also talks about how Malaysian people adopted influences from colonialism as a way of reclaiming colonial food from the colonisers. Toast being the case in point; brought to Malaysia by the British, and now itself a subset of Malaysian street food. Roti john is a kind of omelette sandwich; roti babi is like a toastie filled with pork and tamarind, dipped in egg and griddled; and kaya toast is a traditional kaya curd – like a sweet coconut jam with juiced pandan leaf – served on toast with coddled eggs, white pepper and soy. Julie gets a bit rapturous for a moment. I think she needs to open a Malaysian toast shop in Glasgow. 'We can't deny that colonialism happened,' she says, 'but we can reclaim what we want from it.'

When I say that I cook 'modern Scottish food', no one asks me whether it's 'authentic'. Is it because as a white cook working in Scotland, I have a perceived authority to say this? Is it because in nations that have been industrialised and globally connected as long as Britain has, we're used to absorbing influences from all over – the 'modern' qualifies the cuisine? By these definitions, any person cooking in Scotland today is cooking 'modern Scottish food' if they, the cook, feels they are. And maybe that's the point.

At Inver, I use the excellent produce that's grown and raised around us. But I'll also use ingredients, flavours and techniques that I've encountered on our travels, in other restaurants or in books. When I use dried black lime, however, I'm not trying to reference Iranian cooking heritage. I know little about it apart from what's gleaned from decades of truffling through cookbooks. I couldn't do Persian food justice; I haven't been any closer to Iran than the Bosphorus. There's no particular reason for a free-range guinea fowl, a bird originally from Africa but raised on St Bride's Farm outside Glasgow, to be sharing a plate with creamed nettles and black lime, except that in the prism of my head the flavours work. Black lime is often served in Middle Eastern cuisines with chicken. I marinaded the guinea fowl in a brine made with yoghurt whey, letting the lactic acid tenderise the proteins and add its distinctive fresh tang to the rich, roasted meat. (The thick hung yoghurt itself appeared on the plate.) The rich, mineral nettles full of spring's rising green were what was in the hedgerows and my fridge at the time, and the dried lime's smoky zing added lift and intrigue while marrying with the grassy-green. It was just a reaction to the ingredients we had around at the time. And it's the twenty-first century, so we have ingredients from all countries of the globe who have ever had anything remotely to do with Scotland and its food systems. Plus it was interesting; something different to offer the guests and to engage them with the plate in front of them (and to engage me, the cook, with the process). A kind of Trojan horse with which to usher in a consciousness of all the ingredients presented to them.

It's a familiar format; meat and a vegetable. For creamed nettles think creamed spinach. There was even a bit of nutmeg in the bechamel. So far, so British. The bird was raised in Scotland. So was the cook. The lime came from Aladdin's, a Middle Eastern supermarket in Glasgow, where the Lebanese breakfast has been described as 'an essential Glasgow dining experience'.[18] There is a Middle Eastern community in Scotland several generations old who have opened restaurants and excellent groceries full of vegetables, bags of whole spices and big bunches of herbs more diverse, fresher and cheaper than in any supermarket. It is as easy now to find a pomegranate in Glasgow's 'New Govan' as a turnip.

The alternative approach would be to confine myself to cooking with only stereotypically Scottish flavours like barley, oats, lamb or haggis. But that too is problematic. At this tattered end of colonial history, which flavours are uniquely Scottish? That nutmeg is a spice-rack staple and appears often in many northern European, British and Scots classics, a key building block of the flavours and dishes we know well; there is nutmeg in bechamel sauce, in the parsley sauce with your slice of gammon, or the base of your familiar fish pie. There's nutmeg in bread sauce, to accompany your game in the autumn or a turkey at Christmas. There's nutmeg running through Scots baking like iron through slate: it's in plum duff

(Christmas pudding) and black bun, it's a seasoning for Shetlanders' traditional whipkull at Hogmanay, and a good old custard tart. But no one's ever grown nutmeg in Britain, never mind Scotland.

So back to that black lime. How long does it take for a flavour to be claimed as Scottish? What are the qualities it needs to be accepted? Can it come here of its own accord, in the culinary suitcases of new communities, or must it have been taken from colonial forays past, legitimised by the conquering itself? Is this how we have socialised our flavours? The exclusionary approach to cooking is divisive and derisive. Using only 'traditional Scottish' flavours would be like making the restaurant a theme of itself. Now that is postmodern!

'When identity is determined by a root, the emigrant is condemned (especially in the second generation) to being split and flattened. Usually an outcast in the place he has newly set anchor, he is forced into impossible attempts to reconcile his former and his present belonging.'
　　　　　　　　　Édouard Glissant, *Poetics of Relation* [19]

Young Scottish farmer Col Gordon recently returned from England to his family farm, Inchindown, in the north-east Highlands, where he's grappling with the big questions about what land-ownership in the storied Highlands really means these days, and what a truly inclusive future might look like in the Gàidhealtachd (the traditionally Gaelic-speaking areas of the Highlands). He's experimenting with traditional landraces of wheat, rye and oats which have almost disappeared, but which are well adapted to place and need no 'inputs' to thrive (meaning no destructive chemical fertilisers). A wide and rambling conversation, broad as a glen, ensues. Traversing one of the contours, Col mentions something he's just written, on the cultural roots of these grains and how useful the whole topic is as a metaphor: 'Roots need to live in relation.' He talks about mycelium, that invisible, root-like weave of which mushrooms are the ripened fruit, which connects whole forests underground, allowing trees to communicate, share nutrients and recycle organic matter, even splitting the strong cellulose of a fallen tree back into the carbon and nitrogen of soil.

Roots are not isolated in the ground; they are enmeshed in the whole landscape, through mycelium and soil to microbes, insects, birds, mammals, plants, trees, the air. 'Roots are nothing without relationship,' Col says. Equitable inclusion has to *make* space, physical and cultural, for the people we want to be in it. Col steers me to one of his articles online, where he writes that in Brazil, rather than being called 'heritage' seeds or 'landraces', traditional local seeds are referred to as 'Creole seeds' and have legal protections. Like a recipe, the word 'creole' allows ingredients from disparate cultures and points in time to come together, creating something new to flourish deliciously in the here and now. 'Creolisation is a process which allows for new cultural possibilities to come into being,' says Col. Too much emphasis on heritage or history keeps food trapped in the past.

I hang up on Col and straight away there's Chloe Oswald, chef and chocolatier who worked with us at Inver in the summer between her two years at catering college, when she was eighteen. At twenty-three, Chloe set herself up as a chocolatier, and now Chocolatia has a fine set of awards for her delicious bars and bonbons, which we also serve in the restaurant.

Chloe herself has a diverse background and I'm interested in what she thinks she's doing, how global families are expressed through food in Scotland today. Chloe was born in Scotland, and her dad is from Perth; he's Scottish 'through and through'. Chloe's mum was born in Grimsby, and is half-Danish and half-Trinidadian. Chloe's grandfather on her mum's side, Bestifar ('Grandad' in Danish), is from Trinidad. Bestifar is Arthur Selwyn Frederick, born in Trinidad in 1937, where his family had thirty acres of cocoa and coconut plantation, which is still run by his older brother's wife and children. He went to school in Port of Spain, where he spent time between classes sitting on the docks watching the sailors coming and going, dreaming of being out at sea. So this he did: got his skipper's ticket in Trinidad then worked his passage to England on a Harrison Line ship (following a passenger and trading route from the West Indies via Spain that operated for over 100 years, from 1876 to 1988), and signed up for sailor's school at Fleetwood Nautical College, near Liverpool, where the boat docked.[20] He became one of the UK's youngest skippers, aged twenty-one.

Sri Lankan intellectual Ambalavaner Sivanandan was director of the British Institute of Race Relations for forty years and editor of its journal *Race and Class*. His 2018 obituary describes 'a tireless and eloquent voice explaining the connections between race, class, imperialism and colonialism'.[21] Siva's aphorism – 'We are here because you were there' – captured 'with a simple elegance the relationship between post-war migrants (*we*) now settled in Britain (*here*) on the one hand, and the former crown colonies and other territories of the

British empire (*there*), maintained by Europeans in imperial service (*you*), on the other'.[22]

It was when the young sailor Bestifar was docked at Esbjerg, on the Jutland peninsula in Denmark, that he met Chloe's gran, Ingelise Jensen, who was a chef in a hotel near the port. Mormor ('Grandma') invited him round for Sunday dinner with her family the very next day. Chloe cites Mormor with inspiring her to be a chef, but credits both her grandmothers with teaching her to cook and bake. Mormor used to make them all hot chocolate from a really dark Trinidadian chocolate and good milk. It's because of this link that Chloe is really careful about how she sources the chocolate for her own work, using B-Corp certified Vahlrona to try to side-step the many problems with the global chocolate trade today.

Chloe's Scottish grandad, Ian Oswald, was born in Perth, in 1946. He grew up in rural Perthshire, poaching fish and shooting rabbits. Later, in his garden in Perth, there was a plum tree, apples and pears. When Chloe and her siblings visited him growing up, they picked redcurrants every year from his bushes and he'd make his famous 'RCJ' – redcurrant jelly. 'He taught me how to test the setting point of jam on a frozen plate and he used to hang the berries in an old cloth to get the clear juices from them so the jelly wasn't cloudy.'

I ask Chloe what Scottish food is to her. Straight away she says, 'Well, things that are grown here. What's available.' Her little sister Hailey is studying to be a horticulturist and has just planted up their aunt's garden in Dunkeld with all the berries, fruit and herbs Chloe likes to use in her chocolates. She remembers the five siblings running wild together around the town of Dunoon, where eventually the family settled; the coconut smell of the gorse, and wrists torn picking brambles for a rugged version of bramble jam (berries mashed with sugar and boiled, maggots, twigs and all). The flavours we use at Inver, her first professional kitchen, resonate still: the elderflower and meadowsweet and big deliveries of farm berries. This is all, she says, 'Scottish by association'. And that's the point: these associations are her own. Chloe gives me flavours and ingredients, rather than finished dishes, to describe Scottish food: the berries, wild flowers, Katy Rodgers yoghurt, Isle of Skye sea salt, heather honey for her honeycomb. Prompted, she laughs and says yes of course her Scottish gran taught her how to make lentil soup, stovies, mince and tatties, sausage rolls, fairy cakes and tablet. But as a grown-up professional that's not how she's chosen to interpret 'Scottish' in her own food. 'It's what grows here.' I like this; it makes space in the land for many possibilities.

Most of all, though, she says her family is where she gets her 'flair'. 'Everything has to have a story . . . I have to put a face on everything.' I wonder if this is something she saw a lot of at Inver too, as we started to build a community around the restaurant: Fi with her cheese, Alastair with the halibut, Kate's salad, Bruce's pigs, Fraser's lambs. The people as well as the place itself. Chloe talks about an 'Origins' collection of chocolates which would honour her four grandparents, and of course we talk about what it would be like to be able to buy chocolate from the family plantation. But it's difficult: there are relationships to navigate, different lives to reconcile. It was Chloe's Scottish gran most of all that showed her the role food could have in connecting people; she was always arriving at folks' houses with a pavlova or a pan of stovies. 'That's what she offers. That's what I strive for.'

I remember something Col said in our conversation. His metaphors were diverse – in the seed meditation he quoted jazz musician Charlie Mingus: 'You can't improvise on nothing. You gotta improvise on something.' And I guess this is what Chloe is saying too. You need a starting point for creativity, storytelling, of all kinds. But roots are always just the beginning, not an end in themselves.

Since the early 2000s we've seen the rise and subtle morphing of 'Nordic cuisine'. It's one of the most prominent happenings in global restaurant culture of the early twenty-first century, and a scene in which both reviewers and guests of Inver have liked to site us. If I'm questioning the influences on myself as a modern cook, especially in the context of a restaurant, 'New Nordic' is a presence I must acknowledge. It's also an example of an intentionally constructed food movement with a nationalist identity which excludes as well as binds.

Like movements in arts, sciences or other bastions in the Venn diagram of current culture, shifts in cuisines tend to be reactions against what has previously been the ascendant trend. René Redzepi's restaurant noma is now world-famous. At the beginning, the noma project was a reaction against the then-prevalent Mediterranean hegemony in northern European restaurant and home cooking. Redzepi looked inwards, to the cold clear fjords, the shores and mountains of the politically and culturally related northern European countries of Denmark, Norway, Finland and Sweden. There he found incredible produce and a public ripe for the reimagining of their shared history. The restaurant-going public was then more familiar with French sauces (all floury, fatty roux, cream, butter and concentrates of bone and gelatine),

Italian tomatoes and Spanish olive oil. Now, ancient geoduck clams joined pristine sweet scallops and langoustine on these new northern plates. Simple vegetables were championed; wild herbs, nuts and berries were rooted out of obscurity, and unusual wilder ingredients found their technique and place on the modern restaurant flavour spectrum. (Preserved spruce tips? Sea buckthorn? Seaweeds?) Sauces were lightened; fresh vegetable juices were split with deepest green herb oils, and ferments and pickles replaced the ubiquitous lemon as a source of bright acidity. Chefs themselves foraged, got tattoos and grew beards. It felt so new. One striking change was in the food presentation. When the second noma book, *Time and Place in Nordic Cuisine*, came out, the food didn't look like food. It was more like abstract art, or ikebana, Japanese flower arranging: natural ingredients presented as if they were still in the place in which they had been found. Edible soils, whole tiny herb leaves and edible flowers forced you to look anew at what food could be and remember it had come from the land. Now, these tropes are ubiquitous. You'll find some on the Inver plates too.

We went to Copenhagen in search of a way to articulate our own northern food heritage. Rob and I spent a month working at noma's first incarnation in early 2011, as unpaid 'stagiaires'. At the time we were living on the tiny Hebridean island of Iona, three miles by one mile, population around one hundred people. The restaurant where we worked was open from Easter to October, after which the extreme west coast weather interrupted the ferry service and summer's flow of tourists. We spent those winters 'staging' abroad, learning the language of the northern European landscapes and food histories, like edible storytelling. The New Nordic cuisine then seemed essential for someone fumbling for a way to tell her own story, which includes a food history that intersects with Viking invasions, animals grazing heather-strewn hillsides, dulse on the low tide line and a similar range of wild berries, nuts and herbs in the hedgerows. We share the sea buckthorn and strawberries, forests of pine and birch, game and shellfish. Barley and oats were historically our staple grains too. As in the Nordic countries, dairy has always been a distinct feature of Scots cooking. Rural Scots pickled herring, smoked haddock, cured lamb and foraged mushrooms too.

New Nordic is perhaps the best branding exercise in modern food. It has been hugely influential in the restaurant world (as one commentator says, 'Even if you haven't eaten at Noma, you've eaten at Noma'[23]). But it has also become a unifying idea in the identity of the people of Scandinavia, beyond just 'restaurant world'. In the early days of noma, twelve chefs (including Redzepi) signed 'The New Nordic Kitchen Manifesto', which can now be found on a site belonging to the Nordic Council of Ministers – the official body for intergovernmental co-operation in the Nordic region.[24] Terms like 'pureness', 'freshness', 'simplicity', 'ethics', 'wild landscapes', 'health and well-being' and 'light' all bob to the surface. The effects of the manifesto and of noma's success go far beyond the fine-dining food scene – now, the common wild plants ground elder and wild garlic can even be purchased in several supermarkets in Copenhagen.[25] The same coalition of Nordic governments has just published nutritional guidance for the population which advocates a largely plant-based diet, with no meat, and very little or no alcohol, for the sake of public health and the climate.[26]

The New Nordic crew transferred the French idea of 'terroir', which links the idiosyncrasies of place (weather, soil type, geology, culture) to produce. In France, wine and cheese are perhaps the best-known examples of embodied 'terroir', where certain chateaux have cachet and moulds lavish the Roquefort caves. Although it feels ancient, the whole idea of terroir is traced back only to the nineteenth century, that period of romantic reorientation when a particular group of gastronomes began linking the produce, the place and the taste to a storied past.[27]

It's the stories that do it. Rob and I also spent a few weeks at chef Magnus Nilsson's fabled restaurant Fäviken, on a hunting estate in remote rural Sweden. Magnus's poetic, restrained cuisine seemed to be the very embodiment of the New Nordic principles of simplicity and the veneration of wild nature. Magnus and the Fäviken staff at times hunted, planted and foraged for the menu themselves. Magnus himself is highly conscious of every nuance of the restaurant's presentation. One of his strongest skills is storytelling, of the fisherman's kind; 'telling stories to tell the truth' (as reformed fisherman Bren Smith puts it).[28] Herbs that appeared on the menu as 'dried chives from last summer' were sometimes bought from the Swedish supermarket ICA on the drive to work and dried in the ventilation stream on top of the fridges.

The restaurant itself was an immersive, interactive story of a time and a place that may not have really existed. There was a disconnect between that representation and what I now understand as the realities of running a small rural restaurant. The business was buffered by the wealthy Swedish investment bankers who owned the estate. The game shot on the estate was so plentiful that there was a room-sized freezer so full of meat it would have taken a village several years to get through it (Magnus started a charcuterie business to help). Despite the presentation of a way of living that was intimately entwined with landscape, the human relationship with that land was skewed.

But to focus only on the factual disconnect is to miss the value in the stories themselves. Fäviken did have a kitchen garden, and last summer's chives really were harvested before the frost and rot could waste them. For the guest, the story need not dwindle because the stored herbs did. We were all there to be told the stories and to learn to tell them ourselves. Now, what the best restaurants in Scotland and in the world all talk about is their connection to land, to the source of their food; a farm or a garden of their own, a visit to a winemaker or shellfish diver or a citrus grove abroad. That connection is *the* luxury ingredient. It's aspirational.

The Nordic region does generally identify as a whole, and this everyday tradition of sharing familiar foods is one of the things that unites it. Says Mark Emil Hermansen, researcher and one-time noma employee, 'New Nordic Cuisine to some extent becomes an exercise in nostalgia, an attempt to recapture a bygone era, which allows for the Nordic peoples, now primarily living in cities and towns, to flirt with a lifestyle more representative of the past than of the present.'[29] Food wasn't something that the four countries identified themselves with before – but it is now.

More recently an interesting picture appeared in René Redzepi's Instagram feed: a beautiful basket of chillies, rainbow colours, shapes and sizes from pinkie fingernail to clenched fist, all grown in Denmark. Redzepi's father is an Albanian-born Macedonian who married a Danish woman. René remembers the chillies from childhood visits to this other home. Having taken noma all over the world, including to Mexico, where chilli is an ingredient integral to the experience of food, he was wondering how best to incorporate them into noma's menus. His quest had been first to rearticulate Nordic food traditions, but now it seems he wanted to see his own food history reconciled, the outsider in him coming in.

What is not adequately represented by the New Nordic Manifesto are the foodways and cooks of the Sámi people of Sápmi, one of Europe's oldest ethnic groups. Before national borders existed, the nomadic Sámi inhabited the regions now known as Norway, Sweden, Finland and the Russian Kola Peninsula. Since prehistoric times, they have hunted and fished in the European Arctic, and for centuries have domesticated and herded reindeer. The Earth Island Institute, which documents sacred lands on film, says that 'the Sami practised a shamanistic spirituality rooted in a respectful, harmonious relationship with nature. The land itself was sacred, and it was also marked with specific holy sites.'[30] In the familiar colonial pattern, since around the ninth century and escalating in the seventeenth and eighteenth centuries, the four regional powers encroached on Sámi lands, forcing their assimilation into northern European culture and Christianity, suppressing the use of their languages, using persecution techniques like witch-burning, creating laws that denied access to traditional lands, exploiting land for oil extraction, destroying forests (essential reindeer habitat) and using sacred sites as military bombing ranges. In September 2023 Sámi businesswoman and reindeer herder Maret Ravdna Buljo posted a photo of her own reindeer-milk yoghurt with fermented cloudberries, saying, 'I feel . . . my ancestors dancing around me. I am healing my inherited traumas. It is time to decolonise my wounded soul.'[31] The last four decades have seen a resurgence of Sámi culture, and Sámi parliaments are now operating in Norway, Finland and Sweden. None of the New Nordic Manifesto signatories were Sámi. Rather, they represented a certain kind of restaurant-world, contemporary, 'fine dining' aesthetic. All twelve signatories were white men.

Gastronomy is not synonymous with 'fine dining'. Gastronomy is about good food and its place in a culture. I stopped wondering whether my food was the latest iteration of 'fusion cuisine' or 'postmodern' when I realised it didn't matter and I didn't care. Because, in truth: this is what has always happened to food cultures. They are not static. I cook with integrity and imagination, and with respect for the ingredients, flavours, people and culinary traditions that make it into the kitchen here. We produce food that is delicious, and representative of a particular time and place refracted through the prism of our cooks' diverse heads. That time and place are right here, in a tamed landscape, in a globally connected small country with a deep, resonant history, in the early decades of the twenty-first century AD. And what I choose to stock in my pantry says a lot about what I think 'here and now' means, and my place in it; who belongs here with me, and who doesn't.

The rise of curiosity in cooking for a living might be about more people choosing a life more informed by all the senses, one that is directly connected to nature and landscape in a way that modern lives usually aren't. Sitting writing at a screen all day, I miss the stimulation and immediacy of a kitchen. It's physically hard work, but that physicality is satisfying. It's sometimes mentally challenging, juggling simultaneous orders for multiple dishes, each with their own many components, and coordinating a team of half a dozen cooks to get all those thickening sauces, delicate garnishes, melting ice creams and cooling meats onto plates in perfect condition all at the same time. But it's also immediately gratifying. Cooking in a supportive team satisfies so many aspects of human well-being; the trust, reciprocity, respect, connection and meaning that all of us need to be happy.

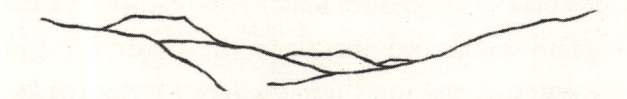

There is so much to celebrate in modern Scotland. There are traditions here deeper and longer than the tartan carpets, and these traditions are relevant to resolving the most current issues in Scotland's normality. A chair pulled back at a shared table. The Scots cook's reverence for all the parts of an animal – bones and blood both. That cook's openness to flavours and ingredients that can make best use of our climate and soil. A love of nutritious grains and kailyards, and for finding innovative, delicious ways to recirculate 'waste'. A communal, equitable use of the best land to see a whole community fed well, using skills that give meaning to lives and their place in a landscape so full of beauty and history. These are the traditions that will see us through, thriving, to the next century. This, now, is the most modern Scotland.

All the symbols and stories we use to create 'Scotland' – the ones that are recognised overseas, or in the tourist shops on the Royal Mile, or on the scenic calendars – create a particular vision of a country that was first articulated as a kind of romantic propaganda for a culture and landscape that had recently been exploited. And under the tartan banners, exploitation of the landscape continues today. The real, enduring experience of 'minority' cultures, who have themselves helped to build the monuments and economy of modern Scotland, is continuously decentralised.

I feel like I've unpicked all the stitching holding my own story together. Now I'm wondering how to mend the patchwork, create a new pattern that better shows off the colours and shapes of my life and our country, at this time in history. If we – I – and our food have been 'colonised' by values I don't share, what would it look like to *de*colonise our food culture? Is there a way of thinking that can give every member of our ecosystem an equitable presence? *Is* there a new story, one that we really can all play a part in?

Chapter Six:

A WAR FOR THE HUMAN IMAGINATION

> . . . the war is the war for the human imagination
> and no one can fight it but you/ & no one can fight it
>   for you
> [. . .]
> history is a living weapon in yr hand
> & you have imagined it, it is thus that you
> 'find out for yourself'
> history is the dream of what it can be, it is
> the relation between things in a continuum
> of imagination
> what you find out for yourself is what you select
> out of an infinite sea of possibility
> no one can inhabit yr world
>
>   from 'Letter #75', Diane di Prima

The signposts are all here. The writers and poets, philosophers and new economists; theorists and activists for decolonisation and environment: the picture they paint is clear. There *are* ways to imagine a planet where we give up nothing that is truly important to us, and yet gain quite literally the whole world. And the food system that serves this world is delicious, healthful, and *enough* – for all.

From the Bolivian Andes to Algerian cities, to the Canadian First Nations and the mountains of New Zealand, to the government of Norway and back to the central belt and Highlands of Scotland: there are other ways of thinking that give all humans and their ecosystems equitable presence on their own land. It is our intertwined senses that unite us with nature and with each other. An economy that reflects the true value of the goods and services that build it already exists. It is this economy that will serve collective interest over individual gain.

The new stories we need are already told; the world we need is already named and mapped. What we must do now is listen and see.

When I asked Col Gordon how we could cultivate a sense of relationship with land, for Scots old and new, he replied, 'People always say policy! But before that, even . . . we need to tell different stories. Storytellers imagine their way in.'

Of course, we *do* need better policies that would (say) redress unequal access to land and curb destructive industry. If we want a fairer food system, we need redistributive taxation, prices that actually reflect *all* the costs of a food's production, and mandatory wage ratios to better distribute profit along the supply chain, especially from the big food corporations and supermarkets. We need subsidies that reward the kind of land management that would allow diverse ecosystems to thrive alongside human beings. We need all guns firing in this war, which is – of course – a battle not solely for imaginations but for the basic survival of the human race. But Col and Diane di Prima echo Gramsci, and in that empower us all: culture shifts first, *before* the big-picture political and economic structures. Food culture is the stories we serve with dinner.

We need to tell and retell the stories that give human beings back their rightful place in nature, in Scotland as elsewhere. At least since Descartes, the great human–nature divide has put us in the position of detached observer. It has enabled us to watch, safe, while icebergs cleave from their great white mass, streams and rivers are emptied of life, the conservation red list grows longer and the mercury rises. But what if this isn't happening to something *other*?

Alicia Kennedy is a cook and food writer whose newsletter 'On Storytelling' appeared in my inbox this summer. 'I also know that those of us with the ability to shift narratives have an obligation to remind people, over and over, of what has occurred... The narrative of foods and cuisines are significant, because they're often the only way many people will experience them. Travel is expensive; time-travel is impossible. What we all have are stories and recipes.'[1] The printing press preserved on paper the highest cuisines, and skewed our perception of what matters in food and cooking, a bias that persists in the carefully lit food mags and socials, the veneration of finest dining, the aspirational brands; and in the luxurious, resource-intense, highly processed meat- and sugar-heavy diet that's now 'normal' to almost all Scots today. But it's the daily practice of humble gestures that matters most: cooking, growing and shopping as connection, sustenance, acknowledgement, empowerment, ritual, prayer. Cooking and the skills for procuring food need to return to their place at our side: our companions, the rope and the bridge to the real world outside our heads.

The Romantic storytellers of the late eighteenth century

were attempting to recreate a world that was in danger of being lost for ever. In doing so they created powerful symbols that still endure, stronger than ever, and codify a kind of Scots identity. But these symbols – the tartan kilt, the haggis dinners – have lost their real referents. The Royal Mile's 'See You Jimmy' hats are unhitched from the things that Sir Walter Scott and Robbie Burns, the musicians, songsmiths and weavers, were really saying. The outlawed Gaelic culture represented a way of being in the land and with people that stood in deeply shadowed relief against the values of the new society rising in Edinburgh, Glasgow and Aberdeen, seeping through the heather and bracken, stealing over the machair and crawling like dark ivy over the ruins.

The word 'romantic' is itself a value judgement. To romanticise something is to present it in a way that is at odds with what's considered 'real'. But in a culture, 'real' is continually negotiated too. There were real problems in pre-industrial societies, not least inadequate and precarious diets for the common people. There has been incredible progress in the last two or so centuries in achieving a diverse and nutritionally adequate diet for many. But it doesn't logically follow that what we have now is ideal. The diet most available and accessible today – most 'normal' – is still precarious and inadequate for people at home and abroad, and jeopardises the natural environment and climate. Real enlightened progress would be to use the technology and knowledge that we have accrued over centuries to make food safe, nutritious and enough, for everyone and everything everywhere. Not just bad in different ways.

The way of thinking that the Gaelic language preserves is not the reserve of Gaelic speakers. It's a local example of what the people who remember our connections to land always say:

it's yours too if you want it to be. Raghnaid Sandilands is a Gaelic translator, writer, publisher and cartographer originally from Lochalsh but now living on Loch Ness.[2] She's been returning stories to the land around her, tracking the tales in online archaeological records, old maps or satellite images, through droving routes, poems, songs and fables; the names that are too long to fit on council road signs. 'Finding stories of people and places and illustrating essays with photos, new maps or recordings, has been a means to make this place feel like home, more vividly our own,' she writes. Raghnaid tells of a packed night in the local village hall, talking land reform with Scots broadcaster Lesley Riddoch. 'At the end of that night a friend said to me, and I think this is the heart of it, "If you know the stories, you love the place, and if you love the place you look after it" . . . Perhaps . . . these are kindly, small radical acts, putting long-forgotten names of people, places and their stories back on the map.'[3] To me, if you read 'place' in its broadest sense – our shared planet – then the stories that reunite humans and nature, and humans with each other, are what we need most right now.

We all live on land. This is not simply a matter for the country dwellers, but for all of us. Mapping a new world starts in your own head and extends a step at a time, out down your close, through your gate, down the streets and into the parks, shops and gardens, fields and beaches around you. You need not wait for anyone else. Leave crumbs. They'll catch up.

Remapping the city, town or area you live in is something you can do yourself – today if you like. Find the community food spots, allotments and food-growing projects. Butchers, fishmongers, bakers of all kinds: real skills connecting you through flicked knife and folded dough to the food you will take home to feed your family. On Scotland's high streets, grocers, cheesemongers, butchers, fishmongers and roasteries, Chinese, Indian, Pakistani and Middle Eastern stores bring communities to scented, delicious, tactile life. The sorrel, elderflowers, meadowsweet and cherry blossoms that grow in so many parks, roadsides and cracks in the pavement are like chinks of light to a world that is still here. You'll start to see your local streets differently. You'll learn people's names, and take some of the edible stories to your own home and family, and tell new stories there. 'We must build networks of meaning and ecologies of knowledge . . . through vital gestures of *compartition* (sharing) instead of competition,' says Bolivian sociologist Silvia Rivera Cusicanqui.[4] Clanship was associated with land before blood. If a family was living on the lands of the clan, they could claim allegiance to the chief and become clan members without any actual blood ties. My Scotland is home for whoever wants to call it home. 'Anyone can connect to a place by learning its stories. Sense of place is not about where you are from but about what you do in a place,' says Col. It's the skills for transforming nature and landscape into food and sustenance that anchor you in place.

In connecting ourselves to the land and people around us, and understanding the longest reaches of our daily needs, we create meaning. We tell stories that help us value, love and protect the land and each other. Right now, some of the most familiar stories this world tells itself have themes of individual entitlement over communal well-being. They say that all humans are not equal. That convenience trumps the pleasure of skills well exercised. The heroes of these tales are those who make the most money or achieve the greatest fame. Other stories, however, tell of the connectedness of all things, and the satisfaction of sacrifice to a greater cause. The oldest tales are of difficult journeys that end in great learning, and the kind of real love that wins out over all. They tell of all of long time, and of our true place in it.

History lives for me here, faced as I am daily with ancient architecture, languages and landscapes only superficially changed over human time. I read the land outside our restaurant to learn new stories for the kind of future I want us all to share. Reading the landscape is also about living in the past. I don't mean we nostalgically try to recreate history, or naively bring back a time that cannot exist again. There is no return: and that is the point. A return implies a linear kind of time, where the past happens once only and is buried all the more deeply by each successive present. Linear time is a difficult kind of time to live in, because all previous versions of you, your family and culture must be discarded; everything that has gone before given a place just out of reach. It is isolating. Each of us must walk alone.

What if we understood that nothing is ever past at all, but rather living today is dependent on life having been lived before? This seems self-evident. Yet sometimes it seems as if every individual lives to create a personal world apart from everything and everyone else. Rather than a mind acting alone in a body to process data received by the senses, human perception is 'immanent in the network of sensory pathways that are set up by virtue of the perceiver's immersion in his or her environment'.[5] There can be no perception without something outside us: trees shushing in cool breezes, the sulphurous scent of drying seaweed on sun-warmed rocks, bundles of kale or lamb fat charring on a wood fire, toasting wheat and heady yeast emanating from a hot oven. We are empty shells without the world around us.

Even human language is codependent on its context, and as environment and custom change, so does language. We see this daily, with new words, turns of phrase and hashtags appearing in dictionaries, on social media and in films. Within Scotland there have always been different heritages and languages to reconcile. Today there are 170 languages spoken here, including Polish, Mandarin, Punjabi, Italian and Arabic, as well as Gaelic, Doric, Scots and English. 'Language celebrates an embodied knowledge of the world that is already shared thanks to people's mutual involvement in the tasks of habitation . . . it is the tradition of living in the land that ensures the continuity of language,' writes Tim Ingold.[6] These 'tasks of habitation' are the skills we use daily to feed and shelter ourselves and each other.

Analogously, this is also what happens to food: as culture and populations shift, different types of fruits, vegetables and grains are planted and traded in different places. Pomegranates are found in Govan mini-markets, and Julie uses wild garlic in her Malay-Scots cuisine. Recipes and names for haggis shift across borders and centuries. Food celebrates an embodied knowledge of the world that is *already* shared. Our senses unite us in the world we create together.

The fluidity of language, human knowledge and food cultures comes from the interplay of history and present, the constant recombination of past and person. 'Just because people are doing things differently now, compared with the way they did them at some time in the past, does not mean there has been a rupture in tradition or a failure of memory,' says Ingold.[7] On the contrary, it's when people are 'forcibly constrained' to replicate precisely the patterns of the past, even when they no longer make sense, that the healthy, liberating flow of human progress is dammed. The constant recombination of tradition is necessary to make sense of the present. The old normals must prepare to change, lest humanity is consigned to an irrecoverable past.

Seeing time as intertwined, rather than mechanistically linear and detached from our influence, means being prepared to think differently about the nature of human beings themselves. If we are constantly living in relation to the past as well as the present, we are part of a transition, as responsible for creating the future as for influencing what is happening now. We are not a passively generated entity, completed at birth with a set of genes ready to puppet our every move, and without agency to change anything around us. Instead, each of us, and our mental and microbiological ecosystems, is 'a site where generation is going on'. There is responsibility in this view of human existence; duty, even, to fulfil our role as best we can. We affect those around us now, and even recreate the past, as we determine the present and future. But there is also empowerment, agency; connection and meaning. There is room for new people and possibilities. If we can see ourselves, our environment and time as intertwined and interdependent, 'there is no opposition . . . between continuity and change'.[8]

Col Gordon talks about the role of mixed-heritage seeds in a food culture of the future. He too considers 'genealogical time' – the idea that time is linear and our future is handed to us like a baton by previous generations. In this imaginative construct of human history, 'first' peoples and their food

A WAR FOR THE HUMAN IMAGINATION

are given 'end points': lines in the sands of time, before which they are entitled to be called traditional or indigenous; after which, not. But these definitions 'also fail to consider the fact that the length of historic time ahead of us could well be equally as infinite as the length of time behind us. If these are the end points in history, where will we be in a thousand years?'

What will our food culture and traditions look like then? Do we imagine them being identical to what is happening now? And what about all the creatures and plants that inhabited the landscape *before* humans did – where are their indigenous rights?

'Ch'ixi' is the name of a colour, grey, in Aymara, a language of the Bolivian Andes. Silvia Rivera Cusicanqui uses 'ch'ixi' to explain how she sees her own indigenous identity persisting in Bolivia, after the country's colonialisation by Spanish people. The colour is created by juxtaposing two different colours, in small points or spots. I imagine it as if viewing a pointillist painting from across the gallery. Rather than being diluted, 'indigeneity is present amongst, but not subsumed by, the modern. Ch'ixi combines the Indian world and its opposite without ever mixing them.'[9] Similarly, mixed racial identity is both the white and the black; not a mid-grey that dilutes both. The concept is empowering. Indigenous individuals have equal rights to both identities and to both ontologies ('ways of being'), not to neither. It is the opposite of compromise or hybridity. In contrast each colour appears the bolder and brighter, and yet from the perspective of distance they form a unified, coherent whole. Rivera Cusicanqui presents a conceptual platform from which to transform the past, present and future.

Ch'ixi can perhaps show us how a modern world can accommodate multiple normals all at the same time without losing coherence and vitality. Understanding how different identities and communities can coexist in the same place could create a vibrant (food) culture that allows space for multiple different contributions and possibilities. A common modern complaint is that 'identities have become increasingly homogenised by the flat-pack patterns of globalisation',[10] leading to a feeling of at least partial disconnect from place by the people who live there. It is true that some land-based practices are changing or disappearing, as new ways of inhabiting place become an appropriate response to new times. But there are more diverse influences on Scotland's food culture now than perhaps ever before. Communities of 'new Scots' have brought recipes, set up shops and restaurants, and are connected through markets, employment and trade (as well as schools, doctors, neighbours and friends) to everything else in the country. When, for instance, Sikh brothers Harry and Jazzy Singh of Glasgow's Punjabi Charing Cross restaurant create haggis pakora, the result is not homogeneity but a mixing of two cultures that creates something new.[11] When the brothers talk of wearing kilts to weddings and loving whisky, I see a role for these traditions in binding peoples across space and time. Combined, we understand each part more.

Multiple layers of meaning have always mapped our country. We each live according to the contours of our own map, and all these maps coexist, overlaid and translucent, common pathways shared and darkened through use, but each still distinct. Perhaps in imagining a ch'ixi world I can see myself more clearly, too. The fragmentary parts of me cohere again when you zoom out. The colours blend into a bright, vibrant whole.

Human beings are not individuals. Our physical bodies are themselves the landscapes of the microbes that sustain us, maps marked with battlegrounds and control centres, sites of dense activity and rolling open plains. Zooming in even further, at the quantum level we are not even solid matter, just vibrating energy; more like a wave than an object.[12] During the course of our lives every atom will be replaced multiple times. By our death we are not physically the same entities as at birth, but the colonies of microbes with us since our first voyage through the birth canal will have unbroken lineage. We and they dissolve into the earth from which we came, a brief congealing of carbon whisked back into the smooth flow of time. From the perspective of planetary history, modern individualism is absurd. We stand or fall together.

At the physical landscape scale, competing uses of land by different people shows how territories are not compromised by coexistence. Different land values are neither separated nor subsumed, but coexist in tension, creating and recreating normality for the people of the land. Scholar Penelope Anthias uses the idea of ch'ixi to understand the indigenous Guaraní community of the Bolivian Chaco, and observes: 'A contested indigenous land titling process, capitalist labour relations, hydrocarbon compensation money, and efforts to maintain relations with spirit beings are all interwoven in the fabric of Guaraní everyday life.'[13] Similarly, in Scotland, competing pressures on land used for game management, carbon-capture schemes, homes, crofts and farming do not dilute the identity of any of these projects or their people, but rather cast light on the peculiarities of each demand. Allowing different peoples and identities access to land and life makes our own self *more* distinctive, not less.

'Food is a matter that goes beyond the modern religion of individual choice. There is such a thing as society and the collective interest,' says food-policy professor Tim Lang.[14] The biggest problems the world faces today are about the 'commons'; the natural environment, biodiversity loss, climate, and the health and well-being of all people are all about shared resources. Food is one of the most significant ways in which we affect each other. We can use it to connect, and we can use it to divide. The way we share common resources like ecosystems, fossil fuels, water, sunlight and land determines whether or not we will succeed as a species on this finite planet.

The New York Times' economics editor Binyamin Appelbaum questions whether the rise of inequality was *really* inevitable; a result of forces beyond human control. He suggests that inequality is instead the result of conscious decision-making by policymakers and the economists who influence them. Appelbaum wrote in 2019 that 'much of the fault lies in ourselves, in our collective decision to embrace policies that prioritized efficiency and encouraged the concentration of wealth.'[15] Economics is mathematical model-making; an attempt at predicting the future. The financial economy is never the only consideration for a society though, and like any other fortune-telling, economic forecasts are not always accurate. Policy makers should use economics as one of a range of tools

A WAR FOR THE HUMAN IMAGINATION

in their policy box, not as an end in itself. If it's only us humans who have caused this problem, however, it means that the solution is within our power too.

A century before, Antonio Gramsci wrote, 'The old is dying and the new cannot be born. This is the time of monsters.'* Slaying these monsters – resolving the intertwined climate, biodiversity and human equity crises – starts with understanding that there *is* a different way of being in the world. And it doesn't mean giving up on the things we love; it might even mean making lives better, for everyone. No single one of us can slay any of these monsters alone, but we are not alone. We are already united, and it is only outdated philosophies that keep us apart. I know this, because our restaurant, Inver, depends on people who think and do like me. The economy and society we need to operate in perpetuity on this blue-green planet already exists.

We procrastinate in making changes in our lives and food habits because that's what people do when a task feels overwhelming. We side-step around problems. It's not laziness, it's self-defence. Facing the enormity of the current climate crisis, overwhelm is the obvious default. Small daily changes seem so futile in the face of the planet-scale forces at work. Plus, if human existence is so precarious, and we're winding down our time on the planet, why bother?

We are not living in the first point in human history where people have felt like this. Back in the nineteenth century German philosopher Friedrich Nietzsche, seeking to overcome this nihilism and give significance to ordinary lives, concluded

---

* This is the popular 'Lego-brick' translation from the Italian. The full translation is: 'The old is dying and the new cannot be born. In this interregnum there arises a great diversity of morbid symptoms.'

that 'One must give value to their existence by behaving as if one's very existence were a work of art.' And what art would see its very referents destroyed? There's not a piece of art or craft in existence that doesn't take influence from the world around us: creative expression that eschews colour and form, composition and texture, atmosphere and subject, is not art. It is not anything. Art itself is a dialogue between artist and subject, artwork and viewer; it depends on connection. In this it is like food and cooking. It seeks to unite us with our own thoughts and to the world onto which they hook. The skills we learn to make our way about the world are what connect us to it, and to each other. Using these daily acts to make changes is not a small shift. You are literally creating a world.

As at Culloden, sometimes it feels like we modern humans fight among ourselves for a win that benefits a minority of us, and in the immediate moment only. It's only from the vantage point of the present that we can see the patterns in history. So it won't be till the end of my life, or my nieces', nephews' and godchildren's lives, that we can be sure that things are changing in the way I see now. But you also can't tell me that they're not.

Colonisation, said Martinican psychiatrist and revolutionary Frantz Fanon, is not merely an economic or political system, but a deeply entrenched structure of power that systematically devalues the colonised people.* *De*colonisation, then, has to be a psychological and cultural transformation, as well as a

---

* Psychiatrist, philosopher and revolutionary Frantz Fanon wrote *The Wretched of the Earth* in 1961, while working as a doctor in (then) French colony Algeria as the country fought for independence.

A WAR FOR THE HUMAN IMAGINATION

political one. Fanon saw that true liberation requires a radical reconfiguration of society, institutions and individual awareness. He urged men and women seeking independence not to adopt the values of the colonising nation, but to create their own culture and identity. Like Gramsci, he believed creating a new national culture was the first step in instigating change. 'A national culture is the whole body of efforts made by a people in the sphere of thought to describe, justify and praise the action through which that people has created itself and kept itself in existence'.[16] Fanon was urging each generation to discover its mission and to fight for it.

In this he echoes John Locke, who said three centuries prior that an elected government's power should be based on consent, and have specified purposes, mainly to protect its subjects. In a well-functioning democracy, said Locke, people enter a covenant with the government; it's a two-way process of obligation.* People do not have to obey a government that no longer protects them, and the consent of an ancestor does not bind the descendants. Each generation must consent for itself.

It should not be up to hard-working parents, teachers, joiners, nurses, designers, computer scientists or anyone else just trying to live a life already full enough, to edit out the damage caused to nature and human well-being from their shopping baskets. There are professional politicians whose job it is to take care of the regulatory framework in which we make our choices. This is the covenant we enter with the state. In

---

* 'The natural state is also one of equality in which all power and jurisdiction is reciprocal and no one has more than another. It is evident that all human beings – as creatures belonging to the same species and rank and born indiscriminately with all the same natural advantages and faculties – are equal amongst themselves.' (John Locke, *Second Treatise of Government*, 1689).

the face of planetary destruction, there is no longer a case for compliance.

Macro-narratives are needed to combat communal problems, but solutions can be micro-narratives suited to local landscapes. Postmodernists were afraid of the 'totalising' narrative of Marx, who wanted to eliminate individualism and for human beings to subserve to the state. But he wasn't thinking big enough. We need really to subserve to the ecosystem. In pursuing something beyond short-sighted party politics, short-term nation-state politics, beyond even national culture and personal identity, we can see humankind's real place from the perspective of planetary time. Human beings all occupy the same niche in the ecosystem. We may be a top predator and a 'keystone species', but we are not omnipotent, and we are at the mercy of the success or collapse of the other species on whose shoulders we stand. Only when the ecosystem is secure are we free to pursue individual will. And perhaps in decentralising ourselves we will find that our own will is not so important after all.

Former director at J. P. Morgan John Fullerton agrees. During a conversation about regenerative economics, Fullerton said, 'This is the era that follows the modern age and [a] reconnection with who we are and where we fit into the bigger picture . . . We are a part of nature, not apart from nature, is the next big development in human civilization that we'll look back on and see as being as big as the shift from the medieval period to the modern age.'[17] I remember Rousseau, who counselled to beware of forgetting our true relationship to the planet that sustains us; that the fruits of the earth belong to us all, and the earth itself to nobody.[18] What instead if the fruits of the earth belong to themselves, only: that nature is *not* a resource, that it belongs neither to an individual person, nor to all? How does that change how we view nature, trade, and each other? What must we give back for what we take?

Our real freedom is the freedom to live in our own small ways. I visited farmer Ian this summer, with some of the Inver team, to see the Highland cattle who live on tiny uninhabited Inchmarnock island, off Bute. The cattle graze the machair grasses and wild flowers, as they have in this place for centuries. Ian told me that the price of lamb had recently gone through the roof, because it had just been Easter and then Ramadan, and everybody was buying lamb. The butcher, Nigel, who relays the animals from the island to the Inver kitchen, had offered him almost double the price that he had expected for the beasts. Ian refused to take the extra, saying he hoped that maybe if the lamb price dipped at some point Nigel might be able to return the favour. And this is how we side-step the 'global' markets, and create intimate networks of our own meaning, in our own time and place. *This* is meaningful freedom of choice.

At the restaurant I tap into an economy that's already here – it already exists. It's always been here, spread like a safety net under us all. In one reading, Inver is a fairly ordinary mid-range restaurant. But perhaps it's in our minds and imaginations that we offer a connection to a different way of being. We are a business, and we make profit in a small way in this capitalist economy. We have never chosen to maximise this profit at the expense of staff, suppliers' or landscape well-being. Rather, we have let ourselves be guided by the concept of 'enough'. This is enough for today. Do you have enough for today?

Change happens. Enslavement was outlawed in 1807. The Crofters Holdings Act for the first time affirmed the rights of crofters to their land from 1886, and today in Scotland 563,000 acres are owned by communities – around three times as much as is owned by the National Trust for Scotland.[19] Women won universal suffrage on an equal basis to men in only 1928. From 'owning' or controlling a full quarter of the planet and 400 million people 100 years ago, the UK now has no official colonies.*

In 2018 New Zealand's Mount Taranaki and the Whanganui River were given legal personhood, meaning their rights can be defended in court against people who want to exploit them. Norwegian campaigners in 2023 won their two-year battle to protect traditional cod-fishing grounds and the fertile seabed around Lofoten, Vesterålen and Senja from the powerful oil industry.[20] The Norwegian government has recently introduced a 25 per cent aquaculture ground-rent tax on salmon farms.[21] France has just banned short-haul internal flights and some private jet flights (measures suggested by a Citizens' Convention on Climate).[22] My new hero is young Dutch inventor and entrepreneur Boyan Slat, who at eighteen dropped out of his aerospace engineering degree and started the Ocean Cleanup, after *creating* the technology to rid the oceans of their 'floating continent' of plastic waste. He's on track to be done by 2040.[23] A recent report from Brazil shows a 60 per cent reduction in the deforestation of the Amazon, after a change in political leadership; the country is now aiming for zero deforestation and 'a new model of prosperity that is less predatory'.[24] Public pressure, boycotts and rebellions, books and media have

---

* It does still have 14 Overseas Territories, 10 of which are inhabited by UK citizens: see UK House of Commons Library, Research Briefing, 20 January 2023, at: <https://commonslibrary.parliament.uk/research-briefings/cbp-9706/>

changed people's minds, changed laws and changed history. That history is less black and white than constantly shifting tides of grey.

Change happens; it is happening now. The question is not *whether* there will be changes to Scots food, diet, culture and the global food systems in which these are all embedded: it is what do we want them to change *to*. It's sometimes harder to be optimistic about the big-time future than to give in to pessimism, but the latter is demotivating, destructive. Optimism is a social duty. If we're going down, I'm going down fighting.

Happily, this fight is delicious.

Nan Shepherd, nature writer and lifelong intimate of the Cairngorm mountains, tells us we should 'use the whole of one's body to instruct the spirit'. Her ode, *The Living Mountain*, is a journey into the being of the mountains; there is no upwards scaling of summits, no battle metaphors or subduing of wild nature. Upon finding herself drenched in the sensations of the mountains, 'one is not bodiless, but essential body'. She explores with all the senses, expecting nothing more than the sensation itself. 'The hands have an infinity of pleasure in them,' she writes. 'The feel of things, textures, surfaces, rough things like cones and bark, smooth things like stalks and feathers and pebbles rounded by water, the teasing of gossamers . . . nothing that I can touch or that touches me but has its own identity for the hand as much as for the eye.'[25] Fellow climber and writer of mountains Robert Macfarlane spots the contemporary relevance in Shepherd's 'bodily thinking'. 'We have come increasingly to forget that our minds are shaped by the bodily experience of being in the world . . . we are literally losing touch, becoming disembodied.'[26]

Walking the hills, fields and shores around Inver, picking the sea herbs and brambles, rosehips and wild flowers, returning to the warm kitchen to fold ballooning dough, rattle seeds onto steel trays and stir gentle custards, we are immersing ourselves in . . . ourselves.

I am writing on the river. This answer holds good today. No edible, social, political or economic system is fixed. Even those that appear to be written in stone can be worn away. As Nan Shepherd's poetic reflection on her mountains tells us, 'The most appalling quality of water is its strength.'[27]

A LANDSCAPE CUISINE

So who am I, then? Who are we, these 'Scots' who make choices on what to eat three times daily but know not which aproned puppeteer tugs the strings? The stories that I have inherited are just that: stories. They are 'true' only in as far as I – we – choose to make them so. National, family and personal identities can be mutually reinforcing or they can disrupt each other. I'd call this edible natural history a palimpsest but nothing has been erased; even species now extinct have informed how we choose to farm and eat. My own narratives are tracked like crumbs scattered through the woods of history. There are uncountable other paths backwards and to the future.

I've looked at the country's more recent history, probing the cultural and social group identity into which I was born. These last few centuries have had an acute influence on who we think we are. Stories and recipes can now be printed, shared and preserved. The land now has a name: Scotland; and we are now Scots. Currently, we are part of a group of countries on the same bit of rock together called Britain and for the last couple of years we have not been part of a bigger group of adjacent countries called Europe. But this situation is so recent as to be impossible to plot on a chart whose axes are all of human time and space. The lines on the graph are constantly redrawn. The shifting allegiances of modernity seem to move the very ground on which we stand.

We Scots live in landscapes constructed with riches wrung from other lands. The violence and destruction of enslavement and colonialisation has contributed to the relatively comfortable, industrialised country we live in today. 'Capitalism' was conceptualised with a false premise stowed away like a landmine, and it has exploded. In addition to the debt owed to the people who built our 'developed' nations, we are in ecological debt over our heads.*

'Nationalism', 'capitalism', 'religion', each with their language and imagery, uniforms and convention; these stories bind us like ropes to the natural world and to each other, and like ropes, they exclude and restrain too. The legacy of Victorian policy and fashion is inscribed on the landscape and mentality of Scotland. People like you tell these stories – politics, philosophy, economics, literature, music, art and food culture are all created first in the human mind and repeated till they are believed. If today's stories no longer make sense, if they do not allow us safe passage through the present to a healthy future, unbind the ropes. Let's weave new stories, invent new –isms,

---

* Jason Hickel and colleagues show that high-income nations and the corporations that dominate them were responsible for 74 per cent of global 'excess resource use' from 1970 to 2017. The two biggest offenders are the US (27 per cent) and Europe (25 per cent), with China at 15 per cent and the entire global south responsible for only 8 per cent. Hickel, J., et al, 'National Responsibility for ecological breakdown', *Lancet Planet Health*, 2022, 6, e342-49, at: <https://www.thelancet.com/pdfs/journals/lanplh/PIIS2542-5196(22)00044-4.pdf>

and tie them to the features of different landscapes. This is what we have always done; perhaps the greatest continuity in history is this fluid storytelling.

Calling my food 'modern Scottish' now feels like trying to pull on an old pair of tights that don't fit any more. My big toe pokes out through a hole in the foot; excess flesh bulges over the waist elastic. 'Scottish' was an important identity and definition for me when I lived in London, and abroad. It was an important anchor when I returned to Scotland to take a risk in opening a business, to put myself out there, to define myself in public. Scottish was an important part of my identity as we opened our restaurant, when I had the audacity to cook on behalf of a country I knew little about.

Now, I see that 'modern Scottish food' is as much an imaginative construct as the nations themselves, requiring qualification to be meaningful: Which Britain? Which Scotland? There's a question open as to whether or not nationalism in food movements is ever helpful, particularly in the country they claim to represent. It's perhaps a wrong turning on our path to an equitable, healthy food culture. Deciding what Scottish food is in the twenty-first century depends on who's cooking, and on which influences they're acknowledging in their life and their refrigerator.

I knew there was something wrong when I set out to determine what was 'modern' about my food and why calling it 'normal' didn't gel for me. The news today is full of the unfolding genocide that one recently constructed nation is perpetuating against another. The only thing that is different to the original colonial expansion by western powers is that now the atrocities are broadcast, live, over the entire world.

A WAR FOR THE HUMAN IMAGINATION

We are all witnesses, and we will see our day in court. Living in modernity isn't optional, but allying myself with the term and all it refers to is now jarring. 'Scottish' – like any nationalism – is a term as dependent on the listener as the speaker.

I have to keep reminding myself that this is a book about food – because, of course, it isn't. Food culture is one facet of *all* culture. How we feed ourselves is informed by values that are in turn shaped by the constant pressure of the people who hold power and purse, and the combined will of the rest of us. The way we live today is the result of conscious decision-making by men over the last 500 years (who in turn have built on the decisions made in the centuries before that). Over the seven centuries since the Assize of Bread and Ale first regulated the production and sale of food in Britain, governments the world over have built the shopping and living environments in which we make our 'free' choice today. We could create a different one.

Capitalism is malfunctioning. It's a 250-year-old, crazed runaway wagon missing a wheel and it's about to crash. You can fix the wagon – screw the wheel back on, address the steering, install modern navigation systems and an electric battery – or you can check the chassis, realise the whole structure is unsound, and write it off before it kills passengers and bystanders both.

The natural world lives to her own rules, her own inarguable system of justice. No matter, really, how we finite beasts chatter among ourselves – it is this justice that will prevail. People, their laws and customs, constantly change. Land endures. Its geological timescale is far greater than a human era. The slow violence of climate collapse is damaging the human landscape most of all. Ecosystems will shift and compensate; certain species will find new biological niches and proliferate at the expense of others. Nature's scales will rebalance. But human beings will not be in the same place. If nature is a woman in chains, every moment that we hesitate to set her free, every moment that we hesitate to atone for our crime, we are convicted.[28]

Through our diet, the Scottish landscape flows from Kirkwall to Kazakhstan, from Kelso to Kenya. Like the land itself, our mindscape has no fixed, immovable borders: our personal, internal landscapes are as frequently redrawn as maps of nations themselves. Food culture morphs with changes in laws and regulations, science and the arts. Wars and economic policy reshape land overseas and in turn migration brings us the seeds of new ideas.

I want a new normal, one that makes room for all the people, creatures and cultures that contribute to my menus, and the landscapes they inhabit – physically and figuratively. A normal that is a fitting place from which to step onwards to an open, equitable future. I want to live in a landscape where all inhabitants have citizenhood: where mountains and rivers, flora and fauna are given an equitable presence in policy and history; where their contributions to our lives as recognised as essential and rewarded as such. I want a government which will make human life more valuable, not less; which will honour its covenant to its people and put the well-being of the many before the wealth of the very few. But I will not wait for it.

I've been wondering if there is a way to stitch together all these landscapes, the natural and cultural, personal and microscopic. I wonder if thinking differently about how to approach growing, choosing and cooking food can lead me into a world where a respect for interdependent ways of being replaces the destructive modern assumption of individual entitlement that seems so normal today.

I think it's worth a shot.

'Landscape cuisine' is an imaginative reconnection of human cooks and eaters to the land where everything starts. The land is a time chariot, connecting us all through time as through space. Scottish food history has plenty to teach us about ways to work with the land, not against it. Landscape cuisine is a conscious effort to articulate principles which will guide me as I cook and serve food for the twenty-first century. It's deliberately broad. There is no prescription – only consequences by which to judge ourselves. Landscape cuisine is bounded only by the natural limits of our ecosystems, and acknowledges and cares for all the landscapes – personal, environmental, cultural – through which we procure the food for our larders. And it's as celebratory of flavour as it is inclusive of influence. I honour and celebrate what I have inherited: the oats and the mince; the butter and its buttermilk; the mussels and kailyards; the soil behind my fingernails; and the little hit of joy at seeing the first green shoots push through the dark. I welcome ways of doing and thinking that are new to me and my kitchen: with these I stay alive, awake, and true to the reality of human life; literally open.

A landscape cuisine is all about how we choose to use land. It's about eliminating waste, and confining our consumption of meat and seafood to that which we know will contribute to local and global ecologies, not dismantle them. Meat must return to its traditional role as an occasional, celebratory food, reflective of the cows', sheep's, pigs' and chickens' (and deer's and game birds') own entitlement to land and the feed that comes from it. All of the animal, from head to tail to bone and blood, must have a place on the plate. Wasting food is wasting land.

The new Scottish cuisine is like the old: we share tables. We honour and acknowledge connection. We choose our own value for the humble. We at Inver use our restaurant to help build supportive and equitable communities, here and far away, and to seat ourselves and our guests in a landscape full of meaning. Traditional foods maintain relevance where they have been solutions that people have found in a particular time and place. On each new today, we acknowledge new people with their own solutions to dinner. We give thanks for sacrifices past and ready ourselves to do the same.

May you have your meal with gladness and health.

ACKNOWLEDGEMENTS

In keeping with the spirit of *Between Two Waters*, I acknowledge the contribution to this book of everyone and everything everywhere. I know that I stand on some very broad shoulders.

More specifically, there are a few critical people without whom the pages would still be blank.

The start of the book and the start of the thanks are with the Maclachlan family: to Jasmine, for giving us the opportunity. To Euan, Charlie and Gina, for being the best landlords we could have asked for. As modern caretakers of storied land and its people there could be few fairer, more welcoming or enlightened. To Lachlan Bay itself, for the sea greens, the scenery and the stories. There would be no Inver without you all.

And to my mum and my dad: 'thanks' is hardly enough. Mum, for making dinner an everyday craft, and Dad, for that first book on Scottish cookery (*Scottish Cookery* by Catherine Brown). 'Adopt, adapt, improve': for once I hope I have done what you told me. To my brother Alan: my first ally. To his partner Hannah and their sons Hamish and Fergus: lights on the path to our future.

To everyone who has contributed time and ideas, on the phone, over coffee, down the pub; especially: Chloe Oswald, Julie Lin, Col Gordon, Ryan Dziadowiec, Alastair Barge, Winston Churchill and Colin Lanyon. And to photographer Mark Cameron for dragging Jo to the wilds of Argyll for the winter photoshoot.

Those of you who know his epic work *The Food of the Scots* know the breadth of gratitude owed to the late Alexander Fenton, who has done all the hard ethnological graft, allowing me to basket the low-hanging fruit. Scots cooks and writers long before me get the credit for knowing the best bits of our landscape to preserve and share with their future colleagues in the kitchen. The brief birl round the rise of capitalism and the enclosures owes much to Dr Jason Hickel. To Professor Tim Lang, Dr David Barling and Professor Martin Caraher of City University, the Food Policy department during my time there: thank you for taking a chance on me on the strength of my chat, rather than my deficient academic qualifications. Kath Dalmeny and Jeanette Longfield at Sustain remain the best people managers of my career, an inspiration in the kitchen and on the page; thank you for the confidence.

To all our family and friends who helped build and create, weave, paint and sew: mums and dads, Gordon and Elaine, Iain and Andrew Foxall, Andrew Wightman and Rebecca Proctor, Ailidh Lennon, Ben Glazer, Adam Gale especially. To the whole team at Inver, from the start. Especially right at the start, when we were less adept employers than we might be now, thank you for bearing with. We couldn't have done it without you. Notably Siobhan Brown, Ally Fisher, Gordy Reilly, Moray Lamb, Chloe Oswald, Matteo Ladas and Sarah

ACKNOWLEDGEMENTS

Bryant; with crucial cameos from Polly Higginson and Ailidh Lennon. Okay, Thomas Dowse, you too. And to the team during the time I wrote the book, thank you for holding the space for me so well: in the kitchen, Matt Smith and Nicky Robinson, with Ed, Rosie, Ruby, Aaron, Ray, Seb, Will, Sarah and Andrea and Clare. And in the restaurant and the rooms, Lisa, Jo, George, Ciara, Georgie, Stephen, Matthieu, Matt and Beth.

To literary agent Rachel, for liking her dinner enough to think I could somehow write too; thank you for seeing me through the menu. To editor Helena for bearing with the raggedy edges of a first book, at first more rag than book, and being the most diplomatic editor. It's been a pleasure watching you work. And the rest of the extended team at Canongate, especially Aisling, Caitriona, Leila and Gill, and Eugenie and Lorraine: thank you so much for all the help, encouragement, efficiency and kindness. You really are an excellent team.

It's important to acknowledge the privileged position I have found myself in: the education and relative financial comfort that has allowed me the room to write this book at all. I hope I am using that privilege justly. To the organisation Land in Our Names (LION), to whom a proportion of the author's proceeds of these book sales will go: thank you for seeing so clearly what needs to be done. Land is power, and reparations should start with the first theft.

To the closest and broadest reaches of my family, genetic and chosen: thank you for everything you've taught me, and everything you've tolerated. To all the other taxonomical families, of which I am also a distant part: for everything you've taught me and everything you have tolerated, too.

And to Rob: partner in life and work, for creating home, with me.

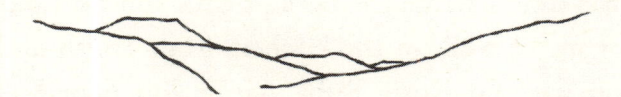

Excerpt from 'Letter #75' in *Revolutionary Letters: 50th Anniversary Edition: Pocket Poets Series No. 27* by Diane di Prima, copyright © the Estate of Diane di Prima 1971, 2021. Published by City Lights Books. Used by kind permission of the Estate of Diane di Prima.

Excerpt from *Scottish Life and Society. Vol. 5, The Food of the Scots: A Compendium of Scottish Ethnology* by Alexander Fenton, copyright © Alexander Fenton, 2007. Published by Birlinn Ltd. Used by kind permission of Birlinn Ltd.

Excerpt from *Poetics of Relation* by Édouard Glissant, translation copyright © by the University of Michigan, 1997. Published by University of Michigan Press. Originally published in French by Gallimard, 1990. All rights reserved. Used by kind permission of University of Michigan Press.

NOTES

Chapter One: The Road Less Travelled

1 Scottish Government, *The Scottish Health Survey 2021: Volume 1*, Ch. 5, at: <https://www.gov.scot/publications/scottish-health-survey-2021-volume-1-main-report/pages/10/>
2 IPCC, 'Climate Change and Land: An IPCC Special Report on climate change, desertification, land degradation, sustainable land management, food security, and greenhouse gas fluxes in terrestrial ecosystems', 2020 revision, at: <https://www.ipcc.ch/srccl/>
3 Lang, Tim, *Feeding Britain: Our Food Problems and How to Fix Them*, Pelican, 2020, pp. 313–314.
4 Good Food Nation (Scotland) Act 2022, at: <https://www.legislation.gov.uk/asp/2022/5/contents>
5 Bradley Ruder, Debra, 'The enteric nervous system that regulates our gut is often called the body's "second brain"', On the Brain lecture series, Harvard Medical School, at: <https://hms.harvard.edu/news-events/publications-archive/brain/gut-brain#:~:text=The%20enteric%20nervous%20system%20that,brain%20when%20something%20is%20amiss>

Chapter Two: Modern

1 According to the *Cambridge Dictionary*, at: <https://dictionary.cambridge.org/dictionary/english/modern>
2 Quoted in Laudan, Rachel, *Cuisine and Empire: Cooking in World History*, University of California Press, 2013, p. 209.
3 Anderson, Benedict, *Imagined Communities: Reflections On the Origins and Spread of Nationalism*, Verso Books, 1983/2006 edition
4 See Worldometers, 'Population', at: <https://www.worldometers.info/world-population/>

5 Hickel, Jason, *Less Is More: How Degrowth Will Save the World*, William Heinemann, 2020, p. 19.
6 Rousseau, Jean-Jacques, *Discourse on the Origins of Inequality*, 1755, at: <https://www.marxists.org/reference/subject/economics/rousseau/inequality/ch02.htm#:~:text=THE%20first%20man%20who%2C%20having,real%20founder%20of%20civil%20society>
7 International Monetary Fund, 'Climate Change, Fossil Fuel Subsidies', 2022, at: <https://www.imf.org/en/Topics/climate-change/energy-subsidies#:~:text=Subsidies%20are%20intended%20to%20protect,come%20at%20a%20substantial%20cost>
8 Lang, Tim, *Feeding Britain: Our Food Problems and How to Fix Them*, Pelican, 2020, p. 374.
9 Kimmerer, Robin Wall, *Braiding Sweetgrass: Indigenous Wisdom, Scientific Knowledge and the Teachings of Plants*, Milkweed Editions, 2013, pp. 169–70.
10 Quoted in Steger, Alex, 'The Capitalist Beast Is Out of Control', Citywire, 11 February 2019, at: <https://citywire.com/pro-buyer/news/the-capitalist-beast-is-out-of-control-jeremy-grantham-takes-aim-at-corporate-culture/a1197044>
11 Jeremy Grantham's 'Race of Our Lives' speech, Morningstar Investment Conference, 25 June 2018, at: <https://www.morningstar.com/sustainable-investing/watch-jeremy-granthams-race-our-lives-speech>
12 Hickel, *Less Is More*, p. 28.
13 See, for example, the account of the enclosures in Hickel, *Less Is More*.
14 Sulan Masing, Anna, 'Pepper Changed the World', *Guardian*, 4 January 2023, at: <https://www.theguardian.com/commentisfree/2023/jan/04/pepper-changed-the-world-but-how-many-people-know-that>
15 Anderson, Deborah, '62 Glasgow Street Names and Areas with Links to Slave Trade', *Glasgow Times*, 29 March 2022, at: <https://www.glasgowtimes.co.uk/news/20030008.62-glasgow-street-names-areas-links-slave-trade/>

16 McCarthy, Angela, 'Bad History: The Controversy over Henry Dundas and the Historiography of the Abolition of the Slave Trade', *Scottish Affairs*, Volume 31 Issue 2, pp. 133–53.

17 Brunache, Peggy, 'Mainstreaming African Diasporic Foodways when Academia is not Enough', in *Transforming Anthropology*, Vol. 27, No. 2, 2019, pp. 149–63.

18 For a fuller discussion, see Col Gordon's podcast *Landed*, Farmerama Radio, 2021, at: <https://farmerama.co/landed/>

19 MacKinnon, Iain, and Andrew Mackillop, 'Plantation Slavery and Landownership in the West Highlands and Islands: Legacies and Lessons', 2020, p. 4, at: <https://www.communitylandscotland.org.uk/wp-content/uploads/2022/08/Report-2020-Plantation-slavery.pdf>

20 MacKinnon and Mackillop, 'Plantation Slavery and Landownership'.

21 Somers, Robert, *Letters from the Highlands: or, the Famine of 1847*, Simpkin & Marshall, 1848, quoted in MacKinnon and Mackillop, 'Plantation Slavery and Landownership', p. 15.

22 Helen, Countess of Sutherland, notebook, Sutherland Estate papers, National Library of Scotland, at: <https://digital.nls.uk/102710709>

23 Laudan, *Cuisine and Empire*, p. 274.

24 See main page of British Sugar, at: <https://www.britishsugar.co.uk>

25 Clover, Charles, 'Tate & Lyle given £127m from CAP', *Telegraph*, 23 March 2005, at: <https://www.telegraph.co.uk/news/uknews/1486231/Tate-and-Lyle-given-127m-from-CAP.html>; for Tate & Lyle's 2022 results, see: <https://www.tateandlyle.com/news/tate-lyle-plc-2022-full-year-results-statement>

26 'Raw truths about subsidies', *Guardian*, 'Letters', 16 December 2005, at: <https://www.theguardian.com/news/2005/dec/16/food.foodanddrink>

27 Written evidence to the UK Parliament from Tate & Lyle, November 2017, at: <https://committees.parliament.uk/writtenevidence/82779/html/> and Hunter, Archie, and Katharine Gemmell, 'UK High Court maintains Brexit

sugar deal', *Bloomberg*, 25 February 2022, at: <https://www.bloomberg.com/news/articles/2022-02-25/u-k-high-court-maintains-brexit-sugar-deal-quashing-challenge>

28 Carter, Lawrence, and Crispin Dowler, 'Brexit-backing sugar refiner gets "Sweetheart Deal" on Cane Imports', *Unearthed*, Greenpeace UK, 8 August 2020, at: <https://unearthed.greenpeace.org/2020/08/08/brexit-sugar-cane-tate-lyle-sweetheart-conservative/>

29 Action on Sugar, 'Will decreasing the availability of sugar in the UK be the key to reducing our intake?', at: <https://www.actiononsugar.org/blog/will-decreasing-the-availability-of-sugar-in-the-uk-be-the-key-to-reducing-our-sugar-intake/>

30 British Beet Research Organisation, 'Agronomic Strategies and the Economics of Organic Beet Production', 2004, at: <https://bbro.co.uk/bbro-research/bbro-research/crop-protection/co-organic-beet-production/>

31 Mintel, 'Nation of Chocoholics: Eight Million Brits Eat Chocolate Every Day', 2014, at: <https://www.mintel.com/press-centre/nation-of-chocoholics-eight-million-brits-eat-chocolate-every-day/>

32 Gayle, Damien, 'Cocoa Planting Is Destroying Protected Forests in West Africa, Study Finds', *Guardian*, 22 May 2023, at: <https://www.theguardian.com/environment/2023/may/22/cocoa-planting-is-destroying-protected-forests-in-west-africa-study-finds>

33 Odijie, Michael, 'Why Does Child Slavery Persist in West Africa's Cocoa Production?', *Africa at LSE* blog, 2 June 2021, at: <https://blogs.lse.ac.uk/africaatlse/2021/06/02/why-does-child-slavery-persist-west-africa-cote-divoire-cocoa-chocolate-production/>

34 Odijie, 'Why Does Child Slavery Persist?'

35 The children were represented by human rights organisation International Rights Advocates, <https://www.internationalrightsadvocates.org>; Balch, Oliver, 'Mars, Nestlé and Hershey to face landmark child slavery lawsuit in US', *Guardian*, 12 February 2021, at: <https://www.theguardian.com/

36 Stempel, Jonathan, 'Hershey, Nestlé, Cargill win dismissal in US of child slavery lawsuit', Reuters, 28 June 2022, at: <https://www.reuters.com/business/hershey-nestle-cargill-win-dismissal-us-child-slavery-lawsuit-2022-06-28/>
37 Paul Schoenmakers quoted in Collins, Tom, 'Ivory Coast Battles Chocolate Companies to Improve Farmers' Lives', Al Jazeera, 22 December 2022, at: <https://www.aljazeera.com/features/2022/12/22/ivory-coast-battles-chocolate-companies-to-improve-farmers-lives>
38 Paul Schoenmakers quoted in Collins, Tom, 'Ivory Coast Battles Chocolate Companies'.
39 Kambhampaty, Anna Purna, 'What We Can Learn From the Near-Death of the Banana', *Time*, 18 November 2019, at: <https://time.com/5730790/banana-panama-disease/>
40 Quoted in Gray, Louise, 'The "pandemic" destroying the world's favourite fruit', 'Follow the Food', BBC, at: <https://www.bbc.com/future/bespoke/follow-the-food/the-pandemic-threatening-bananas.html>
41 The Banana List, Bananageddon, at: <https://bananageddon2018.wixsite.com/home/banana-list>
42 Gray, 'The "pandemic" destroying the world's favourite fruit'.
43 Low, P., 'The Cambridge Declaration on Consciousness', *Proceedings of the Francis Crick Memorial Conference*, Churchill College, Cambridge University, 7 July 2012, pp. 1–2, at: <https://fcmconference.org/img/CambridgeDeclarationOnConsciousness.pdf>
44 Pascoe, Bruce, *Dark Emu: Aboriginal Australia and the Birth of Agriculture*, Scribe UK, 2018, p. 41.
45 Anderson, M. Kat, *Tending the Wild: Native American Knowledge and the Management of California's Natural Resources*, University of California Press, 2005, especially pp. 13–17.
46 Anderson, *Tending the Wild*, pp. 126–7.
47 Pascoe, *Dark Emu*.
48 Pascoe, *Dark Emu*, p. 30.

49 Quoted in Pascoe, *Dark Emu*, p. 7.
50 'Anthropologist: Dr Wade Davis', *National Geographic*, at: <https://education.nationalgeographic.org/resource/real-world-geography-dr-wade-davis/>
51 Hickel, Jason, et al, 'Imperialist appropriation in the world economy: Drain from the global South through unequal exchange, 1990–2015', *Global Environmental Change*, Vol. 73, March 2022, at: <https://www.sciencedirect.com/science/article/pii/S095937802200005X>
52 *World Happiness Report 2023*, quoted in 'Zimbabwe Ranked the World's Fourth Unhappiest Country', *New Zimbabwe*, 3 April 2023, at: <https://allafrica.com/stories/202304030074.html>
53 Mudimu, G., 'Zimbabwe Food Security Issues Paper', ODI's Forum for Food Security in Southern Africa, 31 July 2003, at: <https://odi.org/en/publications/zimbabwe-food-security-issues-paper/>
54 Lang, *Feeding Britain*, p. 363.
55 Lang, *Feeding Britain*, p. 446.
56 Lang, *Feeding Britain*, p. 15.
57 Sen, Amartya, *Poverty and Famines: An Essay on Entitlement and Deprivation*, Oxford Academic, 1983, at: <https://doi.org/10.1093/0198284632.001.0001>
58 Cherniwchan, Jevan, and Juan Moreno Cruz, 'Maize and precolonial Africa', *Science Direct*, Vol. 136, 2019, pp. 137–50, at: <https://www.sciencedirect.com/science/article/pii/S0304387818303195>
59 Redvers, Nicole, et al, 'Molecular Decolonization: An Indigenous Microcosm Perspective of Planetary Health', *International Journal of Environmental Research and Public Health*, Vol. 17, No. 12, June 2020, at: <https://doi.org/10.3390%2Fijerph17124586>
60 Mousseau, Fred, 'Roles of and Alternatives to Food Aid in Southern Africa: A Report to Oxfam', 2004, at: <https://sarpn.org/documents/d0000998/P1121-Roles_and_alternatives_to_food_aid_Mousseau_2004.pdf>
61 Lears, T. J. Jackson, 'The Concept of Cultural Hegemony:

NOTES

Problems and Possibilities', *American Historical Review*, Vol. 90, No. 3, 1985, pp. 567–93, at: <https://doi.org/10.2307/1860957>
62 Gramsci, Antonio, *Prison Notebooks*, Columbia University Press, 2011. <https://www.daas.academy/research/critical-consciousness/>

Chapter Three: Scottish / *people*

1 Burns, Robert, 'Such a Parcel of Rogues in a Nation', 1791, at: <https://www.robertburns.org/works/344.shtml>
2 Pettigrew, William Andrew, *Freedom's Debt: The Royal African Company and the Politics of the Atlantic Slave Trade, 1672–1752*, UNC Press Books, 2013, p. 11.
3 Devine, Tom, *The Scottish Nation: A Modern History*, Penguin, 2012, p. 172.
4 Devine, *The Scottish Nation*, p. 170.
5 Dziadowiec, Ryan, 'Tobar An Dualchais: What Can Proverbs Tell Us About Dùthchas?', 16 March 2022, at: <https://www.tobarandualchais.co.uk/blog/what-can-proverbs-tell-us-about-duthchas?l=en>
6 Gordon, Col, 'Dùthchas: What Are We Actually Talking About?', The Shieling Project, 22 March 2023, at: <https://www.theshielingproject.org/posts/dùthchas-what-are-we-actually-talking-about>
7 Devine, *The Scottish Nation*, p. 25.
8 Devine, *The Scottish Nation*, p. 29.
9 Devine, *The Scottish Nation*, p. 178.
10 Wigan, Michael, *The Scottish Highland Estate: Preserving an Environment*, Swan Hill Press, 1991, p. 17.
11 Wigan, *The Scottish Highland Estate*, p. 16.
12 'The Fife Adventurers', Hebridean Connections, at: <https://www.hebrideanconnections.com/historical-events/65016>
13 Gordon, Col, *Landed* podcast, episode 2, 'The cow or the how?', Farmerama Radio, at: <https://farmerama.co/listen/>
14 Sir Charles Trevelyan to the *Scotsman* in 1852. Trevelyan added that the incoming Anglo-Saxons would more readily 'assimilate with our body of politic'. Widely quoted, including in Devine,

The Scottish Nation, and Silke Stroh's *Gaelic Scotland in the Colonial Imagination*, Northwestern University Press, 2017.
15 Devine, *The Scottish Nation*, p. 299.
16 Wigan, *The Scottish Highland Estate*, p. 17.
17 Trevor-Roper, Hugh, 'The Invention of Tradition: The Highland Tradition of Scotland', in Hobsbawm, Eric, and Terence Ranger (eds), *The Invention of Tradition*, Cambridge University Press, 2012, p. 15.
18 Trevor-Roper, 'The Invention of Tradition', p. 22.
19 Lang, Tim, *Feeding Britain: Our Food Problems and How to Fix Them*, Pelican, 2020, pp. 284–98.
20 Scottish Government, *The Scottish Health Survey 2021: Volume 1*, Ch. 5, at: <https://www.gov.scot/publications/scottish-health-survey-2021-volume-1-main-report/pages/10/>
21 World Obesity Federation, 'Addressing weight stigma and misconceptions about obesity in Europe', at: <https://s3-eu-west-1.amazonaws.com/wof-files/Weight_Stigma_Briefing_FINAL.pdf>
22 Lang, *Feeding Britain*, p. 299.
23 Goody, Jack, *Cooking, Cuisine and Class: A Study in Comparative Sociology*, Cambridge University Press, 1982, p. 151.
24 Johnson, Samuel, and James Boswell, *A Journey to the Western Islands of Scotland and A Journal of a Tour to the Hebrides*, Penguin Classics, 1984.
25 Lawrence, Felicity, 'The exploitation of migrants has become our way of life', *Guardian*, 17 August 2015, at: <https://www.theguardian.com/commentisfree/2015/aug/17/exploitation-migrants-way-of-life-immigration-business-model>
26 Fenton, Alexander, *Food of the Scots*, Vol. 5 of *A Compendium of Scots Ethnography*, Tuckwell Press, 2007, p. 207.
27 Quoted in Fenton, *Food of the Scots*, p. 65.
28 Storhaug, C. L., et al, 'Country, regional, and global estimates for lactose malabsorption in adults: a systematic review and meta-analysis', *Lancet*, Vol. 2, Issue 10, 2017, pp. 738–46, at: <https://www.thelancet.com/journals/langas/article/PIIS2468-1253(17)30154-1/fulltext>

NOTES

29 Fenton, *The Food of the Scots*, p. 100.
30 Fenton, *Food of the Scots*, p. 274.
31 Higgins, David, and Mads Mordhorst, 'Bringing Home the "Danish" Bacon: Food Chains, National Branding, and Danish Supremacy over the British Bacon Market c.1900–1938', Cambridge University Press, 2015, at: <https://www.cambridge.org/core/journals/enterprise-and-society/article/abs/bringing-home-the-danish-bacon-food-chains-national-branding-and-danish-supremacy-over-the-british-bacon-market-c-19001938/6CDCDF0153034821B9D61121E2E405D6>
32 Lang, *Feeding Britain*, p. 322.
33 Cargill–MacMillan family profile, *Forbes*, 8 February 2024, at: <https://www.forbes.com/profile/cargill-macmillan-1/>
34 GRAIN and the Institute for Agriculture and Trade Policy (IATP), 'Emissions Impossible: How big meat and dairy are heating up the planet', 18 July 2018, at: <https://grain.org/article/entries/5976-emissions-impossible-how-big-meat-and-dairy-are-heating-up-the-planet>
35 Mitchell, Ewan, Peter Elwin and Mario Rautner, 'Gran Chaco: The Deforestation Dozen', Planet Tracker, March 2022, at: <https://planet-tracker.org/wp-content/uploads/2022/03/Gran-Chaco-LD-report.pdf>
36 Greenpeace, 'How JBS is still slaughtering the Amazon', 2020, at: <https://www.greenpeace.org.uk/resources/industrial-meat-deforestation-jbs/>
37 The Landworkers' Alliance, Pasture for Life, Sustain and Hodmedod, 'Soy No More: Breaking away from soy in UK pig and poultry farming', 2023, at: <https://landworkersalliance.org.uk/campaigns-advocacy__trashed/soy-no-more/>
38 Lang, *Feeding Britain*, p. 457.
39 McNeill, F. Marian, *The Scots Kitchen*, Birlinn, 2010, p. 251.
40 Fenton, *The Food of the Scots*, p. 263.
41 Fenton, *Food of the Scots*, p. 363.
42 Hawkes, J. G., and J. Francisco-Ortega, 'The early history of the potato in Europe', *Euphytica*, Vol. 70, 1993, pp. 1–7, at: <https://link.springer.com/article/10.1007/BF00029633>

43　Laudan, Rachel, *Cuisine and Empire: Cooking in World History*, University of California Press, 2013, p. 244.
44　Egan, Casey, 'The Irish Potato Famine, the Great Hunger, genocide – what should we call it?', *Irish Central*, 31 May 2015, at: <https://www.irishcentral.com/roots/history/why-we-should-call-it-the-great-hunger-and-not-the-irish-potato-famine>
45　Mann, Charles C., 'How the Potato Changed the World', *Smithsonian Magazine*, November 2011, at: <https://www.smithsonianmag.com/history/how-the-potato-changed-the-world-108470605/>
46　Mann, 'How the Potato Changed the World'.
47　Lang, *Feeding Britain*, pp. 220–21.
48　Lang, *Feeding Britain*, p. 323.
49　Fortune Business Insights, 'Crop Protection Chemicals Market', December 2021, at: <https://www.fortunebusinessinsights.com/industry-reports/crop-protection-chemicals-market-100080>
50　Mann, 'How the Potato Changed the World'.
51　Waste Resources Action Programme 'Save our Spuds' Campaign (2021) <https://wrap.org.uk/resources/campaign-assets/save-our-spuds-potato-storage-video-17-seconds-english-and-welsh>
52　Lang, *Feeding Britain*, p. 315.
53　WRAP, 'Estimates of food surplus and waste arisings in the UK', 2017, at: <https://wrap.org.uk/resources/report/estimates-food-surplus-and-waste-arisings-uk-2017>
54　Lang, *Feeding Britain*, p. 317.
55　Fenton, *Food of the Scots*, p. 76.
56　Quoted in 'Haggis Is English, Historian Says', BBC News, 3 August 2009, at: <http://news.bbc.co.uk/1/hi/8180791.stm>
57　Murphy, Sean, 'Scots fact of the day', *Scotsman*, 19 January 2015, at: <https://www.scotsman.com/arts-and-culture/scots-fact-of-the-day-robert-burns-and-jamaica-1514969>
58　Fenton, *Food of the Scots*, p. 77.

NOTES

Chapter Four: Scottish / land

1 Fenton, Alexander, *Food of the Scots*, Vol. 5 of *A Compendium of Scots Ethnography*, Tuckwell Press, 2007, pp. 25–61.
2 Wilde, Monica, 'Dòigh Nàdair – The Way of Nature', Forest Therapy Scotland, 26 July 2017, at: <https://forest-therapy-scotland.com/doigh-nadair-the-way-of-nature/>
3 Ingold, Tim, *The Perception of the Environment: Essays on Livelihood, Dwelling and Skill*, Routledge, 2022, pp. 67.
4 Fenton, *Food of the Scots*, p. 25.
5 Wigan, Michael, *The Scottish Highland Estate: Preserving an Environment*, Swan Hill Press, 1991, p. 22.
6 Wightman, Andy, Peter Higgins, Grant Jarvie and Robbie Nicol, 'The Cultural Politics of Hunting: Sporting Estates and Recreational Land Use in the Highlands and Islands of Scotland', *Culture, Sport, Society*, Vol. 5, No. 1, Spring 2002, pp. 53–70, at: <http://www.andywightman.com/docs/culture_sport_society_2002.pdf>
7 Wigan, *The Scottish Highland Estate*, p. 83.
8 Wigan, *The Scottish Highland Estate*, p. 84.
9 The Kitchin restaurant, Edinburgh, at: <https://thekitchin.com/menus/> Accessed 15 August 2023
10 Via a phone call with the author, 16 August 2023.
11 Wigan, *The Scottish Highland Estate*, p. 35.
12 The Countryside and Wildlife Act 1981 (UK), at: <https://www.legislation.gov.uk/ukpga/1981/69>; and the amendment in the Wildlife and Natural Environment (Scotland) Act 2011, at: <https://www.legislation.gov.uk/asp/2011/6/contents/enacted>
13 Scottish Government policy, Wildlife Crime, at: <https://www.gov.scot/policies/wildlife-management/wildlife-crime/>
14 Nature Scot, 'Partnership News Release – South of Scotland Golden Eagle Project', 28 November 2023, at: <https://www.nature.scot/pioneering-project-responds-disappearance-merrick-golden-eagle>
15 Nicoll, Ruiridh, 'This land is our land', *Observer*, 12 October 2003, at: <https://www.theguardian.com/observer/comment/story/0,6903,1061116,00.html>

16 Wigan, *The Scottish Highland Estate*, pp. 33–4.
17 According to the Angus Glens Moorland Group. See film at: <https://www.angusglensmoorlandgroup.co.uk/>
18 Lawrence, Anna, and Willie McGhee, Forest Policy Group, 'Woodland Nation: Pathways to a forested Scotland owned by the people', prepared for Andy Wightman, 2021, at: <http://andywightman.com/docs/woodland_nation_mid_res.pdf>
19 Brown, L. E., J. Holden and S. M. Palmer, 'Effects of moorland burning on the ecohydrology of river basins: Key findings from the EMBER project', University of Leeds, 2014, at: <https://water.leeds.ac.uk/our-missions/mission-1/ember/>
20 Anderson, M. Kat, *Tending the Wild: Native American Knowledge and the Management of California's Natural Resources*, University of California Press, 2005, p. 136.
21 Austen, Ian, 'How indigenous techniques saved a community from wildfire', *New York Times*, 27 August 2023, at: <https://www.nytimes.com/2023/08/27/world/canada/canada-wildfires-kelowna-british-columbia.html>
22 Raptor Persecution UK, 'More birds on Angus Glens housing estate than on grouse moor!', 5 August 2018, at: <https://raptorpersecutionuk.org/tag/glenogil-estate/>
23 Smith-Jones, Charles, 'A short history of the shotgun', *Shooting UK*, 1 August 2018, at: <https://www.shootinguk.co.uk/guns/history-of-the-shotgun-101303>
24 Aviva Investors, Company News, 20 December 2021, 'Major peatland restoration, carbon capture & woodland creation scheme announced following acquisition of Glen Dye Moor', at: <https://www.avivainvestors.com/en-gb/about/company-news/2021/12/ai-par-equity-scottish-woodlands-natural-capital-project/>
25 Kempe, Nick, 'BrewDogs Lost Forest at Kinrara: a landscape disaster and abuse of public money', Parks Watch Scotland, 6 February 2023, at: <https://parkswatchscotland.co.uk/2023/02/06/brewdogs-lost-forest-at-kinrara-a-landscape-disaster-and-abuse-of-public-money/>
26 'The price of fast fashion', *Nature*, 2 January 2018, at:

NOTES

<https://www.nature.com/articles/s41558-017-0058-9>; and Ellen MacArthur Foundation, 'A new textiles economy: Redesigning fashion's future', 2017, at: <https://www.ellenmacarthurfoundation.org/a-new-textiles-economy>

27 Lawrence and McGhee, 'Woodland Nation'.

28 Energy and Climate Intelligence Unit, 'Climate impacts on UK food imports', August 2023, at: <https://eciu.net/analysis/reports/2023/climate-impacts-on-uk-food-imports>

29 National Records of Scotland, '91% of Scotland's population live in 2% of its land area', 31 March 2022, at: <https://www.nrscotland.gov.uk/news/2022/91-percent-of-scotlands-population-live-in-2-percent-of-its-land-area#>

30 Wigan, *The Scottish Highland Estate*, p. 154.

31 The Landworkers' Alliance, Pasture for Life, Sustain and Hodmedod, 'Soy No More: Breaking away from soy in UK pig and poultry farming', 2023, at: <https://landworkersalliance.org.uk/campaigns-advocacy__trashed/soy-no-more/>

32 Scottish Government, 'Scottish wild salmon strategy', 14 January 2022, at: <https://www.gov.scot/publications/scottish-wild-salmon-strategy/pages/4/>

33 IUCN, 'Freshwater fish highlight escalating climate impacts on species – IUCN Red List', 11 December 2023, at: <https://www.iucn.org/press-release/202312/freshwater-fish-highlight-escalating-climate-impacts-species-iucn-red-list>

34 'The Salmon of Knowledge', Clan Donald Heritage, at: <https://clandonald-heritage.com/the-salmon/#:~:text=According%20to%20Celtic%20mythology%20the,had%20eaten%20the%20sacred%20hazelnuts>

35 Hope, Annette, *A Caledonian Feast: Scottish Cuisine Through the Ages*, Canongate, 2002, p. 23.

36 'Salmon farming's value to Scottish economy up by almost 20%', *Fishfarming Expert*, 5 October 2022, at: <https://www.fishfarmingexpert.com/gross-value-added-scottish-salmon/salmon-farmings-value-to-scottish-economy-up-by-almost-20/1438303#>

37 Ocean Rebellion, 'Salmon Farming: There Should Be a

Commons Levy', 2 April 2023, at: <https://oceanrebellion.earth/salmon-farming-there-should-be-a-commons-levy/>

38 Quoted in Rowe, Mark, 'Salmon farm threat to Scottish islands', *Geographical*, 17 August 2023, at: <https://geographical.co.uk/wildlife/salmon-farm-threat-in-scotland>

39 Aas, Turid Synnøve, Torbjørn Åsgård, and Trine Ytrestøyl, 'Utilization of feed resources in the production of Atlantic salmon (Salmo salar) in Norway: An update for 2020', *Aquaculture Reports*, Vol. 26, 2022, at: <https://doi.org/10.1016/j.aqrep.2022.101316>

40 Hoyle, Andrew, '20,000 salmon escape from Scottish site', Fish Farming Expert, 7 April 2017, at: <https://www.fishfarmingexpert.com/escape-mull-salmon/20000-salmon-escape-from-scottish-site/1137322>

41 The Spey Fishery Board agrees. See the Spey Fishery Board, 'River Spey Salmon Conservation', at: <https://riverspey.org/about-us/river-management/salmon-conservation/>

42 UK Environment Agency, 'Saprolegnia infections in wild salmon and sea trout', August 2021, at: <https://ifm.org.uk/wp-content/uploads/2021/08/Saprolegnia-in-salmonids.pdf>

43 Fisheries Management Scotland, 'Esk Salmon Fishery Board ends netting for salmon and sea trout on the River North Esk', 9 January 2019, at: <https://fms.scot/esk-salmon-fishery-board-ends-netting-for-salmon-and-sea-trout-on-the-river-north-esk/>

44 Rowe, 'Salmon farm threat to Scottish islands'.

45 See, for example, Instagram, @smith_corin, 8 November and 5 December 2023.

46 According to the anonymous ex-civil servant at Regulation.org, in 'UK Competition Policy', at: <https://www.regulation.org.uk/competition-uk_competition_policy.html>

47 'Down on the fish farm', *Private Eye*, 13 January 2017.

48 Mowi, information for investors, at: <https://mowi.com/investors/>

49 Ocean Rebellion, 'Salmon Farming'.

50 British Nutrition Foundation, 'Protein', at: <https://www.nutrition.org.uk/nutritional-information/

protein/#:~:text=Data%20from%20the%20National%20
Diet,contribute%2016%25%20to%20protein%20intakes>
51 Johnston, Janice, 'Mowi Scotland death – MAIB probe finds failings', *Fish Farmer*, 26 May 2021, at: <https://www.fishfarmermagazine.com/news/mowi-scotland-death-maib-probe-finds-failings/>
52 Furuset, Anders, and Dominic Welling, 'Salmon farming tax of 25% officially adopted by Norwegian Parliament', Intrafish, 31 May 2023, at: <https://www.intrafish.com/salmon/salmon-farming-tax-of-25-officially-adopted-by-norwegian-parliament-ending-8-month-saga/2-1-1459069>
53 Smith, Bren, *Eat Like a Fish: My Adventures as a Fisherman Turned Restorative Ocean Farmer*, Knopf, 2019, p. 57.
54 Smith, *Eat Like a Fish*, pp. 48–9, p. 53.
55 Smith, *Eat Like a Fish*, p. 54.
56 Dowler, Crispin, 'Revealed: the millionaires hoarding UK fishing rights', *Unearthed*, Greenpeace UK, 10 October 2018, at: <https://unearthed.greenpeace.org/2018/10/11/fishing-quota-uk-defra-michael-gove/>
57 Dowler, 'Revealed: the millionaires hoarding UK fishing rights'.

Chapter Five: A Modern Scottish Cook

1 By journalist and writer Clare Finney, interviewing me for her book with Liz Seabrook, *The Female Chef*, Hoxton Mini Press, 2021.
2 Quoted in Wu, Tim, 'The Tyranny of Convenience', *New York Times*, 16 February 2018, at: <https://www.nytimes.com/2018/02/16/opinion/sunday/tyranny-convenience.html>
3 Price, Katherine, 'New data suggests 17% fall in number of UK chefs', *Caterer*, 23 October 2018, at: <https://www.thecaterer.com/news/restaurant/new-data-suggests-17-fall-in-number-of-uk-chefs>
4 Druckman, Charlotte, 'Why are there no great women chefs?', *Gastronomica*, Vol. 10, Issue 1, 5 February 2010, at: <https://gastronomica.org/2010/02/05/why-are-there-no-great-women-chefs/>

5. Giousmpasoglou, C., E. Marinakou and J. Cooper, '"Banter, bollockings and beatings": The occupational socialisation process in Michelin-starred kitchen brigades in Great Britain and Ireland', *International Journal of Contemporary Hospitality Management*, Vol. 30, No. 3, 19 March 2018, pp. 1882–1902, at: <https://doi.org/10.1108/IJCHM-01-2017-0030>

6. Mishel, Lawrence, and Julia Wolfe, 'CEO compensation has grown 940% since 1978', Economic Policy Institute, 14 August 2019, at: <https://www.epi.org/publication/ceo-compensation-2018/>

7. 'The economy would suffer no harm if CEOs were paid less (or taxed more)', in Mishel and Wolfe, 'CEO compensation has grown 940% since 1978'.

8. Percival, Bronwen and Francis, *Reinventing the Wheel: Milk, Microbes and the Fight for Real Cheese*, University of California Press, 2017, pp. 261–2.

9. Ingold, Tim, *The Perception of the Environment: Essays on Livelihood, Dwelling and Skill*, Routledge, 2022, p. 67.

10. Abarca, Meredith E., *Voices in the Kitchen: Views of Food and the World from Working-class Mexican and Mexican American Women*, Texas A&M University Press, 2006, p. 56.

11. Quoted in Abend, Lisa, *The Sorcerer's Apprentices: A Season in the Kitchen at Ferran Adrià's elBulli*, Free Press, Simon & Schuster, 2011, p. 271.

12. Shopsin, Kenny, and Carolyn Carreño, *Eat Me: The Food and Philosophy of Kenny Shopsin*, Knopf, 2008, p. 195.

13. Lyotard, Jean-Francois, 'The Post-Modern Condition, a Report on Knowledge', *Theory and History of Literature*, Volume 10, eds. Wlad Godzich and Jochen Schulte-Sasse, Translated by Geoff Bennington and Brian Massumi, p.79.

14. Henry, Dr. Bernard, 'Jean-Francois Lyotard's Postmodernism and the Contemporary World', *ARPN Journal of Science and Technology*, Vol. 3 (July 2013).

15. Harris, Daryl B., 'Postmodernist Diversions in African American Thought', *Journal of Black Studies*, Vol. 36, Issue 2, 2005, pp. 209–28, at: <http://www.jstor.org/stable/40034329>

NOTES

16 Nunn, Jonathan, 'Crispy bhajia and the golden thread of true quality: A Vittles Review: Tulsi, Maru's Bhajia House and the GOAT of all GOATS', 8 September 2023, at: < https://www.vittlesmagazine.com/p/crispy-bhajia-and-the-golden-thread>

17 Instagram post, @awongsw1, 25 January 2024.

18 Armstrong, Gary, 'Inside Glasgow supermarket Aladdin's', *Glasgow Live*, 18 March 2022, at: <https://www.glasgowlive.co.uk/whats-on/inside-glasgow-supermarket-aladdins-incredible-23409518>

19 Glissant, Édouard, *Poetics of Relation*, trans. Betsy Wing, University of Michigan Press, 1997, quoted in Gordon, Col, 'Meithle: Seed migration, communal improvisation and cultural emergence', *Medium*, 27 April 2023, at: < https://colinchindown.medium.com/meithle-seed-migration-communal-improvisation-and-cultural-emergence-4a9472a55d53>

20 Fleet and routes of Thos. and Jas. Harrison, The Ships List website, at: <https://www.theshipslist.com/ships/lines/harrison.shtml>

21 Younge, Gary, 'Obituary: Ambalavaner Sivanandan', *Guardian*, 7 February 2018, at: <https://www.theguardian.com/world/2018/feb/07/ambalavaner-sivanandan>

22 'Author Interview: Q and A with Dr Ian Sanjay Patel on *We're Here Because You Were There*', *LSE Review of Books*, 16 April 2021, at: <https://blogs.lse.ac.uk/lsereviewofbooks/2021/04/16/author-interview-q-and-a-with-dr-ian-sanjay-patel-on-were-here-because-you-were-there-immigration-and-the-end-of-empire/>

23 Anderson, Rob, 'How Noma Made Fine Dining Far Worse', *Atlantic*, 16 January 2023, at: <https://www.theatlantic.com/ideas/archive/2023/01/noma-copenhagen-fine-dining-unsustainable/672738/>

24 'The New Nordic Food Manifesto', 2004, on the Nordic Council of Ministers' website, at: <https://www.norden.org/en/information/new-nordic-food-manifesto>

25 Hermansen, Mark Emil, 'Creating Terroir: An Anthropological Perspective on New Nordic Cuisine as an Expression of Nordic Identity', *Anthropology of Food*, S7, 2012, at: <https://doi.org/10.4000/aof.7249>

26 Blomhoff, R., R. Andersen, E. K. Arnesen et al, 'Nordic Nutrition Recommendations 2023', Nordic Council of Ministers, 2023, at: <https://pub.norden.org/nord2023-003/index.html>
27 Hermansen, 'Creating Terroir'.
28 Smith, Bren, *Eat Like a Fish: My Adventures as a Fisherman Turned Restorative Ocean Farmer*, Knopf, 2019, p. 50.
29 Hermansen, 'Creating Terroir'.
30 Sacred Land Film Project, 'Lands of the Sami', 2004, at: <https://sacredland.org/lands-of-the-sami-finland-norway-russia-sweden/>
31 Instagram, @maretravdnabuljo, 11 September 2023.

Chapter Six: A War for the Human Imagination

1 Kennedy, Alicia, 'On Storytelling', *From the Desk of Alicia Kennedy*, 16 November 2020, at: <https://www.aliciakennedy.news/p/on-storytelling>
2 Her blog, 'A' siubhal nam frith-rathadan', is at: <https://www.raghnaidsandilands.scot>
3 Sandilands, Raghnaid, 'Tobar an Dualchais: In praise of B-road studies', *West Highland Free Press*, 9 May 2020, at: <https://www.whfp.com/2020/05/09/tobar-and-dualchais-in-praise-of-b-road-studies/>
4 Rivera Cusicanqui, Silvia, *A Ch'ixi World Is Possible: Essays From a Present in Crisis*, Bloomsbury Academic, 2023, p. x, translator's note.
5 Ingold, Tim, *The Perception of the Environment: Essays on Livelihood, Dwelling and Skill*, Routledge, 2022, p. 178.
6 Ingold, *The Perception of the Environment*, p. 183.
7 Ingold, *The Perception of the Environment*, p. 183.
8 Ingold, *The Perception of the Environment*, p. 183.
9 Rivera Cusicanqui, Silvia, *Ch'ixinakax Utxiwa: On Practices and Discourses of Decolonization*, Polity Press, 2019, p. 65.
10 Gordon, Col, 'Meithle: Seed migration, communal improvisation and cultural emergence', *Medium*, 27 April 2023, at: <https://colinchindown.medium.com/meithle-seed-migration-communal-improvisation-and-cultural-emergence-4a9472a55d53>

NOTES

11 Mustefa, Zab, 'Glasgow's haggis pakora is more than just fusion food', *Vice*, 2 May 2016, at: <https://www.vice.com/en/article/kbxpkm/glasgows-haggis-pakora-is-more-than-just-fusion-food>

12 Richard Dawkins, 'Why the universe seems so strange', TEDGlobal, 2005, at: <https://www.ted.com/talks/richard_dawkins_why_the_universe_seems_so_strange?referrer=playlist-the_strangeness_of_everyday_li#t-513026>

13 Anthias, P., 'Ch'ixi Landscapes: Indigeneity and capitalism in the Bolivian Chaco', *Geoforum*, Vol. 82, 2017, pp. 268–75.

14 Lang, Tim, *Feeding Britain: Our Food Problems and How to Fix Them*, Pelican, 2020, Preface.

15 Appelbaum, Binyamin, 'Blame economists for the mess we're in', *New York Times*, 24 August 2019, at: <https://www.nytimes.com/2019/08/24/opinion/sunday/economics-milton-friedman.html>

16 Fanon, Frantz, *The Wretched of the Earth*, Penguin Classics, 2001, p. 118.

17 Fullerton, John, 'Regenerative Economics: A Necessary Paradigm Shift for a World in Crisis', *Economics and Beyond* podcast, Institute for New Economic Thinking, 27 January 2022, at: <https://www.ineteconomics.org/perspectives/podcasts/regenerative-economics-a-necessary-paradigm-shift-for-a-world-in-crisis>

18 Rousseau, Jean-Jacques, *Discourse on the Origins of Inequality*, 1755, at: <https://www.marxists.org/reference/subject/economics/rousseau/inequality/ch02.htm#:~:text=THE%20first%20man%20who%2C%20having,real%20founder%20of%20civil%20society>

19 Figures from Community Land Scotland, 'FAQs', at: <https://www.communitylandscotland.org.uk/our-work/faqs/>

20 For Norwegian speakers, see the campaign website and social media presence: <https://folkeaksjonen.no> | @folkeaksjonen Soldati, Camilla, 'Norway says no to oil explorations in Lofoten', Lifegate Daily, 30 April 2019, at: <https://www.lifegate.com/norway-lofoten-oil-ban#:~:text=One%20of%20the%20world's%20main,and%20home%20to%20unique%20ecosystems>

21 Furuset, Anders, and Dominic Welling, 'Salmon farming tax of 25% officially adopted by Norwegian Parliament', Intrafish, 31 May 2023, at: <https://www.intrafish.com/salmon/salmon-farming-tax-of-25-officially-adopted-by-norwegian-parliament-ending-8-month-saga/2-1-1459069>
22 Limb, Lottie, 'It's official: France bans short-haul domestic flights in favour of train travel', *EuroNews*, 2 December 2022, at: <https://www.euronews.com/green/2022/12/02/is-france-banning-private-jets-everything-we-know-from-a-week-of-green-transport-proposals>
23 The Ocean Cleanup, 'About', at: <https://theoceancleanup.com/about/>
24 Watts, Jonathan, 'Amazon deforestation falls over 60% compared with last July, says Brazilian minister', *Guardian*, 2 August 2023, at: <https://www.theguardian.com/environment/2023/aug/02/amazon-deforestation-falls-over-60-compared-with-last-july-says-brazilian-minister>
25 Shepherd, Nan, *The Living Mountain*, Canongate, Edinburgh, 2011, pp. 103–6.
26 In the Introduction to Nan Shepherd, *The Living Mountain*, Canongate, 2011, p. xxix.
27 Shepherd, *The Living Mountain*, p. 27.
28 Paraphrasing Thoreau, Henry David, *Slavery in Massachusetts*, 1854, available at: <https://www.africa.upenn.edu/Articles_Gen/Slavery_Massachusetts.html>

LIST OF RECIPES

Creamed corn 76
Corn cob custard 77
Chilled tomato and raspberry broth 113
Black pepper oil 115
Hattit kit 122
Skirlie 133
Potato broth 145
Potato milk 147
Hazelnut and beremeal shortbread 160